# WOMEN'S ORDINATION
# IN THE CATHOLIC CHURCH

"Rooted in Vatican II's conviction about the 'pastorality of doctrine' and a related understanding of the critical-constructive role of systematic theological analysis as being in service of the live questions of the church, John O'Brien provides us with an insightful contribution to one such pressing question. Key here is his calling for a revisiting of the relationship between the ordained as standing *in persona Ecclesiae* and *in persona Christi* with a fully representative understanding of ordained ministry. This book is an invaluable resource for any looking for an efficient and substantive treatment of this most contentious of issues within the twenty-first-century Catholic Church."
—Paul D. Murray, Professor of Systematic Theology and Dean of Catholic Studies, Durham University

"O'Brien addresses an important contemporary question with serious academic acumen. Insightfully he notes this is 'a new question that requires a new answer.' From whatever side of the debate one comes, O'Brien will challenge the reader to think differently about this 'new question.' This book is an important contribution to current critical ecclesial debate."
—Fáinche Ryan, Director, Loyola Institute, Trinity College Dublin

"This theologically innovative book is beautifully written and powerfully argued. It focuses on the 'provocative other,' the quasi-silenced voice of women and surveys the ministry of outstanding women in the New Testament, highlights widespread female ministry in the first millennium and argues that the ordination of women represents a necessary pastoral-theological development whose time has come. It is an outstanding volume that challenges the notion that Catholic doctrine on female ordination is immutable and fixed."
—Patricia Kieran, Director of the Irish Institute for Catholic Studies

"This important book is a 'must-read,' irrespective as to one's position on the topic. O'Brien takes seriously Pope Francis' invitation to see the pastoral as having a role to play in understanding doctrine. He brings to bear on the topic a wonderful breath of knowledge, an unapologetic if critical assessment of tradition, and carries us through a discourse that is deeply embedded in faith. The opening chapter is a masterpiece in the hermeneutics of doctrine for our time."
—Thomas R. Whelan, CSSp, Associate Professor in Theology, the former Milltown Institute, Dublin

# WOMEN'S ORDINATION
## *in the* CATHOLIC CHURCH

John O'Brien

CASCADE *Books* • Eugene, Oregon

WOMEN'S ORDINATION IN THE CATHOLIC CHURCH

Copyright © 2020 John O'Brien. All rights reserved. Except for brief quotations in critical publications or reviews, no part of this book may be reproduced in any manner without prior written permission from the publisher. Write: Permissions, Wipf and Stock Publishers, 199 W. 8th Ave., Suite 3, Eugene, OR 97401.

Cascade Books
An Imprint of Wipf and Stock Publishers
199 W. 8th Ave., Suite 3
Eugene, OR 97401

www.wipfandstock.com

PAPERBACK ISBN: 978-1-7252-6804-3
HARDCOVER ISBN: 978-1-7252-6803-6
EBOOK ISBN: 978-1-7252-6805-0

*Cataloguing-in-Publication data:*

Names: O'Brien, John, author.

Title: Women's ordination in the Catholic Church / John O'Brien.

Description: Eugene, OR: Cascade Books, 2020 | Includes bibliographical references.

Identifiers: ISBN 978-1-7252-6804-3 (paperback) | ISBN 978-1-7252-6803-6 (hardcover) | ISBN 978-1-7252-6805-0 (ebook)

Subjects: LCSH: Ordination of women—Catholic Church | Ordination of women—Christianity | Ordination of women—Europe | Ordination—History of doctrines | Catholic Church—Clergy | Ordination | Women clergy

Classification: BV676 O27 2020 (print) | BV676 (ebook)

Manufactured in the U.S.A.                                   JULY 22, 2020

# Contents

*Preface vii*

1. Orientations 1
2. Beginnings 17
3. Women's Ministry in the New Testament 41
4. Ordained Women in the First Millennium 68
5. Women's Ordination in the Middle Ages 105
6. New Answers to a New Question 138
7. A Theology Whose Time Has Come 165

*Bibliography 195*

## *Preface*

THIS BOOK WAS WRITTEN firstly to discharge a debt of gratitude owed to outstanding women I met and worked with over the years, in different countries, in the service of the gospel. Several of these women, often religious Sisters, but sometimes laywomen, married and single, excelled at leading, animating, and spiritually guiding the people of God. Had circumstances been different, I have little doubt that many of them would have made priests of high calibre. This book is dedicated to them, with great appreciation. Had married women and men, and in particular capable women of faith, been in positions of authority in the Catholic Church, its recent history might have been very different. Far from making the church more reasoned, excluding the feminine genius from exercising leadership in the church has made it less coherent. Another reason for writing this book arose from being frequently questioned over the years as to exactly why a dedicated, educated, Catholic woman of faith, quite demonstrably gifted by the Holy Spirit with the capacity to lead, guide, and spiritually animate Christian communities, could not receive Holy Orders. The more closely I examined the reasons put forward for the ban on the ordination of women, the clearer it became that these reasons were rooted in cultural assumptions that lacked binding theological status. Many of these assumptions moreover, never quite exited from the risible assumption of female inferiority and that against the background of a notion of priesthood rooted much more in power than in service. The final shape of the book was worked out in dialog with the Grangecon Group and I am most grateful to them for their fraternal support and for so much more. My thanks go also to Matt Wimer, Robin Parry, and Heather Carraher of Wipf and Stock who expertly guided the book to publication.

J.O'B.
Advent 2019

CHAPTER I

# *Orientations*

ON 29 MAY 2018, the Congregation for the Doctrine of the Faith (CDF) reaffirmed what it regards as the impossibility of the presbyteral ordination of women,[1] asserting that this "doctrine" is "definitive." In a short document of ten paragraphs, it accurately sums up what was put forth on this matter in previous documents by the CDF, by Pope Paul VI, by Pope John Paul II, and by Pope Benedict XVI.[2] The main aim of this present declaration, apart from re-affirming and summing up this teaching, seems to be to seek to add Pope Francis to this list as if to present an unbroken chain of modern, papal, magisterial, teaching on this subject.

In the first paragraph we read:

1. Ladaria, (Prefect of the Congregation for the Doctrine of the Faith), *The Definitive Character of the Doctrine of Ordinatio Sacerdotalis*—about some doubts, [*Il carattere definitive della dottrina di «Ordinatio Sacerdotalis»· A proposito di alcuni dubbi*], 29 May 2018; herinafter CDdiOS.

2. Cf. Paul VI, *Response to the Letter of His Grace the Most Reverend Dr. F. D. Coggan, Archbishop of Canterbury, concerning the Ordination of Women to the Priesthood*, (November 30, 1975); Franjo Cardinal Seper, Prefect, Sacred Congregation for the Doctrine of the Faith, *Declaration Inter Insigniores: On the Question of Admission of Women to the Ministerial Priesthood* (15 October 1976); Paul VI, *Address on the Role of Women in the Plan of Salvation* (30 January 1977); John Paul II, Apostolic Letter *Mulieris Dignitatem* (15 August 1988) and Apostolic Exhortation *Christifideles Laici* (30 December 1988); Pontifical Biblical Commission, *The Interpretation of the Bible in the Church* (23 April 1993); John Paul II, '*Ordinatio Sacerdotalis*' Apostolic Letter "*On Reserving Priestly Ordination to Men Alone*" (1994); Joseph Cardinal Ratzinger, Prefect, Congregation for the Doctrine of the Faith, *Letter Concerning the CDF Reply Regarding Ordinatio Sacerdotalis: Reply of the Congregation for the Doctrine of the Faith to a Dubium* (28 October 1995). See also *Catechism of the Catholic Church*, n. 1577, and International Theological Commission, *From the Diakonia of Christ to the Diakonia of the Apostles* (2002); Pope Francis, *Evangelii Gaudium* (24 November 2013).

> Intimately linked to the Eucharist is the sacrament of Order, in which Christ makes himself present to the church as the source of his life and his work. Priests are configured: to Christ the priest, so as to be able to act in the name of Christ, head of the church.³

The second paragraph states that:

> Christ wanted to give this sacrament to the twelve apostles, all men [*tutti uomini*], who in turn, communicated it to other men [*ad altri uomini*]. The church has always recognized herself bound by this decision of the Lord, which excludes that the ministerial priesthood can be validly conferred on women,

adding:

> that the church in no way has the power to confer priestly ordination on women and that this sentence⁴ [*sentenza*] must be held definitively by all the faithful of the church.⁵

The third paragraph notes the:

> voices that question the definitiveness of this doctrine. To argue that it is not definitive, it is argued that it was not defined *ex cathedra* and that, then, a later decision by a future Pope or council could overturn it. Sowing these doubts creates serious confusion.

The fourth affirms that:

> the church recognizes that the impossibility of ordaining women belongs to the "substance of the sacrament" of order.⁶ The church has no capacity to change this substance because it is precisely starting from the sacraments instituted by Christ

---

3. *Presbyterorum Ordinis*, n. 2.

4. The "official" translation reads "sentence"; perhaps "judgement" might be a better translation.

5. *Ordinatio Sacerdotalis*, (22 May, 1994, n.4. "*deve essere tenuta in modo definitivo da tutti i fedeli della Chiesa*," CDdiOS, 2).

6. With a reference to Denzinger-Huenermann, 1728. But this canon of Trent (Pius IV, 16 July 1562) deals with teaching and canons on Communion under two species as well as the Communion of small children. 1728 reads: "Ecclesiae potestas circa dispensationem sacramenti Eucharistae." It deals with the power of the Church in the administration of the sacraments, but not specifically with the question of women presbyters.

that it is generated as a church.⁷ It is not just a disciplinary, but a doctrinal element, in that it concerns the structure of the sacraments.⁸

The fifth argues that:

> The priest, in fact, acts in the person of Christ, spouse of the church, and his being a man is an indispensable element⁹ of this sacramental representation (cf. Congregation for the Doctrine of the Faith, *Inter Insigniores*, n. 5).

The sixth paragraph turns to the question of infallibility, almost as if to suggest that this doctrine is infallibly taught,¹⁰ without ever clearly saying so:

> It is important to reiterate that infallibility does not concern only solemn pronouncements of a Council or of the Supreme Pontiff when he speaks *ex cathedra*, but also the ordinary and universal teaching of bishops throughout the world, when they propose, in communion with each other and with the Pope, the Catholic doctrine to be held definitively.

The seventh paragraph somewhat loosely argues that:

> Further proof of the commitment with which John Paul II has examined the issue is the prior consultation that he wanted to have in Rome with the presidents of the Episcopal conferences who were seriously interested in this problem. All, without exception, have declared, with full conviction, for the obedience of the Church to the Lord, that she does not possess the faculty of conferring priestly ordination on women.

It continues:

> John Paul II in *Ordinatio sacerdotalis*, referred to this infallibility. Thus he did not declare a new dogma but, with the authority conferred upon him as Peter's successor, he formally confirmed and made explicit, in order to remove all doubt, what

---

7. We will return to this question in chapter 6.

8. "*Non si tratta solo di un elemento disciplinare, ma dottrinale, in quanto riguarda la struttura dei sacramenti.*"

9. "*il suo essere uomo è un elemento indispensabile di questa rappresentazione sacramentale.*"

10. Populist Catholic websites spuriously interpret this present declaration as reaffirming that the teaching on the non-ordainability of women is infallible, e.g., https://www.lifesitenews.com/.../church-teaching-on-male-only-priesthood-is-infallible.

the ordinary and universal magisterium considered throughout the history of the church as belonging to the deposit of faith. Precisely this way of pronouncing reflects a style of ecclesial communion, since the Pope did not want to work alone, but as a witness listening to an uninterrupted and lived tradition.[11]

The eighth notes that:

Benedict XVI also insisted on this teaching . . .

The ninth notes that:

Pope Francis is back on the subject. He, in his apostolic exhortation *Evangelii Gaudium*, reaffirmed: "the priesthood reserved for men, as a sign of Christ the Bridegroom who is consigned (*sic*[12]) to the Eucharist,"

adding that:

Pope Francis reiterated: "On the ordination of women in the Catholic Church, the last clear word was given by Saint John Paul II, and this remains."

The tenth and final paragraph reminds the church that:

it is essential that it remains in Jesus. . . . Only fidelity to his words, which will not pass, ensures our rooting in Christ and in his love.

## AN IMPORTANT DISTINCTION

Everything this declaration—and, as we shall see, all the documents whose teaching it summarizes—claims about the definitive nature of the teaching on the assumed non-ordainability of women (not to mention its strategy of implying that this teaching is infallible), is predicated on the claim that it confirms what the ordinary and universal magisterium considered throughout the history of the church as belonging to the deposit of faith. From the point of view of theology, as distinct from church discipline however, that is something that can be verified only from

---

11. CDdiOS, 6.

12. The official translation of '*che si consegna*,' that first appeared; later, sometimes translated as '*who gives himself*.'" It is a reference to the official(?) Spanish text of EG 104, '*que se entrega*.' These precisions of translation do not impinge on the argument being made.

historical-theological study and not merely by declamation. When this declaration makes a statement such as:

> It is important to reiterate that infallibility does not concern only solemn pronouncements of a council or of the Supreme Pontiff when he speaks *ex cathedra*, but also the ordinary and universal teaching of bishops throughout the world, when they propose, in communion with each other and with the Pope, the Catholic doctrine to be held definitively, . . .

then it becomes equally important to distinguish two realities:

1. Infallibility does indeed pertain to "the ordinary and universal teaching of bishops throughout the world, when they propose, in communion with each other and with the Pope, the Catholic doctrine to be held definitively." That is clearly taught in *Lumen Gentium* 25.2.[13]

2. There remains however, the historical-theological question as to whether a particular teaching or practice is, in fact, one that the ordinary and universal magisterium considered throughout the history of the Church as belonging to the deposit of faith.

   The CDF risks blurring that distinction:[14]

   > In response to this precise act of the Magisterium of the Roman Pontiff, explicitly addressed to the entire Catholic Church, all members of the faithful are required to give their assent to the teaching stated therein. To this end, the Congregation for the Doctrine of the Faith, with the approval of the Holy Father, has given an official *Reply* on the nature of this assent: it is a matter of full definitive assent, that is to say, irrevocable, to a doctrine taught infallibly by the church. In fact, as the *Reply* explains, the definitive nature of this assent derives from the truth of the doctrine itself, since, founded on the written Word of God, and

---

13. "Although the individual bishops do not enjoy the prerogative of infallibility, they nevertheless proclaim Christ's doctrine infallibly whenever, even though dispersed through the world, but still maintaining the bond of communion among themselves and with the successor of Peter, and authentically teaching matters of faith and morals, they are in agreement on one position as definitively to be held. This is even more clearly verified when, gathered together in an ecumenical council, they are teachers and judges of faith and morals for the universal church, whose definitions must be adhered to with the submission of faith."

14. *Concerning the Reply of the Congregation for the Doctrine of the Faith on the Teaching Contained in the Apostolic Letter Ordinatio Sacerdotalis,* 28 October 1995.

> constantly held and applied in the Tradition of the Church, it has been set forth infallibly by the ordinary universal Magisterium (cf. Lumen Gentium, 25).

Thus, the *Reply* apparently wishes to specify that this doctrine belongs to the deposit of the faith of the Church.[15]

> In this case, an act of the ordinary Papal Magisterium, in itself not infallible, witnesses to the infallibility of the teaching of a doctrine already possessed by the church.

It is however, crucial to note that:

1. this is a *Reply* from a Vatican Congregation or Dicastery, and not at all an *ex cathedra* teaching from the Pope;
2. it acknowledges that *Ordinatio Sacerdotalis* is not an infallible declaration;
3. it claims that *Ordinatio Sacerdotalis*: "witnesses to the infallibility of the teaching of a doctrine already possessed by the church."
4. But that simply brings the discussion back to the distinction between the acknowledged reality of the infallibility of the ordinary magisterium and the historical-theological question of whether or not a particular teaching[16] has *in fact* always and everywhere been taught by the church.

---

15. The *Reply* continues: "It should be emphasized that the definitive and infallible nature of this teaching of the church did not arise with the publication of the Letter *Ordinatio Sacerdotalis*. In the Letter, as the Reply of the Congregation for the Doctrine of the Faith also explains, the Roman Pontiff, having taken account of present circumstances, has confirmed the same teaching by a formal declaration, giving expression once again to *quod semper, quod ubique et quod ab omnibus tenendum est, utpote ad fidei depositum pertinens*." That seems to interpret Vincent of Lerins in an extremely reductive way.

16. "Only a baptized man (*vir*) validly receives sacred ordination." "The Lord Jesus chose men (*viri*) to form the college of the twelve apostles, and the apostles did the same when they chose collaborators to succeed them in their ministry. The college of bishops, with whom the priests are united in the priesthood, makes the college of the twelve an ever-present and ever-active reality until Christ's return. The Church recognizes herself to be bound by this choice made by the Lord himself. For this reason the ordination of women is not possible." This quotes CJC 1024: "A baptized male alone receives sacred ordination validly."

An historical question is answered by historical research. Such a question cannot be simply answered in a definitive manner *a priori* by the opinion of a Vatican Congregation.

## PURPOSE OF THE STUDY

This study will examine the assumption that the non-ordainability of women is such a teaching and practice. It will argue that this is *not* the case. In assembling the historical-theological evidence to demonstrate that, it will become apparent that women have been and can be ordained in the Catholic Church.[17]

The specifically historical question of whether or not women have or have not been ordained and the specifically ecclesiological question of whether at this point in the pilgrimage of the people of God, women should or should not be ordained, while intimately linked, are nonetheless distinct. The first is an historical question to be answered through historical research, albeit one that pays nuanced attention to the contextual meaning of terms such as "ordination." The second asks if today, given deeper understanding of gender equality, ordained ministry, spiritual giftedness, and the pastorality (*pastoralidad*) of doctrine, it is or is not theologically and ecclesiologically coherent that appropriately gifted and trained women of faith with the proven capacity and commitment to guide Christian communities, should or should not be ordained to that ministry.

Even if it could be demonstrated that women had never been ordained—an unlikely scenario, as will be demonstrated below—that could be a criterion for present-day decision-making only if the reasons for that previous practice could be received by the *sensus fidei fidelium* as pastorally-theologically coherent in the present context. The systematically theological is always pastorally rooted and destined. It brings the rigor of systematic theology to bear in a consciously critical manner on the ecclesial practice of faith in the hope of enabling and enhancing that practice. In Vatican II the "pastoral" regained its proper standing as something far more than the mere application of doctrine, but as the very context from which doctrines emerge, the very condition of the possibility of doctrine,

---

17. This present study seeks to provide a synthesis of contemporary study of the historical-theological question of women's ordination. Generally speaking, it draws freely and with great appreciation from the scholars cited in the notes and refers the reader to them for further references to primary sources.

the touchstone for the validity of doctrine and the always prior and posterior praxis that doctrine attempts to sum up, systematize, safeguard, and transmit.[18] The pastoral, thus understood, has a specifically hermeneutical and not merely applicative role in understanding doctrine.

## PRELIMINARY ISSUES TO BE CLARIFIED

There are, however, some preliminary issues to be clarified. The first is the notion, articulated in the second paragraph of this Declaration, as well as in the documents of the Roman magisterium, which this paragraph sums up, that: "Christ wanted to give this sacrament to the twelve apostles, all men [*tutti uomini*], who in turn, communicated it to other men [*ad altri uomini*]." That assertion is based on the assumption that we know precisely, or at least in sufficient detail, how the historical Jesus is believed to have instituted the sacrament of Holy Orders. That, in turn, implies that we know with equal certainty, what groups of believers Jesus demonstrably included or excluded as prospective presidents of the Eucharistic memorial of his death and resurrection, inaugurated in the Last Supper, during the life of the historical church down through the ages. That, in turn, is predicated on the assumption that what transpired at the Last Supper is recoverable in the same detail. Such assumptions, we shall argue, are historically dubious and exegetically naive.

The second issue, closely related to the first, is to examine the view that these matters have been definitively resolved by the Council of Trent.

The third issue to be explored, is the contention that any attempt to explore these issues in a deeper fashion constitutes disobedience and the sowing of confusion; a contention based, in turn, on the assumption that the last word has been spoken on these matters. That, however, runs counter to how God, as creator, wishes to be acknowledged and adored precisely in creating the human spirit with an unending desire to know and understand in an ever more unrestricted way—and that precisely as an act of faith in God's creative purpose.

A fourth issue, to be examined in chapter 6, involves demonstrating that while the metaphor of Christ as bridegroom has a scriptural basis, the innovation of appealing to that metaphor as an argument against the capacity of a woman to receive Holy Orders is by no means a conclusive argument.

---

18. O'Brien, "Ecclesiology as Narrative," 150.

Running through many of the discussions that will follow is mounting evidence that the putative non-ordainability of women is a matter of canonical discipline rather than Christian doctrine. That will be explored more amply in chapter 7, where the exploration will conclude that the prohibition on women's ordination is a canonical discipline.

## CATHOLIC THEOLOGY

In seeking to ground itself solidly in the method and tradition of Catholic theology, this study distances itself from two tendencies frequently voiced: one, that the question of women's ordination has been definitively settled, with the matter now closed; the second, that there is no theological basis for the present discipline. The study itself is testament to the fact that the discussion is far from closed. But the responsibility of the Roman magisterium to insist on practical rules of conduct and organization can hardly be said to be without any theological foundation. At the same time, discipline should not be confused with doctrine and neither should a particular discipline, when considered as such, be considered *a priori* unreformable. There is indeed an indisputable, theological basis for Canon Law, but not for insisting that a given law may never be changed, much less cloaking it in the guise of a definitive doctrine of faith.

In line with the tradition of Catholic theology, this study seeks to answer to both faith and reason and to do so in a manner that is historically and hermeneutically aware and self-critical. In respecting the magisterium of the Pope and bishops, it does not gloss over the magisterium of the theologians.[19] There is, of course, also the magisterium of the poor: those denied a voice and the first to be addressed by the gospel. No adequate understanding of church authority can be elaborated that does not give a privileged consideration to their experience.[20] The undeniable silencing of the female voice in the history of theology and canon law amounted to women being "hermeneutically marginalized."[21] Not only

---

19. Aquinas wrote of two kinds of magisterium: The *magisterium cathedrae pastoralis*, which is properly that of the bishop, and the *magisterium cathedrae magistralis*, that of the theologian, Quodlibet III, 9, ad 3 as cited by Y. Congar in "A Semantic History of the Term 'Magisterium,'" in Curran and McCormick (eds.), *Readings in Moral Theology*, no. 3, *The Magisterium and Morality*, 297–313.

20. O'Brien, "The Authority of the Poor," in Hoose (ed.), *Authority in the Roman Catholic Church*, 217–30.

21. Carlson, "Can the Church Be a Virtuous Hearer of Women?" 29–30.

were women unfairly disadvantaged in rendering their experience and perspective intelligible, but equally, as a result, the dominant narrative suffered from a hermeneutical lacuna and significant cognitive disablement in understanding the necessary articulation of an intrinsically important experience and perspective, resulting in the received narrative being skewed and incomplete.

On that basis, the voice of faith-filled, theologically informed female scholars in the ongoing theological dialogue, on this and related questions, merits a privileged hermeneutical status. That hermeneutical privilege consists directly in its therapeutic function in the context of dialogue with other theological perspectives, in that it creates conditions for the latter, for a discovery of methodological self-awareness in relation to their own unobjectified, socio-political rootedness and destination as well as their possible relatedness to structures of exclusion, so as to correct these.[22]

A hermeneutically aware, and therefore self-correcting and developing Catholic theology, does not confuse the core elements of the faith received from the apostles with culturally conditioned propositions designed to express that faith under given, and changing, historical and socio-cultural conditions, especially ones that are now surpassed. The circles of the unexpressed that surround such legitimate, historically necessary, but nonetheless intrinsically incomplete articulations of divine truth are always in need of, capable of, and in the process of acquiring richer expression. Doctrine develops. This self-developing dynamic of Catholic doctrine and theology, far from being some wishful, modernist, hypothesis is part of that theology's very nature and structure. Without it we would not have the Logos Christology of the Fourth Gospel, the Aristotelian mediated theology of Saint Thomas Aquinas, or the ecologically mediated theology of Pope Francis' *Laudato Si'*.

## RECEPTION OF THE TEACHING ON THE NON-ORDAINABILITY OF WOMEN

It is at least arguable that the proposition that women may not validly receive Holy Orders, does not enjoy the *consensus fidelium*. Running through much of what follows in this study is the question of whether or not that proposition has been "received" by the people of God as one

---

22. O'Brien, "Theology and the Option for the Poor," 164.

of those "things without which the deposit [of faith] cannot be properly safeguarded and explained."[23]

There is always a hermeneutical distance between the issuing of a teaching and its "reception," the process through which one ecclesial body makes its own a truth or determination from another.[24] One need only reflect on the historically torturous reception of Ecumenical Councils to realize how nuanced a process that is. Church history provides many examples of non-reception, whether by Rome in relation to various local synods, as well as in the other direction, for example, with regard to the *filioque*. A recent, if less controversial example, might be the non-reception of *Veterum Sapientia* from that most beloved of Popes, John XXIII.[25]

The authority of any teaching is derived not from the power of the hierarchical assembly that promulgates it, but from the conformity of that teaching to the faith received from the apostles. "Reception" is more than blind obedience in as much as its realization involves judgment and consent. The people of God, no more than a local episcopate,

---

23. Bishop Gasser, spokesman for the Theological Commission at Vatican I, explained that the secondary object of infallibility was "truths without which the deposit of faith could not be protected and explained." Schema Primum de Ecclesia, Canon ix, Mansi 51, 552; see also Mansi 52, 1226.

24. Here I draw on Congar, "La *Réception* comme Réalité Ecclésiologique," 369–403.

25. "*Veterum Sapientia*: On the Promotion of the Study of Latin," 22 February 1962. Among other things, at a time when seminary lectures were increasingly in the vernacular, it insisted they should be delivered in Latin. Note the rhetorical flourish of its final paragraph, easily misunderstood as a definitive statement: "Finally, in virtue of Our apostolic authority, We will and command that all the decisions, decrees, proclamations and recommendations of this Our Constitution remain firmly established and ratified, notwithstanding anything to the contrary, however worthy of special note."

One historically significant example of non-reception of a Papal Encyclical and censure, by a local Church, occurred in Ireland during 1888. In April, Rome issued a letter admonishing the Bishops and faithful not to support "Boycotting" and the "Plan of Campaign" in the agrarian struggle or "Land War." On June 24th Pope Leo XIII, in his Encyclical, *Saepe Nos*, (ASS 21 1888 3–5), renewed this admonition and complained of its non-implementation. In September, Cardinal Rumpolla, Secretary of State, wrote yet another letter on the theme, charging the Bishops with disloyalty. In October, the Irish bishops decided on collectively addressing a strong letter to the Pope, effectively informing His Holiness that they understood the situation in Ireland better than he did. It was sent by Archbishop Walsh of Dublin in early December and signed by 28 out of 30 Irish bishops. Thereafter, Rome ceased insisting on opposition to the "Plan of Campaign." E. Larkin, 'The Roman Catholic Church in Ireland and the Fall of Parnell: 1888–1891,' 3–10.

cannot be reduced to passivity. Matthew 20:25–26, Luke 22:25–26, and especially 2 Corinthians 13:10 ("power is given for edification and not for destruction") express a key element in the order that Christ willed for his Church, a communion deeply pneumatological, something eliminated in a solely pyramidal power structure. The hierarchy, whose charism cannot be reduced to juridical power, exercises a ministry of service in regard to that communion. Correlatively, the adherence of faith is not to a power, but to truth, and to the authentic enunciation of that truth.

Animated by the Holy Spirit, Christ's faithful and local churches—as the 2019 Synod of the Amazon has shown—are not purely passive, but are true, living subjects of ecclesial action and free initiative, capable of discernment and cooperation with the Holy Spirit. Because faith implies communion, something not reducible to submission to monarchical authority, consensus is more than obedience. An aspect of the indefectibility of the Church, it is effected by invocation of and guidance by the Holy Spirit and not simply by juridical power. It expresses more the totality of the memory of the church than the numerical sum of particular paths, where each, such as the one under discussion here, might be singly and uncritically considered more or less perfect.

"Reception" does not simply confer legitimacy upon a decision, conciliar or otherwise. In an open process never adequately describable in solely juridical terms, it attests that a decision has truly come from the Holy Spirit and that as such—and not primarily in virtue of its reception—it is of living value for the Church. Thus, "reception" is not constitutive of the juridical quality of a decision and does not refer to that, rather it attests and recognizes whether or how a decision redounds to the good of the people of God. That distinction is paramount in exploring the issue under discussion here. Correlatively, non-reception does not necessarily signify that a decision is juridically incorrect, but rather that the decision taken has little capacity to give spiritual and moral life to the Church; it does not contribute to "edification": to the building up of the body of Christ.

Since it is the Church as a whole that is enlivened by the Holy Spirit, the magisterium, despite its responsibility to nurture the *sensus fidei fidelium* and keep the community faithful to the gospel, is quite demonstrably not *exclusively* responsible for the faith of the Church. The "reception" of doctrine always begins and ends with the magisterium receiving the lived faith and testimony of the people of God prior to giving it official formulation.[26] The process is *dialogical*. That applies in a particular way to those at the margins, undoubtedly including many women, who experience exclusion by the official voice of tradition.

Notwithstanding how the people of God, in the main, accept the present discipline regarding women's capacity to receive Holy Orders as precisely that—a discipline—and do not see its enactment *per se* as juridically incorrect, nonetheless, mounting evidence suggests that very significant tranches of Christ's faithful have not received it as a doctrine that builds up the Church in faith, hope, and love, to the extent that it does not enjoy the *consensus fidelium*.

## CATHOLIC TEACHING: FROM DEFENSIVE TO EXPANSIVE

The experience of faith expressed in the language of doctrine or law has to communicate coherence in multiple, lived dimensions of life rather than be construed simply as a series of logical deductions from presumed immutable, fixed foundations. A frequently held misconception is that doctrine is an abstract, fixed body of knowledge. In reality, doctrine is "open" and expansive.

Pope Francis' concern for how doctrine is presented, how it is systematically ordered, and how it must never be separated from reality,[27] shows important methodological concerns for fruitfulness, renewal, and the otherness of God. These concerns confront the frequently promoted misconception that doctrine is an immutably fixed body of knowledge. Doctrine has to communicate salvifically and emancipatorily with generations and situations impossible to foresee in its original contextualized construction.

Interpretation of Catholic teaching is attentive both to the context and conditioning from which its formulation emerged and to the context and conditioning into which it is being received, where the lived experience of the people of God demands attentiveness to new questions arising in the *present*. Church teaching, never a closed system of propositions, is a historical narrative system open to future development.

---

26. Gaillardetz, "The Reception of Doctrine: New Perspectives," In Hoose (ed.), *Authority in the Roman Catholic Church*, 95–114.

27. Cf. *Evangelii Gaudium* 231 and 241.

The CDF's *Mysterium Ecclesiae* (1973) acknowledged the historical conditioning of doctrine in: the incompleteness of every doctrinal statement; the contextuality of doctrinal affirmations insofar as they are responses to particular questions; the linguistic nature of all doctrine; and the distinction between truth affirmed in a doctrinal statement and the philosophical categories and worldview used to express that truth.[28]

The misconception of fixity gives rise to a particular mental state in believing. A merely notional assent is given to a set of propositions never elaborated in relation to praxis; believers are denied the capacity to infer from their own experience, personal or communal, and are oriented to repeat systematized propositions scarcely understood, from which approved behavior is deduced in a command-obedience mode, to be systematically repeated as a badge of belonging, owning, and approving, often with a view to being approved and promoted. This is at least partly the reason why many in positions of leadership within the Church are slow to engage in deconstructive or even developmental thinking, thereby endorsing conformism.

Pope Francis proposes: "four specific principles which can guide the development of life in society and the building up of people where differences are harmonised within a shared pursuit . . . ." The first, that time is greater than space, "has to do with fullness as an expression of the horizon which constantly opens before us":

---

28. ". . . the hidden mysteries of God: 'by their nature so far transcend the human intellect that even if they are revealed to us and accepted by faith, they remain concealed by the veil of faith itself and are as it were, wrapped in darkness.' (Vatican Council I: Dogmatic Constitution, *Dei Filius*, ch. 4; *Conc. Oec. Decr.* (3), p. 808 (DS 3016). . . . With regard to this historical condition, it must first be observed that the meaning of the pronouncements of faith depends partly upon the expressive power of the language used at a certain point in time and in particular circumstances. Moreover, it sometimes happens that some dogmatic truth is first expressed incompletely (but not falsely), and at a later date, when considered in a broader context of faith or human knowledge, it receives a fuller and more perfect expression. In addition, when the Church makes new pronouncements . . . she usually has the intention of solving certain questions or removing certain errors, . . . even though the truths which the Church intends to teach through her dogmatic formulas are distinct from the changeable conceptions of a given epoch and can be expressed without them, nevertheless it can sometimes happen that these truths may be enunciated by the Sacred Magisterium in terms that bear traces of such conceptions. . . . [I]t has sometimes happened that in this habitual usage of the Church certain of these formulas gave way to new expressions which, proposed and approved by the Sacred Magisterium, presented more clearly or more completely the same meaning." CDF *Mysterium Ecclesiae* (1973).

> Giving priority to space means madly attempting to keep everything together in the present, trying to possess all the spaces of power and of self-assertion; it is to crystallize processes and presume to hold them back. Giving priority to time, means being concerned about initiating processes, rather than possessing spaces. Time governs spaces, illumines them and makes them links in a constantly expanding chain, with no possibility of return. What we need, then, is to give priority to actions which generate new processes in society and engage other persons and groups who can develop them to the point where they bear fruit in significant historical events—without anxiety, but with clear convictions and tenacity.[29]

Doctrines are not freestanding propositions, they are part of a large, dialogical practice whose goal, far from defensive, is progressive and expansive. Tradition requires multiple perspectives to be considered in addition to coherence with the past, such as embodied praxis, transformation, and pragmatic applicability. In addition to established historical reconstructions and reception, there are also horizons of interpretation involving lived Christian experience—some of it new and unforeseen—and the questions that arise there, which open up the question of who interprets and why? That, in turn, focuses on the "provocative other": in this case, the quasi-silenced voice of women.

Only by constantly reinterpreting the tradition, and not discarding it, can fidelity to the tradition's orthodoxy and historicity be maintained. Christian identity is constituted by a relational proportionality between the gospel and cultural-historical contingencies, requiring calibration and rebalancing. Just as the past tradition of faith remains vital, the contemporary situation, not least in its emphasis on the dignity and equality of women in the church, is also theologically significant because, as Pope Francis insists, the pastoral has a specifically hermeneutical role in understanding doctrine.

Christian teaching continues to be catechetically and salvifically performative only through the dynamic process of its production, reception, and communication, and not through a putative, pre-formed, essential meaning waiting to be disclosed or discovered. The dynamics of reception open up a dialogue between the teaching and a new set of questions informed by specific background theories and retroductive warrants from experiences set in the context of a community-of-faith discourse.

---

29. *Evangelii Gaudium* no. 221.

The plurality of pastoral situations, yielding a plurality of such dialogues, allows many kinds of meaning and excludes a singularizing hermeneutic stressing dogmatism, correct reading, and an absolute text.[30]

Without an orientation to fullness, which recognizes that new receptions or re-receptions are continually needed, the church might find herself lacking in the capacity or competency for change even when change is needed. The struggle to overcome the domestication of previous interpretations, seeing reconstructive hermeneutics as one element of a dynamic equilibrium of interpretive factors, is a major challenge in the Church today, not least with regard to the ministry of women.

Pope Francis' magisterium has important implications for interpreting specific doctrines and for the ways in which the nature, development, and interpretation of doctrine are understood.

> The meeting of doctrine and pastoral concern is not optional; interpretation is constitutive of a theology that intends to be ecclesial. The questions of our people, their suffering, their battles, their dreams, their worries, possess an interpretational value that we cannot ignore.[31]

## INSCRIBING MEDIEVAL PRACTICE INTO SCRIPTURAL TEXTS

Methodologically speaking, the present predicament in relation to women's ordination has arisen because canonical positions elaborated in the medieval period were inscribed into the interpretation of scriptural texts to produce, in a circular argument, a series of proof-texts for a canonical position already assumed to be definitive. Nowhere is that more evident than in the interpretations of the New Testament texts concerning the Last Supper that have held sway from the twelfth century until today, and it is to exploring that issue that we will now turn.

---

30. Cf. Gregory A. Ryan, *Hermeneutics of Doctrine in a Learning Church: The Dynamics of Receptive Integrity*.

31. Video Message to participants in the International Theological Congress, Buenos Aires, 3 September 2015.

CHAPTER 2

## *Beginnings*

IT IS COMMONLY ASSERTED that on Holy Thursday we also celebrate Jesus' institution of the ministerial priesthood, or the priesthood of the order of the presbyterate. This assertion is based on an interpretation of Jesus' Gospel command, "Do this in remembrance of me" (Luke 22:19 and parallels), often in an appeal to the Council of Trent, which declared:

> If anyone shall say that by the words "Do this in commemoration of me," Christ did not institute the apostles priests, or did not ordain that they and other priests should offer his body and blood: let him be *anathema*.[1]

The statement of the CDF that: "Christ wanted to give this sacrament (ordination) to the twelve apostles, all men, [*tutti uomini*]," a statement found directly or indirectly in all recent Roman magisterial documents on this question, assumes from a methodological point of view, that we know exactly what happened at the Last Supper in all its particulars, or at least in sufficient detail to know exactly the mind of Jesus at that moment.

These documents assert the reality of priesthood and of ordination and that the twelve apostles were men. But we need to examine the legitimacy or otherwise of the assumption that in regard to the Last Supper we possess an unassailable store of facts from which to argue convincingly the position of *Ordinatio Sacerdotalis*, 1994.

---

1. Council of Trent, session 22, ch. 1.

## THE LAST SUPPER

There certainly was a Last Supper, momentous in what it instituted. But we possess details of the memory of Jesus' institution of the Eucharist and what that may imply for ministry, only in the liturgical formulae of the primitive churches. Although all New Testament accounts of the institution, recognizably dealing with the same event, are substantially in agreement, they are nevertheless different in details through their being enshrined in the liturgies of the churches who transmitted them.

These local churches are effectively tracing and grounding *their* liturgies in the meal celebrated by Jesus. As doctrine and liturgy developed, that is precisely what the Church continued to do, notably at the Council of Trent. This does not at all imply that there is no historical core to the Eucharistic tradition, much less that it is reducible to a later invention by a group celebrating its ritual. A realistic approach incorporating the interdependence of faith and reason, avoids both fundamentalism ("we know with absolute precision what happened at the Last Supper, *wie es eigentlich gewesen ist*, as well as what it excludes, and continue to repeat that exactly") and historical positivism ("we do not know the *ipsissima verba, et acta et intentiones Jesu*—his very words actions and intentions at the Last Supper—and so must simply remain agnostic").

If we do not have the *ipsissima verba Jesu*, the precise words of Jesus, we can certainly catch the *ipsissima vox Jesu*, his authentic voice. The Eucharistic words of Jesus have not been so strongly influenced by the liturgical forms of early Christianity that no historical argument whatsoever can be based on them, but neither do we know precisely what Jesus did and said, or what he included and excluded in such a way as to base with certainty—or even firm assurance—the present discipline of the Roman magisterium regarding the ordainability of women to the presbyterate.

That the memory of Jesus is structured by the concerns of the churches who transmitted it is completely in harmony with the teaching of the church at Vatican II:

> The sacred authors wrote the four Gospels, selecting some things from the many which had been handed on by word of mouth or in writing, reducing some of them to a synthesis, *explaining some things in view of the situation of their churches* (italics ours) and preserving the form of proclamation but always in such fashion that they told us the honest truth about Jesus.[2]

---

2. Dei Verbum 19, which itself resumes First Vatican Council, Dogmatic

Moreover, access to these texts through the formation of the canon of Scripture, to the exclusion of apocryphal texts, follows from the grace of the Holy Spirit precisely as active in the choices of the church. As Origen put it:

> The church has four Gospels. Heretics have very many. One of them is entitled *According to the Egyptians,* another *According to the Twelve Apostles.* Basilides, too, dared to write a gospel and give it his own name. Many have tried to write gospels, but only four Gospels have been approved. You should know that not only four Gospels but very many were composed, but not all have found acceptance (2 Pet. 2:1).[3]

Thus, the theologians of the early church and of the communities of the evangelists have molded received narratives of the Last Supper texts and traditions. Paul gives us the earliest *text* from c. 55 CE, but written some years after he *received* it (cf. 1 Cor 11:2 and esp., v. 23). The generally accepted dating of the redacted, canonical, Gospel texts reveals a pre-Gospel period in Christianity, characterized by early, oral transmission of the Jesus tradition, but with local variations. Since the Eucharist was being celebrated in the primitive church before the redaction of the New Testament texts, as those texts themselves attest, there is clearly an earlier, non-scriptural Jesus tradition about the Last Supper standing behind the present texts. There may even be earlier formulations—not to mention the *ipsissima verba Jesu*—arguably in shorter, laconic, unbalanced, oral traditions that pre-date Paul's conversion, but now inaccessible.

Unquestionably, there is unchallengeable, multiple attestation to the Last Supper.[4] Some of Mark's narrative seems to be pre-Marcan. Matthew seems to follow Mark. But Luke has a more extensive tradition, whether a separate Lukan tradition or a theologically creative redaction of Mark. In the other direction, and a generation later, in John 13 we are presented with a different "sacrament" of the Lord's Supper. Written when an institution narrative was presumably well-known from the liturgy, John sought to stress not simply the "sacrament" as such, but the diaconal implications of sharing in it: a life and community of service as symbolized

---

Constitution on the Catholic Faith, chap. 3, *On Faith.* Denzinger 1789 (3008).

3. In "Homilies on Luke" 1.2. Lienhard, (trans.), *Origen: Homilies on Luke; Fragments on Luke,* 5–6.

4. Whether or not it was strictly a Paschal meal scarcely impinges on the present discussion.

and expressed in foot-washing. Nonetheless, the institution narrative is present in John 6 in a midrash or homiletic re-working.[5]

## LITURGICAL REDACTION

An indication of the primitiveness of the tradition is the manner in which the words of institution of the bread and wine are not as parallel and balanced as might be expected in a later and more elaborated formulary, such as in the present Eucharistic liturgy. Yet note the absence in Mark of "Do this in memory of me," an admittedly important formula, especially in the present debate, but one that does not seem to be part of the Markan tradition. We are left with the question whether that makes it more primitive, earlier, or perhaps later than the Pauline.

Matthew's changes reflect how he redacts Mark, whom he mostly follows. He also creates a closer parallelism and greater balance between the words over the bread and the cup, suggesting how the thrust of the Eucharistic tradition is towards greater inner balance and parallelism within the words of institution. Matthew further adds: "unto the forgiveness of sins," just as earlier, to "you shall call his name Jesus," is added, "he shall save his people from their sins." The forgiveness brought by Jesus continues to be available to the community through the Eucharist.

Luke 22:19–20 contains tiny but still interesting additions. He follows Paul in the words over the cup ("this cup is the new covenant in my blood") but then adds the Markan words "which is being poured out for many/you". This suggests that *Luke* is probably the last of the Synoptic texts to be written down, at a more advanced and more mixed stage of the tradition.

While the Eucharist indubitably has firm roots in the Last Supper, the two are not the same thing *simpliciter*. The suffering of the cross and its divine vindication in the resurrection are anticipated in the one and celebrated with thanksgiving in the other. Clearly, the burden of proof lies on those who would deny a Last Supper during which there were solemn "words of institution" spoken by Jesus, who did and said certain things regarding bread and wine, that provide a firm Christological basis for the celebration of the Eucharist. That, however, is not to import into

---

5. Jesus' statement that "I am the bread of life" (John 6:34–35) parallels the Synoptics' "This is my Body." In verse 51, "The bread that I shall give is my flesh for the life of the world" gives the Johannine form of the words of institution, "given for you," in Luke 22:19.

any reconstructed *ipsissima verba Jesu*, the full theological significance of developed Catholic doctrine, much less discipline, for in any event, the formulation of that doctrine, despite its Spirit-led development, will always fail to express the totality of Jesus' experience, being, and purpose. It would be much less legitimate to import into such a reconstructed *ipsissima verba Jesu* customary but not theologically established attitudes about the implications of such a reconstruction for the non-ordination of women.

## AVOIDING FUNDAMENTALISM

In arguing any theological case from the Last Supper, we must avoid fundamentalist literalism. Whatever Jesus did and said there and then, he did and said once, but we have five canonical versions[6] (1 Cor 11:23–25; Mark 14:22–25; Matt 26:26–29; Luke 22:15–20; John 6:51–58),[7] each filtered through the lens of a local church, worshipping and witnessing in a given context and, sometimes at least, striving to balance different interpretations. Furthermore, in exploring what these words and actions meant at the time of the Last Supper, context is largely defined by a whole series of previous meal fellowships, Jesus' awareness of impending violent death, and expectation of an imminent *eschaton*.

The Eucharistic words of Jesus mediate not some static formula underpinning a fixed canon for millennia to come, but a dynamic reality: the whole saving event of Jesus and the ultimate vindication of good, by its very nature open to deeper readings under new conditions (as the very Eucharistic liturgies themselves, which transmit the memory of the Last Supper, already illustrate). That dynamism is evident in how the temporal non-advent of an imminent *parousia* altered both the consciousness of the Church and the manner in which it read its originating experience, as well as the texts that canonized these experiences. Evidently, those re-readings exhibit the ecclesial concerns and cultural assumptions of their times.

Liturgical texts memorialize the time of origins and inscribe beliefs and practices of the primitive Christian communities onto its beginnings. The Council of Trent did the very same thing, memorializing its

---

6. It is most helpful to study these five texts in parallel. Cf. Aland (ed.), *Synopsis of the Four Gospels*, 284–85.

7. One might also study Didache 9:1—10:7.

canonized, liturgical practise onto the Lukan account of the Last Supper. *Ordinatio Sacerdotalis*, and the latest document from the CDF, continue this, but do so to argue a case that has insufficient basis in these texts. They do so moreover, in an ahistorical and naive manner. That may or may not have been catechetically and canonically legitimate in a different epoch, but it provides no firm basis for arguing that the intention of Jesus at the Last Supper included or excluded appropriately graced women from being validly consecrated to guide the people of God and to preside at the Holy Eucharist as it is celebrated in the Catholic Church today.

## DIVERSE AND VARIEGATED TRAJECTORIES

First-century Eucharistic prayer, moreover, was not at all reducible to formulaic recitation of the supposed *ipsissima verba Jesu* at the Last Supper, but displayed considerable diversity. Its roots may well lie in the intersection of a ritual of sharing one loaf[8] as a memorial of Jesus and the identification of the food and drink ritually consumed with the resurrected body and blood of the Lord, to enact community and to empower resistance to imperial domination. But that developed with considerable interactive diversity. Ignatius of Antioch and Justin Martyr witness to a common cup used in several early Christian communities, but many see the evening-meal section of the Apostolic Tradition as pointing to individual cups. Even this loaf-breaking did not necessarily follow a formal, scripted, invariant procedure. The as-yet-unfinished, historical reconstruction of the developments that occurred demands careful sifting of the evidence through reconstruction or inference.[9] Rather than postulating a linear narrative, considerable divergence is disclosed.

This is equally true of the sacramental motif of identification of the bread and wine in the communion with the resurrected body and blood of the Lord. This occurred in and through different, distinguishable trajectories within primitive Christianity. We can infer that these variegated traditions were received across a spectrum of different ways, from acceptance to modification to rejection. Paul's quasi-technical language of

---

8. The *artos* referred to by Paul in 1 Cor 10:16–17 indicates breaking and sharing of *one loaf*, something diminished in a mass of separate wafers.

9. The massive amount of research on this subject is most helpfully summarized—and with an extensive bibliography—by Shaver, "A Eucharistic Origins Story," Part 1; *The Breaking of the Loaf*, 204–22 and part 2: *The Body and Blood of Christ*, 298–317. Note especially his diagram on p. 311.

"received and handed on" (*parelabon . . . kai paredōka*) is formal and weighty, similar to his effectively creedal language about the death-resurrection of Jesus. He almost certainly "received" this from early leader-confessors, like Ananias, or even from Peter or James. Whether precisely in this form or in a more primitive, less formalized version, this narrative is ancient and probably comes from Syria in the mid-40s CE.

It seems equally clear, however, that not all early communities, including most notably that of the Didache, knew that tradition. Arguably, it reached that community not through the Pauline but through the Matthean community. Without going to the unwarranted extreme of reducing the institution narrative to an interpretative, catechetical etiology, it is nonetheless highly probable that traditions traceable to Paul or Mark or the Didache were not transmitted everywhere at a very early date.

The implied catechetical focus is evident in the text of John 6, which retains the link with the body and blood tradition known to Paul, but does so within midrashic developments that take account of other interpretative tendencies and even rejection of that link, among elements in the Johannine community. Tracing the trajectory through the Lukan tradition is made more complicated by the fact that there is manuscript attestation to a shorter Lukan text, where in 22:19, after "This is my body," we neither find "do this in memory of me" nor the following verse 22 about the cup as "the new covenant in my blood." Today most scholars accept as original—and certainly canonical—the longer text, the one including verses omitted in the shorter text. That, however, points to a group or at least a tendency within the Lukan community that either downplayed, if not eliminated, the prayer over the cup, even if that approach did not in the end, win acceptance.

In reading John 6, it is important to bear in mind that it is not dealing with objections from Judaism as such, but from some groups of Jewish Christians, who, because of rejection of food sacrifice, hesitated to apply sacrificial symbolism to the Eucharistic cup. These, as verses 59–60 make clear, were from among Jesus' "followers," and there were "many" of them. That group who, some have argued, drank water rather than wine in the cup, did not succeed in imposing its ascetic agenda.

## A PROVISIONAL MAPPING

The trajectory from the memory of the Lord's Supper to the Eucharist of the second century is complicated. If, despite the massive scholarship behind them, such reconstructions must be considered provisional, that is even more the case of any vestigial assumption that we actually know in exact detail what happened on the momentous occasion of the Last Supper itself. Here I take as given that the Last Supper was not merely an etiology to provide a basis for emerging Christian table-fellowship, but a real and unique event during which Jesus did speak solemn words of interpretation over the food from an expectation of his impending murder against a background of imminent eschatology. Accordingly:

1. There was a pre-Pauline Last Supper narrative, perhaps with variations.
2. Paul, as he makes clear, "received" this, possibly, though not certainly, from eyewitnesses.
3. Mark receives and transmits this oral tradition, either from pre-Pauline or even Pauline sources.
4. Among proto-Johannine groups, and prior to John's Gospel, oral transmissions from Pauline and/or Markan sources are received in divergent ways.
5. Matthew receives the Markan narrative with only the slightest redaction.
6. "Shorter Luke" receives Mark but deletes the sacrificial symbolism of the cup.
7. "Longer Luke," the canonical text, corrects "Shorter Luke," probably using the Pauline text.
8. The proto-Johannine groups display different tendencies, including: rejection of flesh-and-blood sacrificial symbolism; celebrations using water rather than wine; and importantly, the anti-Docetic tendency upholding sacramental realism. That latter group shapes the canonical Johannine text.
9. At the beginning of the second century there are various combinations and permutations in circulation.
10. These permutations come into contact with each other and mix freely, while allowing for difference.

11. There is a movement towards standardization, but this is never complete or uniform. The Assyrian Church of the East, recognized as having: *"true sacraments and . . . apostolic succession, the priesthood and the Eucharist,"*[10] in one of the most ancient Eucharistic prayers extant, does not have a Last Supper institution narrative.

There is clearly an immense amount of research to be completed before what has been sketched out here can be considered anything close to complete. But for present purposes, it establishes beyond reasonable doubt that we do not know exactly and with certainty the details of the historical Last Supper, certainly not in such a way as to be able to claim that what transpired there rules out definitively the possibility of women being ordained to presidency at the Eucharist.

## INCLUSIVE SOLIDARITY IN JESUS' MEALS

Not only the Last Supper but all the meals celebrated by Jesus in his inclusive solidarity are transmitted to us through the lens of Eucharistic celebrations in the primitive Church. This is particularly evident in Luke, where we finds ten such meals (5:27–39; 7:36–50; 9:10–17; 10:38–42; 11:37–54; 14:1–35; 19:1–10—the Last Supper, where all of these meals are recapitulated in the great meal before Jesus dies—then 24:13–33 and 24:36–49).

The Last Supper encapsulates all the previous meals and at the same time it belongs to eschatology and to Jesus' risen life as a promise of inclusion in the heavenly messianic banquet. By embodying these themes, the Eucharist makes the Church, not abstractly but concretely. These stories tell us little enough about the Eucharist in itself—the canonical preoccupation—rather, they show us what Eucharist tells us about Christian life in the Church.

The first meal story (5:27–39) shows how the Eucharist summons its participants to *metanoia*, change in attitude and behavior, brought about by solidarity with Jesus at table. The second story (7:36–50) relates Eucharist to reconciliation and calls us to welcome one another into true community. In the third meal (9:10–17), there is magnificent, messianic

---

10. *Unitatis Redintegratio*, 15. Intercommunion between Assyrians and Chaldean Catholics is approved, according to pastoral need. Pontifical Council for Promoting Christian Unity, *Guidelines for Admission to the Eucharist between the Chaldean Church and the Assyrian Church of the East*, Rome, 20 July 2001.

hospitality. Luke consciously introduces key expressions from the Eucharistic Liturgy as he does in his Last Supper narrative and will again in that of Emmaus. Use of the term fragments, *klasmata*, in verse 7 suggests not only intertextuality with Didache 9.4 ("Concerning the fragmented bread [*klasmata*], scattered on the mountains but gathered up [*synagein*] to become one") but emerging liturgical practice in various places. The language is liturgical throughout.

In the fourth meal (11:37–54), Jesus, in his corrective to narrow, legalistic thinking, is addressing Christians in the Lukan communities who have a Pharisaic attitude.[11] This is developed in the fifth narrative (14:1–35), which raises the question of who are we going to invite to the Eucharist: with whom do we want or not want to develop solidarity. The dinner described in the parable would be a sign that the Messiah had come, inviting us to see Eucharistic celebration as promise of the messianic banquet.

In the sixth (19:1–10), we again find Jesus addressed as "Lord," this time by Zacchaeus, an indication of post-resurrection Eucharist. By actually doing what Jesus had earlier demanded of the Pharisees (11:41–42), Zacchaeus becomes the *typos* of those who give up all things to follow Jesus.

The Lukan Last Supper recapitulates these seven meals. They unite us in solidarity with the praxis of Jesus. The Last Supper unites us to his passion, dying and rising in solidarity with oppressed humanity, indeed with humanity as a whole in all its moral ambiguity. The Eucharist fulfils this by extending inclusion to all human beings. The evangelists present the received story of the meal in and through early Christian liturgical texts, thereby both enhancing and obscuring the historical event. It is enhanced by showing its relation to the Eucharist and obscured by making the historical situation difficult to reconstruct in its originating details and next to impossible to use as a basis for deciding who may or may not be ordained to preside at its sacramental memorial.

After presenting the Lord's Supper, Luke has Jesus turn to the announcement of the betrayal and denial, which immediately leads into an argument on the familiar Gospel theme about who is "the greater." Judas is not named, because the one who betrays Christ *now* is the one who seeks to be "greater." This, says the Lukan Jesus, continues in the Church because of the desire for power and its exercise in the manner

---

11. The meal described in 10:38–42 with its important Martha pericope will be discussed in detail in the next chapter.

of "the gentiles," especially in the context of the Eucharist, in constructing Eucharistic presidency as power rather than service, not least when self-interestedly trying to control who may or may not preside at it by insisting that it is open only to those who possess *eminentia gradus*, as the medieval theologians would argue, in a construal that shaped the conversation for centuries.

The Emmaus narrative (24:13–33) in its present form seems undoubtedly a Lukan composition, but specific references to Emmaus and Cleopas probably preserve a historical reminiscence. Employing dramatic irony, Luke has these disciples unable to recognize Jesus, while the reader knows what is really going on. The irony comes to a climax when they say "it is now the third day": on the day of hope, they are hopeless. The disciples offer Jesus hospitality still thinking he is a stranger. It is Jesus who takes the bread—it is always the resurrected Jesus who presides at the Eucharist. The whole Eucharistic, liturgical formula is not quoted, but it is unmistakably evoked. In the liturgical act their eyes are opened, the stranger disappears; there are no strangers in the Eucharist. In the tenth and final meal story (24:36–49) the Eucharist is a missionary event proclaiming the forgiveness of sins to the whole world.

It is probably not possible to decide with certainty, *solely* on the basis of these texts, whether or not women may preside at the Eucharist. The notable presence of women in these narratives, however, is indicative of significant women leaders in the primitive Church. Given that the Eucharist unites us to the resurrected Christ—who has transcended gender difference, and summons its participants to change in attitude and behavior (where inner purification counts more than external ritual)—this probably puts the burden of proof on those who would exclude the possibility of women presbyters. This is all the more so when coupled with disavowal of any excluding desire for power and the exercise of it in the manner of the gentiles. Reflection on the Martha tradition, in the next chapter, will strengthen that inference.

## THE COUNCIL OF TRENT

Some might wish to pole vault over all these historical, exegetical, and hermeneutical nuances, by appealing directly to the Council of Trent. Conservative, populist writing frequently claims that the Council of Trent so comprehensively dealt with the question of Holy Orders as to exclude the possibility of women's ordination. Trent, in fact, did not even discuss the issue of women's ordination, which could hardly have even arisen because of the medieval mindset of all the participants[12]—one shared, indeed, by the contemporary Protestant reformers.

The *Preliminary Remark* to Trent's canons on the priesthood reads:

> And because many errors are at this time disseminated and many things are taught and maintained ... in opposition to this ancient faith ... this council, ... after many and grave deliberations maturely touching these matters, has resolved ... to condemn, and to eliminate from holy Church, by means of the canons subjoined, whatsoever is opposed to this most pure faith and sacred doctrine.

Trent did not attempt to say everything about Holy Orders in a definitive way. It aimed at confronting and correcting what it regarded as contemporary doctrinal error.

As regards the priesthood, it focused on affirming it as a reality of the new covenant, a sacrament instituted by Christ. It did that by Pope Pius IV promulgating: *The True and Catholic Doctrine, Touching the Sacrament of Order, Decreed and Published by the Holy Synod of Trent, in the Seventh Session, in Condemnation of the Errors of Our Time*, on 15 July 1558. The first chapter *On the Institution of the Priesthood of the New Law*, reads:

> ... in the New Testament, the Catholic Church has received, from the institution of Christ, the holy visible sacrifice of the Eucharist; it must needs also be confessed, that there is, in that Church, a new, visible, and external priesthood[;] ... this priesthood was instituted by the same Lord our Saviour, and that to the apostles, and their successors in the priesthood.

Nothing is said about whom those successors might one day be. Those crafting the conciliar text almost certainly assumed those successors would be similar to themselves. But that remains an assumption that cannot wholly determine the meaning of the text, something that cannot be simply reduced to the *mens auctoris*.

Something of the memorializing methodology of Trent is revealed in the second chapter *On the Seven Orders*:

> [F]rom the very beginning *(sic)* of the church, the names of the following orders, and the ministrations proper to each one of them, are known to have been in use; to wit, those of subdeacon,

---

12. To be examined in detail in chapter 5.

acolyte, exorcist, lector, and door-keeper.... No one ought to doubt that Order is truly and properly one of the seven sacraments of holy church.

The same methodology is operative in Canon 2:

> If anyone says, that Order, or sacred ordination is not truly and properly a sacrament instituted by Christ the Lord ... let him be anathema.

Similarly, the text *On the Sacrifice of the Mass*, promulgated on 17 September 1557, specifies how it concerns "all errors and heresies being repelled." Chapter 1, "On the institution of the most holy Sacrifice of the Mass," reads:

> He, therefore, our God and Lord, though He was about to offer Himself once on the altar of the cross unto God the Father ... nevertheless, because His priesthood was not to be extinguished by His death, in the Last Supper, on the night in which He was betrayed ... declaring Himself *(sic)* constituted a priest forever, according to the order of Melchisedech, He ... delivered (His own body and blood) to be received by His apostles, whom He then constituted priests of the New Testament; and by those words, "Do this in commemoration of me," He commanded them and their successors in the priesthood, to offer (them); even as the Catholic Church has always understood and taught.

That Jesus is "a priest forever, according to the order of Melchisedech," is affirmed of the Messiah in Psalm 110:4, referred to in Hebrews 6:20 and alluded to in Genesis 14:14–20. The historical Jesus, however, in so far as we know him, never said it of himself. Nevertheless, in accordance with Trent's methodology and textual genre, it is quite legitimate to say that he did: all Scripture is the word of God eternally uttered by the eternal Word and therefore typologically by Jesus, the Word of God incarnate. By extension, since the faith of the Church is continuously guided by the Spirit, what the Church does at Trent cannot be other than what it has always done. That provides a key to understanding Trent's inscriptive appeal to Luke 22:19 in its second canon on the priesthood:

> If anyone says, that by those words, "Do this for the commemoration of me," Christ did not institute the apostles priests; or, did not ordain that they, and other priests should offer His own body and blood; let him be anathema.

How to "receive" such texts today, however, remains an important question.

## NEO-TRIDENTINISM

Semioticians refer to creation and interpretation of texts as encoding and decoding: there being no such thing as an uncoded message. Decoding involves not only basic recognition and comprehension of what a text *says*, but also the interpretation and evaluation of its meaning with reference to relevant codes. Decodings do not follow inevitably from encodings, the process involves interpretation. Is a text received, consumed, or constructed? The *lieu* of the text becomes an *espace* for the *interpretant*. Encoding and decoding are socially contingent practices, not simply *sending* and *receiving*, linked by conveyance of a *message* considered the exclusive vehicle of meaning. One may hardly imagine, as literalists seem to do, a fixed, unalterable meaning wrapped in an encoding, later to be unwrapped or re-wrapped in a decoding.

Trent does not simply re-wrap a scriptural text's supposedly fixed meaning, for us to unwrap it today. It creates a new meaning—as the Church does when it faithfully but creatively reads the text in new contexts. Reception is dynamic and co-creative. One need only read the prologue to the Gospel of John to verify this. Reception hermeneutics focuses on the process and appropriateness of interpretation, rather than on a supposedly fixed, literal text. It takes into account the transformation between past and present horizons of understanding, in contrast to an historical positivism that imagines a text as a kind of fixed, archetypal substance present in a literary work. The key to "reading" "Christ's" institution of Orders is neither to memorialize what Jesus supposedly did in *illo tempore* by inscribing its medieval understanding, nor to dismiss it as ahistorical, but to see it for what it more adequately is: the action in the Church of the resurrected Christ who lives forever to make intercession for us.

After Trent, controversy over how its canons should be interpreted began almost immediately, contributing to an eventual distortion of what it actually legislated and intended, according to a mentality that simplistically and reductively viewed it as having definitively resolved all questions. That Council incorporated, redefined, and updated the norms of the previous centuries to such an extent that it became preferable and common to view these norms and the theology that underpinned them through the lens of the Council's decrees, losing sight, in the process, of context and development. Theological insights and Church practices from the first millennium that could not be so neatly fitted into this schema were de-emphasized, sidelined, and often simply forgotten, as it became obligatory to refer to Trent for solutions to every question, doctrinal or institutional. Neo-Tridentine Catholicism took on a uniformity that scarcely any scholar from an earlier period would have imagined possible.

Pope Paul III had seen Trent principally as a response to what was judged to be the errors of the Protestant reformers. Emperor Charles V had wanted it to be about organizational reform of the church. Paul III feared that would boil down to attacking corruption in the papal court. In the event, it sensibly did both, and in parallel. But "the Council thus did not undertake a comprehensive review of Catholicism."[13] It did not say even a single word about the most impressive Christian undertaking of the time—evangelization outside Europe.

Methodologically speaking, when Trent affirmed that the practice of private confession to a priest had been observed since the beginning, as, so it affirmed, had minor orders, it was exhibiting a principle that underlay almost all its doctrinal pronouncements; manifesting a hermeneutical mindset that insists on unwavering continuity. It was not until the historical writing on Trent by Hubert Jedin in 1946[14] and then that on reform by Yves Congar in 1950[15] that this static misunderstanding of continuity began to be reappraised. Trent memorialized the origins of the Church, inscribing beliefs and practices of the contemporary Church onto its beginnings. At the time, it seemed canonically and catechetically brilliant, necessary indeed, to effect reform in the Church. Never a final, comprehensive statement about all of Catholic belief, but a counter-refutation of a contemporary rejection of some Church doctrines, it said

---

13. O'Malley, "The Hermeneutic of Reform: a Historical Analysis," 531–33.

14. Hubert Jedin was the most important historian in a Church that was finally accepting the historical-critical method as the approach necessary to understand the Church as a historical subject, thereby surpassing the limits of conceiving Church history in primarily theological terms, as "sacred history." The first volume, *A History of the Council of Trent, Volume I: The Struggle for the Council* (1951) in a breakthrough methodology, paid detailed attention to background and context.

15. Congar, *Vraie et fausse réforme dans l'Eglise* (1950).

nothing on many questions, and in particular, never decided the question of women's ordination.

## "DO THIS IN MEMORY OF ME"

Moreover, the institution of the Eucharist is not merely the institution of a sacrament but the establishing of the Eucharist and its presidency as an ongoing, concrete *imitation* of Christ's saving actions, his praxis. Among the various aspects attributable to the Eucharist—memorial; sacrifice; thanksgiving; blessing—*sequela Christi* is the root theological reality coordinating and validating the others. The *imitation* of Christ, the Pauline construction of the Gospel invitation to "Follow me," sees the Christian life as a participation in Christ: life in Christ. The Johannine Last Supper foot-washing narrative and command emphasize that this Eucharistic imitation of Christ is not merely ritual repetition of the words of Jesus, however solemn, but a project both of spiritually living inwardly (in contemplation) and outwardly (in a life of service) the central mystery of Christ's life on earth.

The mandate to "Do this in memory of me," involves much more than ritually repeating Jesus' Last Supper actions in the liturgy—even if it includes that. It enjoins lives that imitate the praxis of Jesus that led to his passion. As such, the Eucharist is the Church's effective memorial of Christ, making *his* saving deeds present through *our* lives. Consequently, debating what is always and everywhere necessary for a true celebration of the Eucharist simply cannot be *exclusively* based on the external actions of Jesus at the Last Supper—even if these were recoverable in detail. Speaking in strictly theological terms, it can hardly be affirmed, much less established, that only a male can preside at the Eucharist: "as if the Church is otherwise unable to express its fundamental faith in the historical events of Christ's life, death and resurrection as the unique source of its salvation."[16]

## IS THIS DECLARATION DEFINITIVE?

There are three main trajectories in seeking to decide on an assumed, definitive status of the position articulated in the 1976 document *Inter Insigniores*, summed up in this Declaration (2018), as well as the earlier

16. Laurance, *The Eucharist as the Imitation of Christ*, 296.

documents it resumes. The first is to agree unquestioningly and uncritically. The second is to dismiss it as historically unfounded, exegetically naive, and of no theological or organizational significance. Some in that camp would dismiss it out of hand as being hopelessly misogynist. The third is to acknowledge the ministry of authority in the Church as having weighty, theological significance, while noting that a statement can be *authoritative* without fulfilling all the conditions necessary to make it doctrinally *binding* and that therefore the practice it enshrines is *open to further development*.

Karl Rahner (1904–84), one of the most influential and faithful, Catholic theologians of the twentieth century, offered an enlightened expression of this third and more nuanced approach. Rahner focuses on the strictly theological aspect of the issue: "whether it is certain that the Christian revelation in its unchangeable substance (*sic*), excludes women from the priestly ministry in the Catholic Church."[17] He examines what he considers the six parts of *Inter Insigniores* (1976):

1. in its first part it postulates a "constant tradition" always and everywhere indisputable and uniformly excluding women from this ministry;

2. in the second part, the conclusion is drawn from the judgement that "Christ did not call any women to be part of the Twelve," that Jesus intended in principle to exclude women from the priestly ministry for all times and under all sociological conditions—notwithstanding the declaration's admission that Scripture has not "made the matter immediately obvious";[18]

3. in the third section, it states that the apostles, convinced of their duty of fidelity to the Lord, never considered conferring ordination upon women;

4. in the fourth section, it draws the conclusion that the Church's practice of excluding women from the priesthood has a normative character.

5. The fifth—and sixth—appeal to the "analogy of fifth" to shed light on conclusions reached in the first four parts.

---

17. Rahner, *Women and the Priesthood*, 35.
18. Rahner, *Women and the Priesthood*, 36.

Rahner accepts this document as an authentic declaration of the "Roman authorities,"[19] one with formal authority that cannot be judged simply as if a statement of other theologians, but nevertheless insists that despite papal approval, it is not a definitive decision: "It is in principle reformable and it can (which is not to say *a priori* that it must) be erroneous."[20]

## WHAT KIND OF TRADITION?

A fundamental question to be faced is whether the uninterrupted tradition to which *Inter Insigniores* appeals is a "divine or merely human tradition." Thus theologians, while attempting to appreciate the decree as impartially as possible, also have the duty of critically examining it so that if a negative result emerged, the declaration can be impugned as erroneous. Its essential argument assumes an intention on the part of Jesus, not historically or sociologically conditioned, that holds for all times. But the argumentation proceeds without it ever being clarified as to where the burden of proof lies. Implicitly, it is shifted onto those who would argue the other way.

*Inter Insigniores* acknowledges that some of Paul's ordinances on women's behavior are influenced by "the customs of the period" and therefore "no longer have normative value."[21] Moreover, in the declaration, the transition from the concept of "Apostle" and "the Twelve" to those of "priest" and "bishop," is too simplistic to accord with present-day knowledge of the origins, structure, and organization of the primitive Church.[22] The declaration jumps over all the difficult but fundamentally important and theologically unavoidable questions about the concrete emergence of the Church and its origin from Jesus. Chief among these is whether the imminent eschatology of the post-resurrection time makes it possible at all to look to Jesus and the apostles for an unalterable blueprint in regard to the structure of the emerging communities that could really be related to later times, unambiguously and forever. Moreover, the declaration does not offer a comprehensive concept of priestly ministry, effectively restricting it to the sacramental power of consecration. That

---

19. We shall return to this issue in chapter 7.
20. Rahner, *Women and the Priesthood*, 37.
21. Rahner, *Women and the Priesthood*, 40.
22. To be discussed in more detail in chapter 7.

limitation, one may add, has bedevilled both sides of the contemporary discussion of women's ordination.

Rahner insists that a practical rule of action can be socio-culturally conditioned and open to change as a result of a changed socio-cultural situation. Polygamy and war in the Old Testament, slavery in New Testament times, the ban on usury until the eighteenth century—not to mention the insistence on women being veiled in Church down almost to today—are examples of concrete rules of action coexisting with moral principles to which they were opposed in the abstract, but where the contradiction could not be perceived in earlier socio-cultural situations. If, in the past, there were socio-cultural reasons for not electing a woman leader of a congregation, it needs to be clearly proven that these reasons of themselves are insufficient to explain the presumed attitude of Jesus and the apostles.[23] If it is assumed that Jesus and the apostles had more substantial reasons for allegedly doing so, then it would need to be demonstrated what these were, something the declaration does not do.

To Rahner's thinking, the mere fact that Jesus was male is no answer to the question of women's ordination, since it is not clear that a person fulfilling Christ's mandate and "in that sense, but not otherwise," acting *in persona Christi*[24] must at the same time represent Christ precisely in his maleness.[25] If that cannot be clarified, the "conclusion seems inescapable that the attitude of Jesus and the Apostles is sufficiently explained by the cultural and sociological milieu in which they acted."[26] Discussion may and must continue, especially with the regard to the theological and especially ecclesiological implications of the consequences of women's sociological emancipation and how that may change the consciousness of the Church as a whole. The declaration insists that in this question,

---

23. The later "Christ as Bridegroom" argument attempts to do this. It will be discussed in chapter 6.

24. The connection of *in persona Christi* with the exclusive competence of the priest to consecrate the Eucharist was underlined in post-Conciliar documents: the synod of 1971 stated that: "*solus sacerdos in persona Christi agere valet ad praesidendum et perficiendum sacrificale convivium,*" Ench. Vat. 4, 1166; the letter of the Congregation for the Doctrine of the Faith, Sacerdotium ministeriale, 1983, stresses that "*munus tam grave conficiendi mysterium eucharisticum adimplere valeant [episcopi et presbyteri] . . . ut ipsi . . . non communitatis mandato, sed agant in persona Christi,*" AAS 75 (1983): 1006; this is recalled in the 1983 CIC: "*Minister, qui in persona Christi sacramentum Eucharistiae conficere valet, est solus sacerdos valide ordinatus,*" can. 900, 1.

25. Rahner, *Women and the Priesthood*, 43.

26. Rahner, *Women and the Priesthood*, 44–45.

the Church must remain faithful to Christ, but what fidelity means in connection with this problem remains an open question.[27] Exactly the same may be said about the tenth and last paragraph of the most recent document.

## *ROMA LOCUTA EST?*

Attempts to close the discussion for the sake of discipline, but in doing so, claiming that the present position of the Roman magisterium is definitive, can scarcely be considered theologically coherent. A moratorium, even if canonically or organizationally realistic or desirable, cannot be declared in theology. Like all believers, theologians seek, however haltingly, to love God with their whole heart, soul, mind, and strength (Mark 12:30). Engaged in *fides quaerens intellectum*, faith seeking understanding, they seek in a particular way to love God with "their whole mind." They seek to understand infinite, unrestricted being and love, something only possible—and even then in an ever incomplete way—because the Holy Spirit has been poured into the heart of the believer (Rom 5:5). God having created us for Godself, has endowed us with "a pure, detached, disinterested desire simply to know." Since the object of this intellectual desire is God, this "eros of the mind" is unrestricted. For theologians, not to respond to that would be to deny God's purpose in creation.

The desire to understand cannot be reduced merely to assent to teaching, since it is a never-ending intellectual quest to understand that teaching in all respects, including its possible limitations. Without it there would arise no inquiry, no wonder, no questioning, and ultimately no adequate understanding. Without it there would never have been an Athanasius, an Augustine, an Aquinas, a Newman, a Rahner, or the creative feminist theologians of today. "The immanent source of transcendence in man is his detached, disinterested, unrestricted desire to know. As it is the origin of all his questions, it is the origin of the radical, further questions that take him beyond the defined limits of particular issues."[28] This is not reducible to a merely objective quest. Faith as the knowledge born of love proceeds from falling in love in an unrestricted manner:[29] falling in love with God.

---

27. Rahner, *Women and the Priesthood*, 47.
28. Lonergan, *Insight: A Study of Human Understanding*, 97, 659.
29. Lonergan, *Method in Theology*, 105–6.

As to the future: the process of questioning and developing traditions continues indefinitely, precluding any static interpretation of Christianity or any contextually constructed formulation of a Christian praxis-doctrine as final and irreformable. Part of its very structure is the realization, at once humbling and liberating, that after us will come people who will understand and articulate all that we hold dear in a more adequate manner than we do.

As to the past, it provides "the *Wirkungsgeschichte* possibilizing the text-interpreter conversation."[30] It is not simply a fixed object of study but a source of possible meanings. Reason is always rooted in historicity. One can neither leap over tradition, nor freeze it in ideology.

> Our historical consciousness is always filled with the variety of voices in which the echo of the past is heard. Only in the multifariousness of such voices does it exist; this constitutes the nature of the tradition in which we want to share and have a part.[31]

To access past meaning in totality is not possible. Even less possible is the notion that having once accessed it, one may contain its fullness in an unalterable formula or law.

## BEYOND DOCTRINAL LITERALISM

As soon as the Church grasped the necessity of a hermeneutically aware, historical approach to the meaning of Scripture,[32] it applied with great sophistication the tools of redaction and form criticism to scriptural narrative, highlighting the contextual nature of meaning. This was partly influenced by the need to explain the meaning in context of its own dogmatics at the time of the classical articulation of those dogmas. Ironically, it hesitates to do the same to the narratives that enshrined, transmitted, and canonized the interpretations that shape its own ecclesial practice.

---

30. Gadamer, *Truth and Method*, 258.
31. Gadamer, *Truth and Method*, 284.
32. This may be said to have begun with *Divino Afflante Spiritu* (30 September 1943), the encyclical of Pope Pius XII, on promoting biblical studies, commemorating the fiftieth anniversary of *Providentissimus Deus* (1893) of Pope Leo XIII and to have been solidly established by *Dei Verbum* of Vatican II (1965) before reaching a new level of hermeneutical sophistication in *"The Interpretation of the Bible in the Church,"* presented by the Pontifical Biblical Commission to Pope John Paul II on 23 April 1993. Literalism, whether in exegesis or theology, forms no part of Catholic theological method.

We bid farewell to scriptural literalism but cling to doctrinal literalism. Joseph Ratzinger, later Pope Benedict XVI, expressed this very clearly:

> The point of view which sees only Scripture as what is unclear, but the teaching office as what is clear, is a very limited one and that to reduce the task of theology to the proof of the presence of the statements of the teaching office in the sources, is to threaten the primacy of these sources which ... would ultimately destroy the serving character of the teaching office.[33]

Theology deals with the Absolute: through the analogy of faith it can discourse meaningfully about it, but it does not possess any absolute language with which to do so. Ecclesiology does not first have an extra-linguistic understanding of the Church that subsequently expresses itself in doctrine. Consequently, conversations between narratives are intrinsic to retaining this basic identity of signification that happens through the emergence of meaning in the conversation.

An example may illustrate our problematic. The insistence in 2001 by the ecclesial center of authority, on a rigid adherence to literalist translation of liturgical texts, over a balanced search for dynamic equivalence,[34] not only masks a deeply conservative and ideologically driven mindset, but also cuts off the very branch of the living ecclesial tree on which the liturgical texts themselves first grew. A new narrative transmitting a new synthesis is always possible, because narratives and the words that construct them always have around them a "circle of the unexpressed" drawing the conversation into the "infinity of the unsaid"—surely a desirable scenario for any ecclesiological narrative that wishes to communicate how the infinity of God's love is ever at work among God's people.

What then is the genre of statements claiming that an ecclesial practice (as distinct from the Tradition of the Church), which although shaped by changeable socio-cultural contexts and their presuppositions, claims for itself a definitive and unchangeable status? I suggest that it is *rhetoric*, a genre that intends to persuade and that may be analyzed as

---

33. J. Ratzinger (later Pope Benedict XVI), "The Dogmatic Constitution on Divine Revelation," in Vorgrimler (ed.), *Commentary on the Documents of Vatican II*, vol. 3, 197.

34. *Liturgiam Authenticam* (2001), with its unworkable insistence on a literal translation of Latin liturgical texts, subject to a *recognitio* by the Vatican, in a process requiring a line-by-line translation review, produced dismal results in the imposed, Latinized English translation of the Eucharistic Prayers. This was largely abrogated by Pope Francis in his *motu proprio Magnum Principium* (2017).

such. Classically, rhetoric—not just stylistic ornamentation but persuasive discourse—cultivated the art of persuasion. Renewed interest in the epistemological implications of rhetorical tropes reflects a reappraisal of objectivism. Epistemology, and with it theology, is emerging from the hegemony of objectivist language when it used to draw on its premises to produce statements alleged to be incapable of modification. All discourse is unavoidably rhetorical. This reflection is likewise rhetorical: it attempts to persuade readers that constructing an assumption of the non-ordainability of women as unchangeable does scant justice to the profundity and nuance of the Catholic intellectual tradition.

Words are also signs. They signify levels of meaning. Beyond its dictionary meaning, its denotation, a word will have connotations. Meaning includes both. Denotation offers the putatively definitional, literal, obvious, commonsense meaning of a sign—what dictionaries attempt to provide. Denotation may seem to lead to a chain of connotations as if it were an underlying and primary meaning, but denotation is not the first meaning, although it often pretends to be. It is no more than the last of the connotations; one that seeks both to establish and close the reading; the superior myth whereby the text "pretends to return to language as nature."[35] Connotation produces the illusion of denotation; of language as transparent, of *signifier* and *signified* as identical: the illusion that a widely repeated and shared *signifié*—as when the CDF continually repeats that women cannot receive Holy Orders—is the natural meaning of a text.

Denotation and connotation combine to produce ideology, a third order of signification, in the shape of myth. Myths are not simply fables, but dominant ideologies of their time and place. They point out and make us understand something; but impose that something on us through the ideological function of "naturalization." They make dominant historico-cultural values, attitudes, and beliefs seem "natural," "normal," "obvious," and thus "objective" and "true." Social groups tend to regard as "natural" whatever consolidates privilege and power. That, in turn, raises the question of who gains or retains privilege and power and, correlatively, who is disempowered by a given ideological construction of a theological problematic such as the one under discussion here.

Who, one may ask, is empowered and who is disempowered by excluding women from Holy Orders? From this perspective, the putative non-ordainability of women may be considered myth, not only because

35. Barthes, S/Z, 21.

it contains unscientific elements, such as unsustainable assumptions regarding women, but in the sense that it has organized a shared way of seeing the relationship between women and Holy Orders within ecclesial discourse, and seeks rhetorically to make this so dominant as to appear "evident" and "natural," thereby camouflaging an unacceptable dynamic of disempowerment.

## MEMORIALIZING PRESENT PRACTICE

The arguments brought forward by the ecclesial center involve a form of memorializing present practice by inscribing it onto the practice of the primitive Church. To see the limitations of such an approach demands a closer examination of the actual ministry of women in New Testament times. We will explore such ministry in our third chapter.

CHAPTER 3

# Women's Ministry in the New Testament

IN NEW TESTAMENT TIMES, gifted Christian women exercised important leadership ministries in the emerging churches. In their own context, many of these ministries would have been considered diaconal, presbyteral, or episcopal, even if the understanding of those terms and the ministries they referred to were initially, even if Spirit-led, somewhat functional and practical and lacked degrees of definition they would later acquire. But that is also true for the men who exercised such ministries, at least up to the third generation of Christians. The work, ministry, and responsibility involved were effectively the same for both men and women,[1] and in the case of men, these ministers are correctly considered the forerunners of deacons, priests, and bishops, as these ministries and offices came to be understood.

The question then arises in the case of women serving in those ministries, whether considering them as not having exercised a real and true ministry as forerunners of deacons, priests, or even as bishops can be given any strictly theological basis, or whether that discrepancy is primarily a matter of the consequences of a gradual patriarchalization of Church structures.

## FROM PROOF TEXTS TO FEMINIST EXEGESIS

The fruits of the massive amount of New Testament research, both by women exegetes as well as male exegetes who have sought to respond to their findings, raises the question for many as to what blocked

1. Cf. Acts 1:14, 8, especially Acts 2:18, citing Joel 2:29.

theologians from grasping so many now seemingly obvious angles of interpretation of New Testament passages dealing with the ministry of women. Whether in spirituality, apologetics, ecclesiology, or liturgy, the approach to Scripture was one of *dicta probantia*: proof texts. A range of quotations from both Old Testament and New Testament was amassed to justify a preferred understanding or established practice. That was eisegesis: the *status quo* was *read into* the text, which was then cited as proof of the presuppositions already in place. The text was not allowed to interact with existential issues. This, of course, did not arise in a vacuum, since methodologically speaking, groups and tendencies favoring different sets of conclusions and priorities were doing exactly the same thing.

Under those circumstances, the profile of leadership ministry for women in the New Testament—and *a fortiori*, in the historical church—was gradually reduced almost to invisibility. Exegesis was done by men for an undeniably male-dominated Church. Texts, especially those found in the concluding epilogues of Pauline letters, were scarcely read, much less mined for what they said directly or implied indirectly about women's ministry. The reception of Vatican II with its emphasis on the laity, and that in a changing world and Church more appreciative of women,[2] especially as illuminated by ground-breaking research, would change that, though there were notable, earlier attempts to do so.[3]

One important development was the rise of women theologians and exegetes. A significant text from The Pontifical Biblical Commission, *The Interpretation of the Bible in the Church*,[4] speaks of three principal forms of feminist biblical hermeneutics, which it terms: the "radical," the "neo-orthodox," and the "critical" forms. In the commission's view, the first denies all authority to the Bible, maintaining that it has been produced by men simply with a view to confirming age-old androcentrism. The

---

2. In *Laudato Si*, n.103, Pope Francis writes, "The Church acknowledges the indispensable contribution which women make to society through the sensitivity, intuition and other distinctive skill sets which they, more than men, tend to possess . . . ." We need to create still broader opportunities for a more incisive female presence in the Church. Because "the feminine genius is needed in all expressions in the life of society, the presence of women must also be guaranteed in . . . settings where important decisions are made . . . in the Church and in social structures."

3. Already in the nineteenth century, female scholars had challenged Church- and academy-based gendered bias in the interpretation of Paul's female colleagues, especially Lydia, Prisca, and Phoebe. Marshall, *The Recovery of Paul's Female Colleagues in Nineteenth-Century Feminist Biblical Interpretation*, 21–36.

4. Presented to Pope John Paul II on 23 April 1993.

second accepts the Bible as prophetic to the extent that it takes sides on behalf of the oppressed—and thus also of women. The third seeks to rediscover the status and role of women disciples during the life of Jesus and in the Pauline churches. At that historical period, it maintains, equality prevailed. But this equality, it is claimed, has for the most part been concealed in the writings of the New Testament, as a tendency toward patriarchy and androcentrism became increasingly dominant.

To its employment of the historical-critical method, feminist hermeneutics adds two criteria of investigation. A hermeneutic of suspicion requires that one does not simply depend literally on texts as they stand, but, cognisant of the ecclesial *Sitz-im-Leben* in which they were redacted, one looks for indications that may reveal something quite different. Secondly, the study of societies in biblical times notes their social stratification and the position they accorded to women. It emphasizes historical reconstruction and comparison of different situations of woman in the first century. Relative to the norm in Jewish and Greco-Roman societies, the innovations that took shape in the public life of Jesus and in the proto-Pauline Churches, indicate that all disciples of Jesus formed "a community of equals." In this way, one aims to rediscover for today the submerged history of the role of women in the early Church.

Such exegesis has brought many benefits, especially in detecting the presence, significance, and role of women in the New Testament, in Christian origins, and in church office. It helps to unmask and correct certain commonly accepted interpretations that were tendentious and at least unconsciously sought to justify male domination of women in Church and society. In promoting that text, Cardinal J. Ratzinger, then Prefect of the CDF, wrote:

> In the meantime, this methodological spectrum of exegetical work has broadened in a way which could not have been envisioned 30 years ago. New methods and new approaches have appeared, from structuralism to materialistic, psychoanalytic and liberation exegesis.

## HOSTING THE EUCHARISTIC ASSEMBLY

The changes may be illustrated in reading the Martha tradition in the New Testament, at different levels. Pastorally speaking, the hospitality that Jesus receives at the house of Martha poses the problem of how Eucharistic communities are constantly distracted by secondary considerations, with presbyters diverted from what is necessary and critical to the meaning and efficacy of what they do. The dynamic of the Martha pericope operates to lead the reader towards the realization that in the absence of a contemplative dimension, the Eucharistic celebration can become just another duty carried out in a purely functional, if not complaining, manner. There is transubstantiation of the species but no transformation of the people.

In the Lukan meal narrative (10:38–42),[5] Martha is the pivotal character; it is to *her* home (v. 38) that she welcomes Jesus. Mary is *her* sister. Throughout the pericope Jesus is called "Lord" to emphasize that this is a story about believers—it is a catechesis for the Church. For some, this would have seemed no less culturally problematic in those times than in ours. The story of Lydia, the dealer in the purple dye trade in Acts 16:14, also a Lukan narrative, is illuminative. She says to Paul, "if you consider me *a believer* in the Lord, come and stay at *my house*." Among believers, and in contrast to cultural assumptions, a woman can be a full and significant disciple, as both Martha and Mary are here: a woman may host the Eucharistic assembly, as Martha seems to do here. The gospel reverses many cultural values. The inference seems clear.

This Eucharistic hostess is "bothered about many tasks"—literally: much service (*periespato peri pollēn diakonian*). *Diakonia*—service—seems to have two levels of meaning here, referring both to the tasks in hand, as well as to the ministry at the Eucharistic table itself. Luke alludes to these two levels also in Acts 6:2–4. In responding to Martha's complaint, "the Lord"—a Christological title indicating a post-resurrection, ecclesial narrative—effectively ignores her assessment of the situation. Her problem was *not* that she had too much ministry but that *she was neglecting the one thing necessary;* the contemplative base of all action that gives meaning to and puts everything into perspective. The Lord calls Martha by name and indeed repeats it: "Martha, Martha!" We recall "Samuel, Samuel!" in 1 Samuel 3:10, "Simon, Simon!" in Luke 22:31, and "Saul, Saul!" in Acts 9:4. This literary device focuses the attention on the one who is calling, alerting the listener to an important announcement: activism without contemplation results in exhaustion, dissipation, and endless complaining.

---

5. O'Brien, *The Danger in Dining with Jesus*, 258–76.

## LUKE'S MARTHA

But one must look more closely. The inscribed historical situation of Luke 10:28–42 is that of the early Christian missionary movement gathering in house churches. Martha welcomes the resurrected Lord of the Eucharist and his people into her house. She is preoccupied with *diakonia* and *diakonein*, already in Luke's time, technical terms for ecclesial leadership.

From the Pauline literature, one can discern that some women were travelling missionaries and leaders of house churches providing space for the preaching of the word as well as for Eucharistic meal celebrations. Paul fondly mentions many women, and especially their ministry, in his letters: Apphia (Phlm 1:2), Chloe (1 Cor 1:11), Claudia (2 Tim 4:21), Euodia and Syntyche (Phil 4:2), Julia (Rom 16:15), Lois and Eunice (2 Tim 1:5), Mary (Rom 16:6), Nereus' sister (Rom 16:15), Nympha (Col 4:15), Persis (Rom 16:12), Phoebe (Rom 16:1-2), Priscilla (Rom 6:3-5; 1 Cor 16:19; 2 Tim 4:19), Rufus' mother (Rom 16:13), Tryphena and Tryphosa (Rom 16:12), and Junia (Rom 16:7). These women were actively involved in significant ministry and at least some of them, quite unmistakably, were leaders. In early Christian usage, *diakonia* refers to this Eucharistic table service in the house church, though not restricted to it, since it could also include proclamation of the word.

This is still evident in Acts 6–8, despite Luke's redactional interest.[6] The seven Hellenists are appointed to devote themselves to the *diakonia* of the tables, while the Twelve dedicate themselves to the word, but the deacons nevertheless become initiators of the Christian missionary movement and founders of communities. The structural and linguistic affinities between Acts 6:1–6 and Luke 10:38–42 leave traces of the problematic. Just as Martha complains that Mary leaves (*katalipein*) the serving (*diakonein*) to her in order to listen to the word (*ton logon*) of the Lord (*Kyrios*) so the twelve apostles maintain that they cannot leave (*katalipein*) the word (*ton logon*) of God in order to serve (*diakonein*) at tables. In Acts 6:1–6, Luke separates the *diakonia* of the word from that at tables, restricts them to different groups, and subordinates one to the other.

The indispensable function of the deacon is of two sorts. Ignatius of Antioch (c. 35–107) calls the deacons "servers of food and drink" (Ign. Trall. 2:3), principally providing for the poor. They received and administered the offered gifts and distributed them to the needy. Ignatius,

---

6. Fiorenza, "A Feminist Critical Interpretation for Liberation," 30–32.

however, emphasizes that they are "not only servers of food and drink" but "servers of God's church." The deacons are the "servants of the mysteries of Jesus Christ" (Ign. *Trall.* 2:3), clearly implying that they have a ministry at the celebration of the Eucharist. It is also said expressly of deacons that they "serve in the Word of God" (Ign. *Phld.* 11:1); preaching also seems to come within their field of activity.

These two functions, charitable and liturgical, are not separable. Worship and service form an indivisible whole. A *diakonia* not rooted in worship, or a liturgical service which does not develop into *diakonia*, are unthinkable for Ignatius. The deacons appear in their duties as subject to the bishop; Ignatius calls them his fellow-servants (*syndouloi*). He understands the bishop as both the one who presides over worship and who exercises oversight over acts of charity. So the activity of the deacons could not possibly take place apart from a dependence on the bishops.

In 10:38–42, Luke stresses that the *diakonia* of Martha, in its multiple activities, is not the "one thing needful" and is subordinate to "listening to the word." This corresponds to Luke's picture of the role of women in Luke-Acts, which despite its overall, markedly positive tone, whereby Jesus shows a preferential concern for women, never presents a woman preaching the word or leading a house church. Luke nonetheless knows of such female leadership activities since he emphasizes that the married couple Priscilla (often named first) and Aquila took Apollos "aside" in order to instruct him in the way of God (Acts 18:26). Yet he avoids portraying Priscilla as a missionary preacher.

## JOHN'S MARTHA

That Martha and Mary were well-known in the early churches can be seen from the Fourth Gospel. Martha, Mary, and Lazarus are characterized as Jesus' friends whom he loved (John 11:5). In Johannine terms, they are his true disciples and he their teacher. This Evangelist took for granted the Church situation of his time, which included both structure and what would become known as sacrament; yet counteracted some of its tendencies with perceptive correctives to some contemporary, ecclesial attitudes.[7]

The Fourth Gospel, redacted in the 90s, treats of women in Church office when we are told that Martha served at table, *diakonein* (12:2). By

---

7. Brown, *Roles of Women in The Fourth Gospel*, 689–95.

then, the office of *diakonos* already existed in the post-Pauline churches. Waiting on tables was a specific ministry to which the community or its leaders appointed individuals by laying on hands (Acts 6:1–6); originally done for the selection of leaders for the Hellenist Christian community. We do not know precisely how titles were used at this early period, but Raymond Brown suggests that the closest parallel, in the titulary of later Church structure, would be "bishop."

Today we hear and read and use words like deacon, presbyter, and bishop through the prism of two thousand years of their *Wirkungsgeschichte*. The original resonance of "bishop" would have been like that of the word "overseer" today. It meant the one or ones who looked over the community or community of communities. Before Ignatius and even during his lifetime, and in some places later, it was a ministry often exercised by a group rather than an individual. The monarchic episcopate did not prevail in the West before then. It should not be assumed, for example, in Philippi before the middle of the fourth century. In a presbyteral church, the role of women deacons may well have been even more significant.[8]

Martha, in her time and place, was probably one such local "overseer." Luke looks back on the scene from the eighties, and he may have thought that their work was comparable to that done by the deacons in his time, especially if he had begun to think of the apostles as bishops—implicit in the developing notion of the bishops as successors of the apostles.

In the narratives of the angel(s) at the empty tomb, the women are given a message for the disciples. In John, as in Matthew, Mary Magdalene is sent by the risen Lord himself, and announces the standard apostolic proclamation of the resurrection: "I have seen the Lord." Mary Magdalene therefore comes close to meeting the basic Pauline requirements of an apostle; and it is she, not Peter, who is the first to encounter the risen Jesus, according to a tradition that, in all likelihood, is historical. The priority of the manifestation of the resurrected Jesus given to Peter, in Paul and Luke,[9] constructs him as first among "official" witnesses to the resurrection. For that very reason, the secondary place given in the tradition to women disciples, makes the *invention* of a first appearance of the risen

---

8. Abrahamsen, "Women at Philippi: The Pagan and Christian Evidence," 27–29.

9. Writers mostly refer to Paul and Luke in regard to women disciples, but the theme is powerfully present also in *Mark* even if less systematically theologized, Montes-Peral, *El comportamiento de las mujeres discípulas en la pasion de Marcos*, 3–44.

Christ to a woman most improbable. In Western tradition Magdalene was considered "the apostle to the apostles," *apostola apostolorum*.[10]

## MARTHA AS CONFESSOR

Giving a woman, Martha, a role traditionally associated with Peter, seems intentional on John's part. As exemplified in the story of Lazarus, Mary, and Martha, it impinges on how we understand the ministry of Martha. The most striking incident in which Peter witnesses during the ministry of Jesus, besides that of witnessing the first appearance of the risen Jesus, is his confession at Caesarea Philippi (Matt 16:16): "You are the Christ, the Son of the living God." It wins Jesus' praise as reflecting divine revelation. The closest parallel in all the four Gospels is found in John 11:27: "You are the Christ, the Son of God"; found on the lips of Martha in the context of a major revelation to her of Jesus as "the resurrection and the life" and coextensively, of her firm faith in him, confessed and canonically remembered in an ecclesial, creedal formula attributed to her.

Just as other Christian communities thought of Peter as the one who made a supreme confession of Jesus as the Son of God, and the one to whom the risen Jesus first appeared, the Johannine community associated comparable memories with Martha and Mary Magdalene. This does not denigrate Peter's ecclesial authority, any more than the presence of the Beloved Disciple alongside Peter might be wrongly imagined to do so. When the "twelve apostles" were becoming paramount, John wished to recall how other disciples, including women, had also played important apostolic roles in the Jesus movement as well as in the emergence of the primitive Church.[11] Martha is constructed here as exemplifying in her context, the ministry that would later be described as "confessor," often in the title "bishop and confessor," which is to say, she exercised a comparable leadership as overseer (*episkopos*) of the creedal formulation of the faith.

---

10. Calling Magdalene "apostle" is frequent in the famous ninth-century life of Magdalene by Rabanus Maurus: "eam ad apostolos instituit apostolam digna mercede gratie et gloriae, primoque et praecipue honoris privilegio . . . quam ante modicum instituerat resurrectionis evangelistam et ait illi: 'Vade ad fratres meos et dic illis . . .'" Migne, *Patrologia Latina*, 112, 1474B. This emphasis is now included–since June 3rd 2016–in the Roman Missal in the Preface for the feast of St. Mary Magdalene on June 22nd.

11. This point will be further developed in chapter 7.

Discipleship is the primary Christian category for John, and the disciple *par excellence* is "the disciple whom Jesus loved." "Now Jesus loved Martha and her sister [Mary] and Lazarus" (11:5). That John reports first that Jesus loved Martha and Mary, seems to suggest they were either better known than Lazarus, or exercised a more significant ministry than he did; perhaps after his death, but maybe even before that. In the allegory of the Good Shepherd, John compares the disciples of Jesus to sheep whom he calls by name (10:3-5). In the appearance of the risen Jesus to Mary Magdalene, she recognizes him when he calls her by her name, "Mary" (20:16).

The point is all the more important since in 10:3-5, the "sheep" are twice identified as "his own," an almost technical expression used at the beginning of the Last Supper: "Having loved *his own* who were in the world, he loved them to the end" (John 13:1). In this way, the Johannine redaction places a woman in the same category of relationship to Jesus, as it placed the Twelve at the Last Supper.

In the Fourth Gospel, Jesus' public ministry climaxes in the revelation that he is "the resurrection and the life" (11:1-54). As a "beloved disciple," Martha becomes a spokeswoman for the messianic faith of the community. That Martha "served at table" could be an allusion to Luke 10:40, but importantly, in John 11 and 12, she is characterized as fulfilling *both* the ministry of the word and of the table.

This indicates how some women might have appealed to female leadership in the primitive Jesus movement to legitimate their own ministry. Luke's redactional interest is not dissimilar to that of the Pastoral Epistles, which also distinguish between ministers who labor "in preaching and teaching" (1 Tim 5:17) and those who "serve" (1 Tim 3:8ff). Luke's rhetorical interests, as in 10:38-40, are, according to Fiorenza, to silence women leaders of house churches who like Martha might have protested at their gradual exclusion. Comparison with the Fourth Gospel's depiction of Martha and Mary helps clarify Luke's prescriptive rhetoric in a situation of women's struggle against the gradual patriarchalization of the Church, shown in the restriction of women's ministry and the separation of the *diakonia* of the word and the *diakonia* of the table.

## PHOEBE

The New Testament *of itself* yields no decisive, explicit, textual answer offering any once-and-for-all-time understanding of the nature, order, and function of the spiritual or ministerial offices of the Church, including those of bishop, deacon, and priest. That is acknowledged in the second part of *Inter Insignores*. Regarding deaconate, exegetical and historical difficulties are evident in examining three classical passages: Acts 6:1–15, Philippians 1:1, and 1 Timothy 3:1.[12] Contemporary understanding of Holy Orders moreover, whether of presbyterate, deaconate, or episcopate, cannot be simplistically inscribed into first-century texts.

But if substantial continuity since New Testament times is assumed and argues for the male deaconate, can this not also be true for women deacons? What is sauce for the gander is sauce for the goose. In Romans 16:1–2, Paul writes: "I commend to you Phoebe, our sister, who is also a deacon (*diakonon*) of the church in Cenchreae, that you might welcome her in the Lord in a manner worthy of the holy ones and assist her in whatever matter she may have need of from you; for she herself has been a patroness for many, indeed for me as well."

Paul describes her as: Phoebe (*Phoibēn*), sister (*adelphēn*), deacon (*diakonos*), and patroness (*prostatis*).[13] Phoebe (*Phoibēn*) is identified first as a believer, then as "our sister" (*tēn adelphēn hēmōn*), then thirdly, as a "deacon" (*diakonos*)—the word is in the masculine gender. The translation "deaconess" is a paraphrase, in as much as there is no evidence of the feminine form of the word, *diakonissa*, deaconess, until the third century (Apostolic Constitutions 8.19, 20, 28). But funerary inscriptions, as we shall examine in the next chapter, even well into the Byzantine period, indicate widespread use of the masculine form, *diakonos*, to refer to women who ministered in official capacities as "deacons." One of them, Sophia, is not only called *"the* deacon" (*hē diakonos*), intriguingly, a masculine noun with the feminine article, but also called "the second Phoebe."[14]

Similar terminology is used of other important women ministers. Saint John Chrysostom[15] (349–407) believed that Euodia and Syntyche

---

12. Viecher, *The Problem of the Diaconate*, 84–104.

13. Perry, *Phoebe of Cenchreae and "Women" of Ephesus*, 13–18.

14. Perry, *Phoebe of Cenchreae and "Women" of Ephesus*, 16 n. 22.

15. "Do you see how great a testimony he bears to their virtue?... [S]o Paul testifies to them, saying, whose names are in the book of life. These women seem to me to be the chief of the Church which was there, and he commends them to some notable man

were leading women in the Philippian church and compared them to Phoebe. If, as seems likely, Phoebe is being commissioned as an envoy by Paul, then she clearly exercises the ministry of deacon as it would come to be understood theologically in the Church. The deacon was ordained to serve the ministry of oversight, *episkope*. The ministry of deacon must thus be understood in terms of public service to the ministry of *episkope* exercised by the bishop or presbyter—and not at all merely as a stage on the journey to priesthood. *Diakonia* had as its foundational biblical meaning, the sense of being publicly commissioned on behalf of another. The deacon is the one who is "sent forth" by the bishop in a ministry explicitly placed at the service of the episcopal ministry of overseeing.

That word *diakonos*, deacon, may be situated in four different semantic domains: interpersonal care or help (Mark 10:45; Matt 20:26, 28; 25:44; Acts 20:24; Rev 2:19); household service, especially food service (Mark 1:31; Luke 10:40; 22:26–27); religious roles (1 Tim 3:10; Rom 16:1; 1 Tim 3:8); and the transfer of possessions in financial support of others (Acts 6:1–2; Rom 15:31). The general idea of *diakon-* words in the New Testament is *service humbly rendered*, as distinct from merely humble tasks to others while under someone's authority, as clearly exemplified in the case of Phoebe.

Uses outside the New Testament reveal an expanded semantic domain that cuts across lines of social status, from a *diakonos* who acts as a "slave" or personal "attendant" to one who acts as a king's or as a god's messenger or emissary or ambassador. *Diakonon*, as used in Romans 16:1, is made emphatic by the feminine participle *ousan*, "being [a deacon]." That implies that Phoebe was known as and characteristically ministered or functioned as a deacon (*diakonos*). Though trusted to deliver Paul's letter to the Romans, she is not merely Paul's personal attendant or ambassadress, but a διάκονος of "the church in Cenchreae."

Paul's choice of language is telling. "I commend to you" is a technical, epistolary expression to introduce a friend or acquaintance. The term "sister" assures the Romans she is not an interloper. "Please receive her in

---

whom he calls his yokefellow, to whom perchance he was wont to commend them, as to a fellow-worker, and fellow-soldier, and brother, and companion, as he does in the Epistle to the Romans, when he says, I commend unto you Phoebe our sister.... For they laboured with me in the Gospel.... Laboured with me. What do you say? Did women labour with you? Yes, he answers, they too contributed no small portion.... The Churches then were no little edified, for many good ends are gained where they who are approved, be they men, or be they women,... but observe that he gives his orders, that these women should enjoy much protection." *Homilies on Philippians* 13.

the Lord," means "welcome her into the community as one of its members." The phrase "in the Lord" indicates a close relationship in Christ. The last of the terms with which Paul describes Phoebe is *prostatis*. In its feminine form, as here, it referred in ancient literature to a woman (or goddess) who acted as a "patroness," providing material support, indicative of a person of prominence. If a reference to one who is a contributor to charity, it refers to the fifth in Paul's list of Spirit-bestowed charisms (Rom 12:8; cf. also 1 Cor 12:28), "the one contributing with generosity," and in this case, seems closely aligned with the sixth charism in that list; "the one governing in diligence (*ho proistamenos*), the one standing in the lead" (cf. also 1 Thess 5:12; 1 Tim 5:17). Phoebe is thus a superior or at least a wealthy, influential leader in the service of the church at Cenchrae. She is a deacon-minister, and, for Paul, "to minister" is something weighty. Speaking of her patronage, Paul adds: "and of I myself too," acknowledging the debt he owes to Phoebe's diaconal ministry.[16]

That description of Phoebe stresses her role as an advocate for Paul and others among élite circles of Corinth and Cenchreae. Paul includes Phoebe's commendation in part because she embodies the social ethic he outlines in Romans 12–15. By choosing and arranging this distinctive, even ironic, set of nouns to describe Phoebe as sister, patroness, servant, Paul continues his challenge to Roman notions of social status and Jewish notions of religious purity, which threatened the formation of egalitarian Christian identity and relationality in the churches.

## WOMEN DEACONS IN EPHESUS

When churches in a given locality grew (1 Tim 3:8–13; cf. Acts 6:1–7), they required "deacons" to ensure that the ministry of service continued without interruption, in conjunction with that of the word and prayer. Close reading of 1 Timothy, especially chapters 2 and 3, suggests that the "women" of 1 Timothy 3:11 are being evaluated for diaconal service. The repeated syntax of 1 Timothy 2:9 and 3:11 is noteworthy: "similarly, women" (*hōsautōs gynaikas*) in 2:9 and "women, similarly" (*gynaikas hōsautōs*) in 3:11. As in his instructions on worship (1 Tim 2:8–9), Paul[17]

---

16. Fitzmyer, *Romans*, 728–33.

17. Many exegetes argue on linguistic and theological grounds that Paul is not the actual author of 1 Timothy, in the modern sense of authorship. Here I prescind from this question and speak of Paul as author in a colloquial way.

addresses the men, then the women, in his instructions about suitable qualifications for leadership. The absence of pronouns and articles alongside *gynaikas* (women) in both 1 Timothy 2:9 and 3:11, suggests that here Paul is not addressing the wives of male deacons. This use of *gynaikas* (women) in 3:11, stands out: it has no parallel in Paul's instructions about overseers/bishops. That in turn, may indicate that while patriarchalization had begun to restrict candidature for episcopacy, it had not yet done so regarding the deaconate, something that would not occur for several centuries.

If, as is frequently suggested, Paul were listing character requirements for the "wives" of deacons in 3:11, the question would immediately arise as to why there are no such requirements for the "wives" of overseers/bishops in 3:2–7, especially since 1 Timothy 3:2 clearly implies that at that point, bishops were married. Given that bishops/overseers must be "hospitable" (3:2); willing and financially able to open their homes to the church, providing food for the gathering, and hosting travelling Christians, requirements for their wives would be an important consideration. Neither in the case of bishops nor deacons is 1 Timothy speaking about "wives" of these officeholders. It is speaking about women who are candidates for the deaconate.

Paul's use of *gynaikas* in 3:12: "let deacons be of one wife" (i.e., married only once) has indeed led some commentators to translate *gynaikas* as "wives" in 3:11. But the transition from 3:11 to 3:12 is better explained by what otherwise would seem the remarkable omission of "man of one wife" (*mias gynaikos andra*) in 3:8–10. Paul would be likely to omit the one-woman-per-man policy in 3:8–10 if he were referring there, as indeed he is, to character requirements for both male *and female* diaconal candidates. He makes this point explicit in 3:11 by repeating the character qualities of 3:8–10 for those candidates who are "women." In 3:12, for those candidates who are men, he underscores their fidelity to "one woman" (3:12) even as he calls women to be "faithful in all things" (*pistas en pasin*), including their marriages (3:11), and to be "a wife of one man" (*enos andros gynē*), i.e., married only once (5:9).

Paul's alternating pattern of addressing "men" then "women" in 1 Timothy 2, and the syntactical parallel between 2:9 and 3:11 *hōsautōs gynaikas / gynaikas hōsautōs* ("similarly the women"/"women, similarly") strongly imply that the "women" of whom he writes in 3:11 are *women candidates for diaconal service*: women deacons. Not only did Paul not prohibit diaconal ministry by Christian women, he dignifies it by commending Phoebe and by recognizing women among the candidates who were being evaluated for diaconal office at Ephesus.

## THE WOMEN ACCOMPANYING THE APOSTLES

In 1 Corinthians 9:5 we read: "have we not the right to take along a sister-wife (*adelphēn gynaika*), as even the rest of the apostles and the brothers of the Lord and Cephas?" The phrase *adelphēn gynaika* exhibits many interesting textual variations, probably witnessing to early debate as to what it signified. Some twelve sources witness to a plural use, as in "women" (*gynaikas*), and later other Latin manuscripts give renderings such as *mulierem sororem, mulierem, sorores mulieres* (Jerome) and *sororem mulierculum*.[18] The phrase was obviously found problematic as to its precise meaning. Clement of Alexandria held that the apostles, totally dedicated as they were to the ministry, were accompanied by these women, not as wives (*gametas*), but as fellow ministers/deacons (*syndiakonous*).[19]

Protestant reformers, influenced not least by their rejection of clerical celibacy, generally insisted on these women as principally wives. In recent Catholic writing, the phrase has often been used to argue for voluntary celibacy for priests. Others emphasized an assumed role of providing material support. Yet Priscilla, one of the most significant of such woman, is never defined as "providing material support," as others have been, with that designation even generalized to a total description of the group. If in Greek culture women apostles were necessary to minister to woman, issues of public propriety were less an issue in Rome where working-class and lower-middle-class women circulated and labored publicly. Romans 16 refers to up to sixteen women, and it seems clear from the vocabulary that these in the main were fellow-workers, Priscilla quite explicitly so (v. 3). She and Aquila were people who risked their

---

18. Cook, "1 Cor 9:5, The Women of the Apostles," 352–68.

19. "But the [apostles], in accordance with their ministry, devoted themselves to preaching without any distraction, and took women with them, not as wives, but as sisters, that they might be their co-ministers/deacons (*syndiakonoi*) in dealing with women in their homes. It was through them that the Lord's teaching penetrated also the women's quarters without any scandal being aroused." *Stromata* Book 3, chapter 6, 53, Clement continues, "We also know the directions about women deacons which are given by the noble Paul in his second letter to Timothy." Accessible at www.earlychristianwritings.com/churchfathers.html.

very lives for the gospel (v. 4); they hosted a house church in their home (v. 6), just as 1 Corinthians 16:10 suggests they also did so in Asia.

Even if not conclusively so, these facts certainly point towards understanding 1 Corinthians 9:5 as speaking about missionary partnerships. Priscilla is most likely an example of one such partnership where the woman was the principal party. The relationship Paul refers to is possibly but not necessarily conjugal; *gynē* can mean "woman" as well as, though not necessarily, "wife." Moreover, "wives" does not necessarily preclude "missionary partner." The women referred to in 1 Corinthians 9:5 are missionaries.

## SHOULD WOMEN KEEP SILENT IN CHURCH?

In 1 Corinthians 14:33b-36 we read:

> For God is not of disorder but of peace. As (*hōs*) in all the assemblies of the saints, the women should keep silent in the assemblies; for it is not permitted for them (*autais*, fem. pl.) to speak, but they should be in submission, just as the law says. But if they desire to learn anything, let them ask their own husbands at home; for it is shameful for women to speak in an assembly.

For centuries, these words have been appealed to as a standard proof text by those who wish to exclude women from authority in the Church. That text however, clearly contradicts Paul's fundamental position on women spelled out in Galatians 3:27: ". . . there is no longer male or female for you are all one in Christ Jesus."

The force of this becomes clearer when we consider that verse in its entirety: "There is not Jew or Greek, there is not slave nor free, there is not male and female, for you are all one in Christ Jesus." There is an equivalence of cogency in deconstructing the three binaries, each deconstruction equally foundational to Paul's vision. He has devoted huge sections of the letter to the Romans explicating how there is no longer "Jew nor Greek"; just as in the letter to Philemon, the latter is to take back Onesimus: "no longer as a slave, but more than a slave, a beloved brother, especially to me and how much more to you, both in the flesh and in the Lord" (Phlm 1:16). The phrase "in the flesh and in the Lord" signifies that this is brotherhood, not only in purely religious terms, but in the realities of daily life. That "there is no longer male nor female," is surely to be understood with like cogency. The grace of Christ meant that salvation is offered to Jew and gentile alike; Christian faith makes a Christian slave one's brother/sister in social reality and not just in religious terms. Baptism makes all disciples, irrespective of gender, one in Christ, and one in Christian dignity and responsibility for ministry.

The difficulties to which 1 Corinthians 14:34–35 gave rise are illustrated by many Western manuscripts that transpose verses 34–35 to follow verse 40. Evidence from Codex Fuldensis (541–546) is intriguing. Following verse 33, a scribal siglum directs the reader to a note in the margin that provides the text of verses 36–40. Without completely deleting verses 34–35, the scribe seemingly intends them to be omitted while the passage is being read in the liturgy.[20]

One significant response to difficulties posed by these verses, contends that it is an interpolation into an earlier text, made by someone other than the author, since it clearly expresses a non-Pauline sentiment with which Paul would have sharply disagreed. That 1 Corinthians 14:33b–36 is an interpolation, may be tested by reading 1 Corinthians 14 carefully and noting the jump of discontinuity in the subject, half-way through verse 33, until the end of verse 36. Readers who skipped verses 33b–36 and continued from verse 33a directly to verse 37 would notice that it reads much more smoothly and continuously. That finds a degree of support in some ancient manuscripts, where some or all of verses 33b–36 come at the end of the chapter after verse 40.

By the time the Pastoral Epistles were redacted to their canonical form, there seems to have been a culturally-conditioned hardening of attitudes towards the role of women in the communities. The Augustan and post-Augustan imperial reforms of family life had sought both to strengthen and to refocus the patriarchal family around the husband and wife relationship, and further, around the predominance of the husband. 1 Timothy 2:8–15 and Titus 2:3–5 give summaries of the consequences of this acculturation of the gospel to contemporary, social reality, often referred to as *Haustafeln*. Women should be quiet; they have no permission to teach; or to have authority over a man. Previously some feminist exegetes had sought to soften this apparent prohibition in 1 Corinthians 14:33b–36 of women speaking, by arguing that the verb *lalein* in this context, means "to talk" rather than "to speak," as if Paul was simply trying to cut down on idle chatter. But the use of *lalein* throughout the chapter,

---

20. Metzger, *A Textual Commentary on the New Testament*, 499–500.

both in relation to the gift of tongues and that of prophesy, would argue against that reading.

Redaction criticism suggests to some that the verses in 1 Corinthians 14:33b-36 are deutero-Pauline. This is supported by their vocabulary, and especially the appeal to "the law" (*ho nomos*)—as in: "women . . . should be subordinate *as the law also says*" (v. 34); a most unlikely Pauline line of argument, given his deconstruction of "law," and probably reflecting nascent, misogynist developments represented in 1 Timothy 2:9-15, in an attempt to harmonize the earlier tradition with them. That tendency in turn, appeals to Genesis 3:28 as a pseudo-scriptural basis for a subordinate position for women. In that text, however, domination-subordination between the genders is a consequence of the fall, and not at all an expression of the originating, divine will.

## SILENCING WOMEN OR CORRECTING MEN

Interpolation, however, is one of two possible explanations for the presence of these ill-fitting verses.[21] The other is that Paul is quoting the standpoint of the Corinthians from their letter to him, in order to refute it.

With the exception of Codex Vaticanus, manuscript evidence would be deemed by most scholars sufficient to establish 1 Corinthians 14:33b-36 as almost certainly belonging to the original composition. It is true that when Clement of Alexandria (c. 150-215) discusses the behavior of women in church, he cites 1 Corinthians 11:5, 13 ("is it becoming for an unveiled woman to pray?")[22] but *not* 1 Corinthians 14:34-35. That, however, is better explained, not by assuming he possessed a manuscript without these verses, but by inferring that Clement and the Apostolic Fathers before him, well knew that 1 Corinthians 14:33b-36 was not at all Paul's position, but rather, a quotation from the Corinthians' letter to Paul, outlining their position—one that he proceeded to refute.

A quotation-refutation device begins in verse 33b rather than verse 34 because of the break in thought marked by "As" (*hōs*), which begins verse 33b.[23] Verse 33b is most naturally taken as the first clause of the sen-

---

21. Payne, *Man and Woman, One in Christ*, 217-67.

22. *Paedagogus* 3:11, Paedagogus accessible at http://www.ccel.org/ccel/schaff/anf02.html.

23. MacGregor, "1 Corinthians 14:33b-38 as a Pauline Quotation-Refutation Device," 23-28.

tence continued in verse 34. But note carefully, how the text continues in verse 36: "Or (*ē*) did the word of God originate with you (*humas*, pl.), or (*ē*) to you men only (*humas monous*, masc. pl.) has it come?" Verse 37: "If anyone seems to be a prophet or spiritual, let that one recognize that what I write to you (pl.) is a commandment of the Lord"; and verse 38, "but if anyone disregards this, let that one be disregarded." Paul introduces both rhetorical questions in verse 36 with "or" (*ē*), something that he does six times elsewhere in 1 Corinthians, either to argue against the Corinthians' position (1:13; 6:16; 9:6, 8, 10; 11:22) or to express disapproval of a Corinthian practice (6:2; 9, 19; 10:22; 11:13).

If Paul had meant to direct verse 36 to women in particular, he would have used the feminine plural *monas*, "[women] only." Instead, he employs the masculine plural *monous*, either "[men] only" or "[people] only." If 14:33b–36 is not an interpolation, the meaning of *monous* is "[men] only," since this alone furnishes a coherent grammatical contrast between the women referred to in 14:33b–35 and the men rebuked in verse 36. *Humas* in verse 36 is masculine as well, denoting "you [men]." These observations disclose Paul's intended meaning in verse 36: "Or did the word of God originate with *you men*, or to *you men only* has it come?" The contrast between women addressed in verse 34 by the feminine plural "they" (*autais*) and the "you men [only]," censured in verse 36 for their position in 14:33b–35, further demonstrates that 14:36–38 stands as a rejection of 14:33b–35.

Far from attempting to silence women, Paul is rebuking Corinthian men for prohibiting women from speaking in church. For Paul, such a restriction would be tantamount to alleging that the word of God is addressed properly to the men and merely derivatively to their wives. The shift of verses 33b–36 interrupts the chiasm spanning verses 26–40. By means of it, Paul clarifies that verses 33b–35 are not his own thoughts and that he strongly *opposes* the ideas expressed there.[24]

## QUOTATION-REFUTATION DEVICE

A device of quotation-refutation is demonstrably a feature of 1 Corinthians, where it is used many times (6:12–13; 7:1–2; 8:1, 8; 10:23). Paul will quote a position from the Corinthians' letter, with which he disagrees, and then refute it. The most explicit instance is 7:1–2, the recognition of

---

24. On this approach to the passage see Peppiatt, *Women and Worship in Corinth*.

which led to the scholarly discovery of the other four: "But concerning (*peri de*) that which you wrote about; 'It is good for a man not to touch a woman (*gynaikos mē haptesthai*) . . . .'" Here Paul clearly identifies the extra-Pauline source of this topic's discourse as "that which you wrote about" (*hōn egrapsate*), and shifts to his refutation with the interjecting phrase *dia de*, "but because." 1 Corinthians 14:33b–38 features both of these two kinds of grammatical indicators used in 1 Corinthians' quotation-refutation devices; an introducer of new discourse governing the Corinthian quotation and an interjecting term governing the Pauline refutation. Each of the other four established quotation-refutation devices in 6:12–13, 8:1, 8:8, and 10:23 contains only one of these species. The foundational one in 7:1, as in 14:33b–38, features both, along with the unique, explicit acknowledgment of the Corinthians' correspondence as its source material.

Paul did not need explicitly to identify 14:33b–35 as an unacceptable Corinthian statement. The Corinthians knew well what they themselves had written. Contextual evidence led the Apostolic Fathers, who had no access to the Corinthians' epistle to Paul, to the same conclusion. In 11:3–16, Paul argues—presumably for reasons of contemporary decorum—that women should have their "heads covered" when praying or prophesying in church, which covering he identifies as "long hair" (v. 15). Thus, while insisting on decorum, he explicitly states that women should indeed pray (aloud) and prophesy in church. That demonstrates *the impossibility that 14:33b–35 expresses his own opinion*. Moreover, it contradicts Paul's central point in 1 Corinthians 14, whereby everyone in the church, regardless of gender, should be instructed by everyone else: "What is the outcome then, brothers?"—surely used inclusively given what follows—"When you assemble, each one has a hymn, has a teaching, has a revelation, has a tongue, or has an interpretation. Let all this be done for edification. . . . For you can all prophecy one by one, so that everyone may be instructed and encouraged" (14:26, 31).

The Corinthians' stance in 14:33b–35 flies in the face of one of Paul's dominant themes: the freedom of believers from the "law"—which among many other prescriptions and restrictions, was widely interpreted as forbidding women to speak in the assembly. Paul goes so far as to state that embracing the latter implies rejection of Christ (Gal 4:9–11; 5:1, 4). Far from forbidding women to speak in church, Paul is insisting that women may exercise the same ministries in worship as men and is reprimanding Corinthian men for attempting to silence their female equals.

## EUODIA AND SYNTYCHE

Paul recognized women as exercising leadership in the Church. In Philippians 4:2–3, he writes: "I urge Euodia and I urge Syntyche to think the same thing in the Lord. Indeed, I ask you, my true companion [yokefellow], to help them—these women who have contended together with me in [the cause of] the gospel, along with Clement and the rest of my co-workers, whose names are in the book of life." The *New Jerome Biblical Commentary* describes Euodia and Syntyche as "Two women, prominent in the community, otherwise unknown to us."[25] While at face value true, that statement may nonetheless conceal their significance.

Paul uses two terms about them that he had employed previously regarding Timothy and Epaphroditus. Euodia and Syntyche had contended together with him (συνήθλησάν) "in the gospel." That verb is used twice in Philippians (1:27 and 4:3) and means "to contend on the side of someone; to cooperate with; to make every effort with." Thus, Paul is effectively referring to Euodia and Syntyche as his "co-workers" (*synergoi*) as earlier he had referred to Epaphroditus (2:25), and elsewhere to many significant Church leaders, both male and female. In both proto- and deutero-Pauline literature, "co-worker" is a term of some weight. By implication, the ministries of the women Euodia and Syntyche were comparable to those of Timothy and Epaphroditus.

Philippi was the chief city of Macedonia and a Roman colony (Acts 16:12). Macedonian women apparently enjoyed greater freedoms, rights, and powers than many other women of that time and played a significant part in public affairs. Significantly, in Philippi, Paul's first contact was at a meeting for prayer by a riverside, when he spoke to the women gathered there, one of whom, Lydia, seems to have been a leading figure. This wealthy woman was Philippi's first Christian convert—some like to claim her as the first European Christian. It is likely that Lydia hosted and led something akin to the first house church in Philippi when Paul and his colleagues moved on from there (Acts 16:13–15, 40).

What was the relationship of Euodia and Syntyche with Lydia? Some have speculated that "Lydia" was a kind of nickname drawn from her place of origin—Thyatira in Lydia—and her real name was Euodia or Syntyche. True or not, the key point is that Paul specifically addresses them personally and individually, together with Clement, indicating that these women were influential members of the Philippian church

---

25. Byrne, "The Letter to the Philippians," 797, col. 2.

and making it likely that they exercised ministry comparable or equal to Clement's. It is certainly credible that Euodia and Syntyche possibly hosted house churches where they ministered as overseers (*episkopoi*).

Despite a common assumption that Euodia and Syntyche were quarrelling, Paul does not explicitly state that. He is rather, urging each of them: "to *think* the same thing in the Lord." "Think" (*phroneō*) is a key word in the letter to the Philippians. Paul had been encouraging mature people to have the same thinking as himself, that of reaching out for the goal of spiritual perfection (3:14–15; cf. esp. 2:5). John Chrysostom did not see any sign of a quarrel in Paul's plea to Euodia and Syntyche; he saw only praise and wrote: "Do you see how great a testimony he [Paul] bears to their virtue?"[26] But even if they were disagreeing, that might indicate their importance in the leadership of the community, it may suggest they are the people who can alleviate the problem of disunity and possibly put an end to it.

## NEW TESTAMENT UNDERSTANDING OF DEACON

Revaluation of the New Testament understanding of "deacon" draws from the research of Anni Hentschel and John N. Collins.[27] Their work is independent, but largely concurs.[28] Hentschel observes that: "New Testament occurrences of *diakonia* and its cognates . . . express neither lowly service nor merciful concern."[29] Her emphasis is on restoring to the Pauline text values arising from *diakonia* as a divinely commissioned ministry, insisting that "helping" cannot be established as its basic meaning. For Collins, Paul received the word of God and, under mandate, transmitted it to the Corinthians. Doing that is what Greeks would call *diakonia*. Interpretation of the *diakonia* of Paul solely or merely as humble service for the sake of the community is no longer possible. It is the *quality* of the service, not its socially perceived importance or unimportance, that in imitation of Jesus, must be humble.

In recent years, women theologians have tended to criticize Luke's attitudes in his use of *diakonia* words for a post-Pauline exclusion of

---

26. *Homilies on Philippians*, 13, see above.

27. Collins, *Diakonia*; Collins, *Are All Christians Ministers?* Collins, *Deacons and the Church*, 21.

28. Collins, "Reinterpreting *Diakonia* in Germany," 69–81.

29. Hentschel, *Diakonia im Neuen Testament*, 1.

women from ministerial roles in the community. At the heart of such argumentation is the linguistic connection between the Martha and Mary scene in Luke 10:38–42, and Acts 6:1–6. Those scholars, however, although writing in the 1990s, were interpreting *diakonia* in terms of apparently demeaning tasks reserved to slaves and women, drawing attention to the predominance of such roles for women in the Gospel narrative, while in Acts, the same word took on an altogether different color as applied exclusively to men in designated ecclesial tasks.

Hentschel refuses to interpret "the daily *diakonia*" (6:1) and the *diakonein trapezais,* "service of tables" (6:2), as simply expressing practical charity. For her, dividing the responsibility of the Twelve for "word" and "deed" into separate ministries for the Seven (deed) and the Twelve (word) is a Lukan redaction disguising a previous ministry of the "word" carried out by the Seven among the Hellenists. These seminal studies of Collins and Hentschel insist that pertinent New Testament texts are to be read differently from the caritative way modern exegesis had, until very recently, generally interpreted *diakonia*.[30]

The semantic approach convinced these authors that they could not interpret *diakonia* without a rigorous re-reading of those sections of the New Testament where *diakonia* contributed to ecclesiology. Interesting corollaries include *diakonia* usage in relation to Romans 15:25 and passages about the collection for Jerusalem and parallel usage at Acts 11:29 and 12:25. This is also illustrated, as we have seen, in Phoebe's being entrusted with the text of Romans[31] and arguably, in the implied importance of Chloe in 1 Corinthians 1:11–12, as well as in the qualifications required for deaconesses in Ephesus and very widely in the historical role of many women deacons.

## DIACONATE AND PRIESTHOOD

The restoration of the permanent diaconate after Vatican II, deeper semantic exploration of the New Testament, and historical reconstruction of early church practice, have led to ongoing reflection on the theology of

---

30. The modern renewal of the female diaconate began among German Lutherans in the 1840s. It focused on caritative ministries such as nursing and social work, endorsing a notion of diaconate as humble service rather than service, of whatever kind, even socially important, humbly rendered. It declined with the professionalization of such professions.

31. This point will be further developed in chapter 7.

the diaconate. As discussed, Scripture of itself yields no decisive answer regarding the nature and order of the spiritual offices of the church and a homogeneous structure of church ministry cannot be deduced from Scripture alone. The *episcopoi* are, to a certain extent, related to the *presbyteroi*, important in Jewish church constitutions. The terms are at times, almost synonyms, usable interchangeably (e.g., Acts 20:17). Offices of *episcopos* and *diaconos* probably first arose in Hellenistic churches and *episcopoi* were later linked with *presbyteroi*. Some early Christian writings mention *episcopoi* and *diaconoi* but not *presbyteroi* (Didache 15:1).

The deacons are subordinate to the bishop, but we cannot textually deduce what precisely their ministry was. Their relationship to the elders (*presbyteroi*) remains somewhat obscure. Ignatius of Antioch (50–117) is the first to prescribe expressly these three offices as an essential structure in the church. "You should honour all the *deacons* like Jesus Christ, the *bishop* like the image of the Father, and the *elders* as the council of God and the gathering of the apostles. Without these one cannot talk of the church" (Ign. *Trall.* 3:1). While the evidence for ordained female deacons in the early Christian period, especially in parts of the Eastern Church, seems clear and unambiguous, the literary record does not give a detailed, comprehensive picture of their liturgical ministry. At one period, one of the most important ministerial duties of the deaconess was conducting the physical anointing and full immersion of (scantily clad) adult women catechumens, who were then "officially" baptized by the bishop's prayer after they were robed. That specific ministry became obsolete with the increasing rarity of adult baptism from the end of the fourth century on.[32] Rather than defining the women's diaconate in terms of a fixed liturgical role, to be immutably preserved and repeated, that illustrates how deacons are at the service of the bishop's ministry of oversight.

The *Traditio Apostolica* of Hippolytus tells of diaconal ordination:

> When one ordains a deacon he should be chosen in the way already mentioned, and the bishop alone should lay hands on him in the same way. We ordain in the following way: the bishop alone lays on hands at the ordination of the deacon; for the latter is not ordained to the priesthood, but to the bishop's service, to do what the latter tells him.

That will prove of basic importance for later canon law. Deacons belong to the clergy, but differently from the *sacerdotium*. The bishop and the

---

32. Karras, *Female Deacons in the Byzantine Church*, 273–77.

priest have what will come to be called priestly-sacramental functions; the deacon is assigned to the bishop as a helper.

For the *Didascalia*, the deacon is first of all a servant of the bishop; his executive organ. The bishop is the administrator of the gifts. Deacons collect and distribute them according to the bishop's instructions. They have the function of a helper at the celebration of the Eucharist; to recall the command to forgive one another; to care for right order. They have a part in the pastoral tasks of the bishop, for example, in dealing with legal and similar matters.

In the late patristic Church, as the presbyter's office was becoming more prominent, the deacon's was being minimized. Nicene and post-Nicene councils restricted their administrative and cultic functions, and several authors in the West wrote tracts upbraiding deacons for their self-importance. By the Middle Ages and *a fortiori* today, the diaconate no longer possessed the importance it knew in the first centuries. In the West it was restricted more and more to liturgical functions, finally becoming merely a step on the way to priesthood, effectively ceasing as an independent office.

The pastoral-theological context of the diaconate in the contemporary Catholic Church has been described as a "confluence of three realities":[33] the growth of lay ecclesial ministry since the council; the restoration of the permanent diaconate; and the decline in the numbers of presbyters. The acceptance, at least in principle, of the equality of men and women in the Church now raises the question of the restoration of the female deaconate—and much more.

## INADEQUATE THEOLOGIES OF DIACONATE

The dominant ministerial path, particularly for diocesan clergy, is one culminating in ordination to the priesthood. This *cursus honorum* traditionally took the form: porter, lector, exorcist, acolyte (the minor orders), followed by sub-deacon, deacon, presbyter, and bishop (the major orders). But the ancient tradition never presupposed that one must advance from one ordained ministry to the next. The sequence of deacon, presbyter, bishop, was not firmly in place before the Middle Ages. The

---

33. Gaillardetz, "Towards a Contemporary Theology of the Diaconate," 419–38.

Church may well consider abandoning the transitional deaconate as a sacramental prerequisite to presbyteral ordination.[34]

In practice, the present approach, especially in the case of married deacons, seemingly suggests that deacons participate, albeit in a subordinate degree, in the ministerial priesthood. That sacerdotalist view of deacon as effectively a "junior priest" leaves many deacons' ministry filled with baptisms, weddings, and funerals: a clear, but unwarranted, theological shift in the ministerial meaning and shape of deaconate. Such pastoral accommodationism provides no solid foundation for a theology of the deaconate. Sacraments are celebrated within the Eucharistic community under the presidency of its pastor. Better to develop a theology of deaconate truly distinctive of the deacon's ministerial relationship within the Church.

The early Church's developing theology of ministry focused not on powers conferred, but on the ecclesial relationship into which the ordinand was configured. Eucharistic presidency followed from pastoral leadership over a community. Now it is virtually the opposite. Leadership of the community follows ordination, often without reference to any community. Quite clearly, this raises ineluctable questions where women, even if not sacramentally ordained, have been selected, nominated, installed, and received as pastoral leaders of church communities where there is no ordained priest.

It is deacons' explicit service to the pastoral oversight of the bishop and presbyter that justifies their share in apostolic office. Ordination does indeed place the deacon in a new ecclesial relationship, characterized by the unique bond between the deacon and bishop, expressed in the formal promise of obedience that a deacon makes to his bishop. This close relationship to the one responsible for pastoral oversight, is reflected in the way in which the deacon's liturgical ministry is visibly aligned with the one who presides.

Deacons did not ever, as an ordinary dimension of their ministry, exercise pastoral oversight over a local Eucharistic community. When deacons engaged in this ministry, they did so as an exceptional accommodation to a shortage of presbyters. That is a crucial distinction. The presbyter and bishop are ordained to minister *in persona Christi capitis*, "in the person of Christ as head," albeit in *persona ecclesiae*, but not the deacon. The appropriate ecclesial response to a situation in which a

---

34. Wood, *Sacramental Orders*, 166-71.

community is deprived long-term of a presbyter, is to ordain its *de facto* leader to the presbyterate, whether deacon or lay person. Consequently, a thoroughgoing discussion on the future of the diaconate requires the same for the presbyterate, and likewise, any discussion of women deacons implies a discussion about women presbyters.

## NOT JUST A STEP TOWARDS PRIESTHOOD

Transitional deacons intend to become priests but are required to be ordained deacons as a step toward priesthood. However, historically all the orders were meant to be permanent. A lay person could be elected bishop without having first been a deacon or presbyter. There is clearly plenty of evidence both for sequential ordination as well as for the absence of it. Ample precedent can be found on both sides of the discussion, but sequential ordination is a canonical convention and has never been a universal tradition in the Catholic Church.

Perhaps the most famous Western example of such direct ordination is Ambrose of Milan (340–397). When elected as bishop he was still a catechumen.[35] The tide of recent scholarly opinion leans towards the position that Ambrose, without any preparatory ordinations to the diaconate or presbyterate, received no other ordination than that to the episcopate.[36] In the early centuries of the Church we find "instances of deacons becoming bishops, members of the laity becoming bishops, members of the laity becoming presbyters, and presbyters becoming bishops."[37] During the late patristic period, candidates for the episcopacy in Rome were drawn from the deacons, not from the presbyters. When Church growth required many more clergy, the quality of bishops declined: hence the perceived need for probation and the testing of candidates through a *cursus honorum*; one of the reasons why sequential ordination was introduced. That sequential pattern became normative only in 1073.[38] The diaconate does not, of its nature, have the character of a step to the priesthood. Sequential ordination met a pastoral need

---

35. "Ambrose," in Cross and Livingstone (eds.), *The Oxford Dictionary of the Christian Church*, 42–43.

36. Gibaut, "Sequential Ordination in Historical Perspective," 378.

37. Gibaut, in *Sequential or Direct Ordination?* 17–21.

38. The presbyteral ordination of the deacon Hildebrand in 1073 prior to his sequential ordination from the presbyterate to episcopal consecration as Gregory VII, was the pivotal indication that sequential ordination had become a canonical norm.

rather than a theological or sacramental concern. The Church can ordain to various offices without prior ordination to other offices.

This gives rise to a strange irony on both sides of the present discussion about women deacons. Both the conservatives who oppose women deacons, as well as many, though not all, of those who propose it, seemingly do so while considering it as a step towards priestly ordination. But deaconate is a ministry in itself and not merely a step towards the presbyterate, nor is it an arguably superfluous, liturgical adornment, nor is it a way of filling in for the shortage of priests which avoids tackling the question of who may be ordained presbyter. At its heart, the deaconate is being commissioned and ordained by the bishop for delegated tasks in the service of his *episcope*. But what this confusion does highlight is that there can be no serious discussion of the deaconate without an equally serious discussion about the presbyterate, both for women and men.

## COULD WOMEN BE PRESBYTERS?

If women could be deacons could they also be presbyters?[39] Time now to look for more evidence of both, especially during the first five centuries of the Church.

---

39. Rahner, *The Theology of the Restoration of the Diaconate*, 272.

CHAPTER 4

# Ordained Women in the First Millennium

THERE IS A VERITABLY massive amount of literary and epigraphic evidence of ordained women in the Catholic Church during the first millennium, especially during its first five centuries. This is especially the case in relation to women deacons, but the literary and epigraphic evidence also points to women presbyters and, in some cases, to women exercising some form of the ministry of *episcopos*.

## EPIGRAPHIC EVIDENCE OF WOMEN DEACONS

From an inscription in Palestine near the Mount of Olives, we learn of deacon Sophia. After a cross, it reads: *"here lies the servant and bride of Christ, Sophia, deacon, the second Phoebe, who fell asleep in peace on 25 March . . . ."* Description of bishops, presbyters, and deacons as *"servant of Christ"* is a motif widely found from the third century onwards. Sophia is called *diakonos* and "second Phoebe."[1]

The ministry of other women deacons is epigraphically attested in the Jerusalem area. For one, the inscription reads: *"Here lies Maria, deacon, the daughter of Valens, who lived 38 years and died in 548."* "Deacon" is abbreviated to *dk* so *diakonos* and *diakonissa* are equally possible readings. Contrary to the Council of Chalcedon (451), which set forty as the lowest age for ordination (*cheirotoneisthai*) of deaconesses, she was clearly younger. The age of forty had been set to ensure that deaconesses would not re-marry after widowhood, a prohibition most likely pointing

---

1. Eisen, *Women Officeholders in Early Christianity*, 158–98.

to ordained office (1 Tim 3:12; 5:9). The inscription indicates that this lower age-limit for women deacons could not always be sustained.

The many Christian inscriptions in Asia Minor are often signalled by a cross or a pair of peacocks, a symbol of immortality and renewal. In one, at Krykos in Cilicia, we read: *"Grave chamber of the diak... Timothea of the 'monastery?' of..."* Once again, it is uncertain if the title is διάκονος or διακόνισσα. It seems likely from what remains of the inscription that Timothea was a monastic deaconess. In the travelogue of a Western nun called Egeria, there is mention of a διακόνισσα named Marthana. Other Korykos inscriptions refer to women deacons, including a Maria, a Theodora, a Theophilia, and a Charitina.

At Archlais in Cappadocia, an inscription reads: *"Here lies Maria of pious and blessed memory who according to the word of the Apostle, raised children, sheltered guests, washed the feet of the saints and shared her bread with the needy...."* Of significance is how three lines of this inscription quote 1 Timothy 5:10, even if stylistically, thus implicitly arguing the historical reality of women's diaconal ordination from 1 Timothy, as we have sought to do in the previous chapter. That text, as does this inscription, refers to the qualifications for office holders in the Church, clearly implying that Maria too held office.

At Iconium in Lycaonia we read of a deaconess Basilissa: *"The first man of the village, Quintus son of Heraclius, with his wife Matrona and his children Anicetus and Catilla, all four lie in this grave. The wife of Anicetus, the deacon* [the word is spelt *deiakonos*], *Basilissa has erected this pleasant tomb together with her only son Numitorius who is still an immature child."* The text suggests that Basilissa was a young widow, thus providing evidence of married women deacons—unless she became a deacon after her widowhood. Other women holding Church office, attested to in Phrygia, include Strategis, Aurelia Faustina, Matrona, and many more. At Laodicea Combusta in Phrygia, we read of: *"Paula, the most blessed deacon [diakonos] of Christ +. She built me the tomb of her dear brother Helladius...."* In the same place another inscription attests a woman deacon (διάκ), Masa.

Near Nicomedia in Bithynia, an intriguing but undated inscription reads: *"In memory of the deacon* [genitive: *diakonou*] *Eugenia, we the poor of Geragathis have restored the coffin we decorated."* It is all but impossible to know who these restorers were. Of note is a letter of Pliny (Ep. X, 96) from around 112 CE, speaking of him torturing two Christian slave women (*ancillae*) who are called ministers/deacons (*quae ministrae dicebantur*) to obtain information about Christian worship. While open to debate, for some that text provides early witness to women deacons. Women deacons in Asia Minor were called both *diakonos* and *diakonissa*. Their ministerial activities are not mentioned on the inscriptions. Some were mothers and wives and some monastic deacons. Several of a very extensive number of surviving inscriptions were dedicated by women.

Similarly, abundant inscriptions are found in Greece. An inscription to a clergy family found at Melos in Cyclades reads: "*The presbyters worthy in every memory, Asclepis and Elpizon and Asclepiodotos and the deacon [(d)iakonos] Agalliasis . . . .*" It is not introduced by the third-century formula "in Christ," indicating probable fourth-century provenance.

## INSTALLED BY THE BISHOP

At Patras in Achaia, an inscription reads: "*The best beloved of God, the deacon [diakonos] Agrippiane, has laid this mosaic in order to fulfill her vow.*" There is another surviving fourth-century votive inscription from Macedonia for a deacon, Matrona. A caption at Delphi reads: "*The most pious deaconess* [the word is used three times] *Athanasia, . . . who was installed as deaconess by the most holy bishop Pantamiano[;] . . . if anyone dares to open this tomb where the deaconess has been buried, may he suffer the fate of Judas . . . .*" This inscription is noteworthy because it explicitly mentions the installation (*katastathisa*) of a deaconess by a bishop. In the same area, there is an inscription to another deaconess, Neikagore.

Bonitsa in Macedonia furnishes an inscription that reads: "*Here Theoprepia the slave of the Lord, eternal virgin and deacon [diak] of Christ, who has finished an ascetic life . . . .*" Theoprepia is shown to hold office in the Church not only by the designation "deacon" but by being called "slave of the Lord," a quasi-technical term for an ordained minister. At Philippi in Macedonia, we find the inscription: "*The graves belong to the deacon Posidonia and to Panchareia, the least of the canons.*" That bears witness to two officeholders, though one cannot determine with certainty the meaning of "canon." Basil of Caesarea addressed two letters to "canons," one to a canon called Theodora. The term probably implies an ascetic and may be the forerunner of the medieval title "Canoness." The former may have had responsibility for burials. Another inscription at Philippi writes of "*the deacon Agathe and the cashier and linen weaver John . . . .*" On the all but certain assumption that John was Agathe's husband, this hints at further evidence of married, women deacons.

At Edessa in Macedonia, we find: *"Monument of Agathokleia, the virgin and deacon."* Juxtaposition of the two titles may indicate that Agathokleia was a consecrated virgin before she became a deacon. Another inscription at Edessa gives: *"Monument of the deacon Theodosia and the virgins Aspelia and Agathokleia."* The wording demonstrates that the vocation of virgin, while sometimes linked, was not identical with that of deaconess. Neither necessarily implied the other.

In the West, there is epigraphic evidence of women deacons in Gaul, Italy, and Dalmatia. At Rome one inscription reads: *"By the gifts of God and the blessed Apostle Paul, Dometius, the deacon [DIAC] and manager of the holy, apostolic and papal chair, together with Anna the deacon [DIAC], his sister [EIUS GERMANA], has presented this vow to the blessed Paul."* Note how both are designated deacon with exactly the same abbreviation.

At Doclea in Dalmatia there is an inscription: *"The deacon [diac] Ausonia for her vow and that of her sons."* This Ausonia was both a deacon and a mother. At Ticini in Gaul we read: *"Here rests in peace, in happy memory, Theodora the deaconess [diaconissa] who lived 48 years more or less. Buried 22 July 539."*

## PROHIBITION IMPLIES PRACTICE

The epigraphic witness to women deacons ministering in Gaul in the sixth century, discussed above, makes a point of some importance, given that local church synods there—from the end of the fourth to the middle of the sixth century—sought, with mixed results, to eliminate the ordained, diaconal ministry of women. The Synod of Nimes (396), in Canon 2, forbade cultic ministry of females (*ministerium feminae leviticum*). The word *leviticum* certainly connotes cultic service: ministry at the altar, and probably that of a deacon. When the presbyter became associated with the "priest" of the Old Testament, the deacon was associated with the "Levite," considered his subordinate, liturgical assistant. Writers saw the diaconate as foreshadowed by the Old Testament Levites.

The Synod of Orange (441) forbade the ordination of women deacons entirely (*omnimodus non ordinandae diaconae*). The prohibition was repeated at the Synod of Epaon (517) and again at Orleans (533). Repeated reiteration of this prohibition almost certainly indicates that it was largely ignored, not only by the women deacons themselves, but by the local bishops and churches who were ordaining them. That, moreover, indicates that local churches, as well as those who ministered in them, saw such prohibitions in a *purely legal sense* relating to imposable or non-imposable discipline, and *not as a theological statement declaring these consecrations and ministries to be invalid*, as that term might be used today. Certainly, it indicates that ordained women deacons only became a problem to some church officials in the fourth century. From that time onwards, prohibitions are found, in that way making more visible an office and ministry that until then, in all probability, was simply a matter of course.

Not everyone is memorialized in an epigraph or a book. Incidences of women's liturgical ministry were probably significantly more numerous than those found in literary and epigraphic testimonies. Studies attest to the continuity with which the church hierarchy and local church councils confronted the problem of women in the priesthood. A significant influence on the attitude of the church was that some heretical groups admitted women to the priesthood and the episcopate. But this is not so in nearly all the cases mentioned here, as well as in the letter of Gelasius, who as Pope is writing to Catholic bishops (see below).

The mere fact of a woman-presbyter and her ministry may, but does not *per se* necessarily, connote either her heterodoxy or that of the church in which she exercised her ministry. In a comparable way, this present study does not directly examine the validity or otherwise of the ministry of individual women or groups of women who claim to have been ordained priests among various ecclesial groups. It deeply respects the excellent ministry of many women in various ecclesial communities but without prejudice to such ministry, the precise question studied here is whether or not women have been properly ordained in the Catholic Church. The indications are that many were.

Nonetheless, the Catholic Church, committed as it is to ecumenism, considers with receptive appreciation the action of the Holy Spirit among Christians and ecclesial communions outside the Roman Catholic Church: "Nor should we forget that whatever is wrought by the Holy Spirit in the hearts of our separated brethren can contribute to *our own edification*."[2] There are two points here: firstly, we have something to *learn* from the "other"; secondly, the Holy Spirit works in the "other," not

---

2. *Unitatis Redintegratio*, 4 (italics ours).

only for the "other," but also for *our* sake. The Catholic Church may not be simply indifferent to women's ordination in the Anglican, Lutheran, and other communions, but must examine it theologically in the context of receptive ecumenism.

## A DEACONESS—AND A SAINT

Many Eastern churches venerate Saint Theosebia as a saint and a holy deacon—her feast day is celebrated on January 10th. The sister of Basil and Gregory of Nyssa, and extolled by Gregory Nazianzen, she ministered in Cappadocia in the second half of the fourth century from where several ordained women are known. While many of those other women seem to have been deacons, Theosebia, in the opinion of Illiaria Ramelli, was more likely a presbyter.[3] In the time of Origen, in the early third century, the *Didascalia Apostolorum* also mentions female presbyters (πρεσβύτιδες), together with virgins and widows, as ecclesiastical orders. They are ordained by the bishop through consecration, with χειροτονία, the technical, theological term for the consecration at the heart of ordination, just like male deacons and presbyters, and are included in the clergy.

Gregory Nazianzen's Letter 197 consoles Gregory of Nyssa on the death of Theosebia, his *syzugos*. Lexically, *syzugos* means "colleague." But it sometimes referred to a spouse and probably due to a later, widespread assumption that women called deacons and presbyters in antiquity were wives of deacons and presbyters—an assumption itself based on an insufficiently examined, anterior presumption that women could not have been ordained—it is often incorrectly maintained that Theosebia was Gregory's wife.[4] Examination of the evidence indicates she was his sister and colleague; like their sister Macrina, a consecrated virgin, but not his wife. While it is highly likely, if not certain, that Gregory of Nyssa was married at some point, his wife was not Theosebia. He states in *De Virginitate* that he is far removed from "the glory of virginity." In the same work, he describes deep grief for the death of a young wife in childbirth, with such intensity as to suggest personal experience.

For Ramelli, Letter 197 and Epigrams 161 and 164 indicate that Theosebia was not Gregory's wife but his colleague in church ministry.

---

3. Ramelli, "Theosebia: A Presbyter of the Catholic Church," 79–102.

4. An assumption so widespread that Brown, *The Body and Society*, 296 and 503, does not challenge it.

Theosebia is clearly said to have been one of the children of Emmelia, and therefore a sister of Gregory of Nyssa, Macrina, Basil, and Peter, and the *syzugos*, colleague, of a presbyter and bishop, Gregory of Nazianzen, a great friend of Basil. Moreover, Gregory Nazianzen writes things about Theosebia that cannot refer to the death of a young wife: he remarks that she died at "an appropriate age"; "at the right moment" (*kata kairon*); and therefore not before her time when she was still a young woman. Gregory Nazianzen also declares both that Theosebia was a *syzugos* of Gregory of Nyssa during his priesthood, and that she was his sister, speaking of her with reverence as "your holy and blessed sister." Here, "sister" cannot simply mean "sister in the faith," since Nazianzen specifies that Theosebia was the daughter of Emmelia.

Furthermore, in Letter 197.5, he differentiates his own spiritual kinship (πνευματικὴ συγγένεια) with Theosebia from the bodily kinship (*sōmatikē*) she shares with Gregory of Nyssa. Nazianzen's statement that Gregory of Nyssa lived together with Theosebia ("to have lived together with such a woman" [*toiautē syzēsai*]; Letter 197.4), cannot be explained by a hypothetical marriage: they were siblings.

## THEOSEBIA THE PRESBYTER

Gregory Nazianzen's Epigram 164 praises Theosebia as "the support of pious women" (*erma gynaikōn eusebeōn*) and designates her as "the courage of women" (*tēn gynaikōn parrēsian*) in Letter 197.5. In Letter 197.5-6, Nazianzen celebrates her: "Theosebia, the truly sacred" (*tēn ontōs hieran*), and "truly colleague of a priest and endowed with a dignity equal to his" (*hiereōs syzygon kai omotimon*) and "worthy of the great Mysteries" (*tōn megalōn mystēriōn haxian*). The latter phrase, "worthy of the great Mysteries," suggests Eucharistic presidency.

Nazianzen was a presbyter and bishop, just like Theosebia's brother and colleague, Gregory of Nyssa. That he spoke in such high terms of Theosebia, whom he called "my Theosebia" (*Theosebian tēn hemēn*), because of her "life consecrated to God" (Letter 197.5), is remarkable. More remarkable still, he deems Theosebia the most outstanding among her illustrious siblings, declared more outstanding even than Gregory and Basil.

Even if one wished to interpret *adelphōn* as indicating siblings, Nazianzan's words would imply that Theosebia was more illustrious than

Macrina, the firstborn, deeply respected by Gregory of Nyssa. Given Macrina's status as the founder of a great monastery, that eulogy, if not dismissed as exaggerated hyperbole, is explicable only if Theosebia's ministry was that of a presbyter. Notable among Gregory Nazianzen's words is the description of Theosebia as "truly sacred and truly colleague of a priest and endowed with *a dignity equal to his* and worthy of the great Mysteries" (italics ours). Theosebia is said to have been ἱερά and a colleague (*syzygos*) of a priest (*hiereus*), and a priest herself. Taken together, these remarks indicate that in Gregory Nazianzen's letter, *syzygos* means not "wife" but "colleague in the priestly office." *Syzygos*, meaning "colleague," frequently occurs in the writings of Gregory Nazianzen. In all cases, the term indicates equality.

That Theosebia was a priest-colleague is confirmed by Gregory Nazianzen stating that she was not only the colleague of a priest but was invested with a dignity, and enjoyed an honor, equal to that of a priest (*hiereōs homotimos*). Basil, also her brother, uses the term ὁμότιμος to indicate the equality of dignity and honor between woman and man. That *hiereōs homotimos* must be understood in this sense of equality is confirmed by Nazianzen's statement, immediately following, that Theosebia, evidently by virtue of her ecclesial office, had such a dignity (*axia*) as to be worthy to participate in the celebration of the "great Mysteries," a term that had indicated the celebration of the Eucharist since Clement of Alexandria (150–215 CE).

Nazianzen's words referring to Theosebia, priestly colleague (ἱερέως ὁμότιμος), indicate at least a woman presbyter. He uses this wording twice. Remarkably, in Epigram 164, Nazianzen, immediately after the three bishops, Basil, Peter, and Gregory, does not mention other brothers of theirs, not even Naucratius, who was an exemplary ascetic, nor does he cite their eldest sister, Macrina, whom Gregory of Nyssa profoundly revered and who was the founder of the Annesi monastery;[5] instead he mentions Theosebia. Although Macrina, superior of a monastery, and the eldest among her siblings, was a consecrated virgin; Theosebia had received presbyteral ordination.

Gregory of Nyssa, Theosebia's colleague and brother, is praised by Gregory Nazianzen soon after her and in close association with her,

---

5. A single monastic unit of men and women where Macrina served as leader. In 787 the Seventh Ecumenical Council approved these structures and their statutes, which became known as the rule of Saint Basil. Sunberg, *The Cappadocian Mothers*, 161.

celebrated because he was a great priest or bishop (ἱερεύς μέγας). In the eyes of Gregory Nazianzen, presbyteral and episcopal ordination were his most important attributes. Theosebia's ministry, as described by Gregory Nazianzen, involved participation in the presidency of the Eucharist and the spiritual and perhaps material support offered to pious women of her church. It is noteworthy that the functions of a presbyter or bishop (*hiereus*) that Gregory Nazianzen indicates in *Carmina*—the celebration of the Eucharistic sacrifice and care of souls—are identical to those which he ascribes to Theosebia, the colleague and equal (*homotimos*) of a presbyter. Theosebia was certainly ordained and on the basis of what can be inferred from Nazianzen's writings, it is reasonable to conclude that she had been ordained a presbyter.

## ORDAINED WOMEN IN CAPPADOCIA

There is all but indisputable evidence of ordained women deacons. Three daughters of Terentius, the governor of Cappadocia in the early 370s, were deacons. Their orthodoxy was crucial in support of Basil, Gregory's and Theosebia's brother, an important anti-Arian and anti-Macedonian Catholic bishop, who in Letter 105, (dated c. 372 CE), when he was bishop of Caesarea in Cappadocia, praised their orthodox (Nicene) faith as crucial in a time of hostile debate. Theosebia, like her brothers, was doctrinally Catholic; she was anti-Arian and anti-Macedonian and her presbyteral ministry required of her to be a doctrinal guide. Even abstracting from her presbyteral ordination, it is legitimate to infer that she exercised a form of authority and governance, not only in her local church, but more widely in Cappadocia.

This is confirmed by Gregory Nazianzen's words of praise in Letter 197 that she was "the advantage of the generation" of the Cappadocians, "the adornment of Christ," and "the glory of the Church." Nazianzen moreover, is unmistakably speaking of the orthodox, Catholic Church. Analysis of Theosebia's office with those of contemporary, ordained women in Cappadocia seems to corroborate that Theosebia, whom Gregory Nazianzen repeatedly describes as colleague and *homotimos* of a *hiereus*, was certainly ordained, and probably a presbyter.

## ORDAINED DEACONESSES IN THE WEST

In the West, opposition to women's diaconal ordination became widespread, even conventional, as exemplified by a letter of Pope Zachary to Pippin and the Frankish bishops and abbots (747), who writes concerning nuns: "that it is a sin for women to serve at the altar"; his letter ostensibly quoting that of Pope Gelasius *(see below)*. In the other direction, a letter from the bishops to Louis the Pious (829) declares that they: "Have attempted in every way possible . . . to prevent women from approaching that altar as it is forbidden, . . . women are not allowed to enter the sanctuary."[6] The context may suggest that both these letters are speaking of diaconal rather than presbyteral ministry. But it also suggests that the practice of ordaining women deacons had not completely disappeared in the West as late as the ninth century.

There are certainly examples of women co-officiating at the altar of the Eucharist in early sixth-century Brittany, "*le ministère diaconal proprement dit,*" as evidenced by a letter from three bishops, Licinius of Tours, Melanius of Rennes, and Eustochius of Angers, forbidding it.[7] The women ministers, "*ces femmes que vous appelez conhospitae,*" evidently women deacons, administered Holy Communion from the chalice in Eucharistic celebrations on portable altars, which these presbyters wheeled from house to house. Thus, the bishops were prohibiting two practices that they considered irregular. That, however, must be viewed against the background of Celtic migrations into Brittany and the emergence there of a missionary church.[8]

Speaking of the women ministers as *conhospitae* probably intends to be derogatory, but it is important to note that the *virgines subintroductae* of the Celtic church were ascetical, spiritual women[9] of standing and agency, and in the main not at all the *mulieres subintroductae*, effectively

---

6. Cited by LaCelle-Peterson, *Liberating Tradition*, 159.

7. "Cet abus, consistait à confier à des femmes la distribution de l'Eucharistie sous l'espèce du vin, et, en général, l'assistance du prêtre à l'autel, le ministère diaconal proprement dit." Duschene, *Lovocat et Catihern; Prêtres Bretons du temps de Sainte Melaine*, 6.

8. Bailey, "The Strange Case of the Portable Altar," 31–51.

9. This is especially evident in the Irish church of that period. Cf., Reynolds, *Virgines Subintroductae in Celtic Christianity*, 547–66. This practice, typologically drawing on the apocryphally constructed *Acts of Paul and Thecla*, was a key element in Christian asceticism of the Eastern Empire, cf. Brown, *The Body and Society*, 267–75. A famous example, in modern times, is illustrated in Mahatma Gandhi's practice of Brahmachariya.

concubines, of later controversy. Such ascetical, spiritual women formed a notable aspect of first-millennial Irish Christianity.[10] J. Lodt, while anachronistically dismissing this women's liturgical practice as the heresy of Pepundius,[11] infers that it was widespread in Britain and Ireland.[12]

## POPE GELASIUS WRITES OF WOMEN PRIESTS

In 494 Gelasius I, Pope during 492–496, wrote an epistle:[13] "to all episcopates established in Lucania, Bruttium, and Sicilia," which furnishes evidence that there were women priests being ordained at the end of the fifth century. This epistle, addressed to three episcopal conferences and not just to one single bishop, contained twenty-seven decrees, one of which explicitly confronts the question of women priests: "Nevertheless we have heard to our annoyance that divine affairs have come to such a low state that women are encouraged to officiate at the sacred altars, and to take part in all matters imputed to the offices of the male sex, to which they do not belong."[14]

The clear basis of the letter was that Pope Gelasius had learned that women were being admitted "to officiating at sacred altars" (*sacris altaribus ministrare*), an expression that unmistakably indicates ordained, priestly ministry. The term "officiate" (*ministrare*) corresponds to the Greek *leitourgein*, adopted from canonical Christian Scripture, as found in Acts 13:2 and Hebrews 10:11.

Whether the expression "that women are encouraged to officiate at the sacred altars" (*ut feminae sacris altaribus ministrare firmentur*), if taken on its own, refers to deaconesses or presbyters, is inconsequential.

---

10. Harrington, "The Virgin Consort in Hagiography," in *Women in a Celtic Church*, 256–70.

11. The letter of Licinius et al. speaks of a "*secte abominable qui n'avait jamais été introduite dans les Gaules.*"

12. Haddan and Stubbs, *Councils and Ecclesiastical Documents Relating to Great Britain and Ireland*, 271, but cf. especially p. 292 and also Lodt, *Un Ancien Usage de l'Église Celtique*, 92–93.

13. Ep. 14, in Thiel, *Epistulae Romanorum pontificum genuinae*, 360–79, as cited in Otranto, *Note sul sacerdozio femminile nell'antichità in margine a una testimonianze di Gelasio 1*, 341–60. Otranto's study in translated by Rossi, *Priesthood, Precedent, and Prejudice*, 73–94.

14. "Nihifaminus impatienter audivimus, tantum divinarum rerum subisse despectum, ut feminae sacris altaribus ministrare firmentur, cunctaque non nisi virorum famulatui deputata sexum, cui non competunt, exhibere." (As cited by Otranto)

For Gelasius immediately adds that he has known that women were performing *all* the functions (*cunctaque... exhibere*) that had been assigned to the ministry of men only, and not to the female sex. Elsewhere in this letter, Gelasius adopts "ecclesiastical service" as a synonym of presbyteral ministry. Thus, *"virorum famulatui"* indicates the ministry of presbyter, and, as is clear from the word "all" (*cuncta*), it comprises *all* the aspects of [male] priestly services: liturgical, juridical, and magisterial.

Pope Gelasius intended to condemn what he regarded as a serious abuse: that of women presbyters performing duties he would insist should be reserved to men. This reading clarifies not only *"tantus divinarum rerum despectus"* ("such disrespect for divine affairs") but also the insistent wording of the decree, in which Gelasius condemns those bishops who either commit such putative abuses, or appear to favor them by not denouncing them.

He does all of that however, without ever specifying scriptural or theological foundations for rejecting admission of women to the priesthood. He writes juridically, canonically. He refers to rules and canons: to the *regula Cristiana, regulae ecclesiasticae,* and *canones* that some bishops had either violated or ignored. Evidently, he regarded a repeated call to canonical decisions and laws as sufficient to reveal the gravity of the condemned abuse. In so doing, even when quoting the canons of a local synod, he engages in a *canonical* rather than a *theological* discourse.[15]

Insistent reference to the responsibilities of the bishops "who commit these [errors]" (*qui ista committunt*) and "who dared to carry out these acts" (*qui haec ausi sunt exercere*) probably indicates a relatively wide extent of the phenomenon in question. *Committere* and *exercere* suggest active participation of some bishops in the perpetration of what Pope Gelasius considers an "abuse." His judgment referred to a mandate specifically conferred by some bishops on women for the exercise of sacerdotal ministry. These bishops, he writes, have "brought great destruction

---

15. The canons to which Gelasius was referring were probably 19 of the Council of Nicaea, 11 and 44 of the Council of Laodicea, 2 of the Council of Nimes (394 or 396), 25 of the First Council of Orange (441), which prohibit women from being a member of the clergy. Nicaea 19 is arguably the most important of these. It laid down rules regarding deaconesses who converted from the heresy of Paul of Samosata, whose baptisms and *a fortiori* whose ordinations were judged invalid since they denied the Trinity. Nicaea ruled that such deaconesses, if they were worthy, should be rebaptized and reordained by the bishop. (The council fathers belatedly realized that this rule made no sense with regard to Paulianist deaconesses, because in their sect, deaconesses were not ordained.)

upon the church," "with various motives" (*multimodis impulsionibus*), the gravest of which is the conferring of Holy Orders on women.

Those ordinations were probably not isolated phenomena. Gelasius sent the same epistle to other local churches concerned with the same problems. One may infer that at the end of the fifth century, some women, ordained by Catholic bishops in communion with Rome, were presbyters exercising the ministerial priesthood in a fairly wide area of southern Italy and in other regions too. Southern Italy was culturally connected with Byzantine areas where, from the third century on, women exercised the diaconate. But "all episcopates established in Lucania, Bruttium, and Sicilia" went beyond this in conferring priesthood on women. There undoubtedly were ordained women priests in Southern Italy and Sicily at this time. Otherwise, why would Gelasius I have prohibited the practice of ordaining them?

## PRESBYTERS LETA AND FLAVIA

In this light, some intriguing ancient inscriptions take on added significance. On one of them we read: *"Sacred to her good memory: Leta the Presbyter* [presbytera] *lived 40 years, 8 months, 9 days, for whom her husband set up this tomb. She preceded him in peace on the day before the Ides of May."*[16] The epitaph explicitly refers to a presbyter, Leta, who died aged just over forty, for whom her husband had constructed a tomb. In the light of the Gelasian epistle, one may infer that the Leta of the epigraph of Tropea was an actual *presbytera*, exercising sacerdotal ministry among the Christian community of Tropea—today a municipality in Calabria.

If Leta had been simply the wife of a presbyter, one would have to draw the rather unlikely inference that her husband, who built the tomb, declined to designate himself as a presbyter in order to confer this designation upon his wife. But every recorded time a presbyter prepares a tomb for his wife, he always refers to her by the term *coniux*—wife, or sometimes *amantissima*—most loving. Moreover, the coupling of words *presbyter-presbytera* to identify *presbytera* as the wife of the presbyter, has been found, but not the coupling *maritus/coniux/vir-presbytera*. Another

---

16. "B(onae) m(emoriae) s(acrum). Leta presbitera vixit annos XL menses VIII dies VIIII (sic) quei (seil, cui) bene fecit maritus Precessit in pace pridie idus Matas." 54CIL10. 8079; De Rossi in *"Bollettino di Archeologia Cristiana"* (1877): 88 tav. 7 4; Diehl, *"Inscriptiones Latinae Christianae Veteres,"* 1192.

*presbytera*, Flavia, is recorded in a comparable inscription on a sarcophagus from Salona in Dalmatia.[17]

## ARCHAEOLOGY

Just as archaeology has significantly illuminated biblical studies, so has it shed considerable light on the historical study of significant women leaders, including female presbyters, in the church of the first five centuries.[18] At Uçak in Phrygia there is a tombstone, one of a series of the same type, on which is inscribed: *"Bishop Diogas in memory of Ammion the presbyter."* Ammion is a woman's name frequently found in Asia Minor. Diogas a bishop in the early third century, probably erected this tombstone for a women presbyter of that name. Her only attribute mentioned is that she was a *presbytera*.

Although it does not contain the distinguishing term *"pneumatikos,"* that inscription may possibly point to Montanist provenance. Certainly Epiphanius, in his *Panarion* (c. 377), mentions such heretical groups who ordain women as bishops and priests. His negative view of such behavior is illustrated in his discourse on the Collyridians,[19] whose syncretist practices he examines to argue that women have never properly ministered in a priestly role. Epiphanius concludes that the only official church office for women is that of deaconess, whose activities he endeavours to depict as minimally as possible. In so doing, he argues that older deaconesses and widows were called *presbytides* or eldresses. In the present study, however, in line with its focus, examples refer overwhelmingly to ordained women in the Catholic Church.

Epiphanius' minimalism may be read against the background of canon 11 of the Synod of Laodicea, which attests to the existence of women presbyters called *presbytides*, who acted as presidents of congregations, even if only to order that such *presbytides* should not be installed.

---

17. This stone coffin bears the consular date of 425: "*Ego Thaeodo(sius) emi a Fl(avia) Vitalia pr(es)b(ytera) sanc(ta) matro/na auri sol(idis) III. Sub d(ie). . . .* The inscription reads that Theodosius had acquired for three golden solids, a plot in the cemetery of Salona from the *presbytera* Flavia Vitalia. Here a *presbytera* has been invested with an official duty, which during a certain period was appropriate to a presbyter.

18. Eisen, *Women Officeholders in Early Christianity*, 116–142.

19. *Panarion*, 375 AD, VII:1,6 cf. Bareille, "Collyridiens," in *Dictionaire de Theologie Catholique*, and Salmon, "Collyridians," in Smith and White (eds.), *A Dictionary of Christian Biography*, who suggests the term κολλυρις is cognate with 2 Sam 8:68.

Although this canon survives only in summary form, it seems clear that its employment of the term *presbytides* is not in relation to older women as such, but in the sense of church office, leadership within the community, leading the assembly and presiding at the Holy Eucharist. The term used, *prokathésthai*, is also used of bishops, presbyters, and deacons by Ignatius (Ign. *Magn.* 6.1.2) to mean "preside."

The phrase *"en ekklesia kathistasthai"* is the technical term for the installation of a cleric and in the Synod of Laodicea it is used exclusively to mark the installation in office of higher clergy. Restriction of the office of *presbytides* with the intent of excluding women from any service of the altar, indicates that *presbytides* belonged to the higher clergy. If theirs had been only a marginal ministry, one of little note, it would scarcely have been necessary to forbid it by a synodal canon. That *presbytides* were women presbyters, is supported by the reception of this canon. Isodore (365–435) and Dionysius Exigus (497–545) effectively translate *kathistasthai* as *ordinare*: to ordain. Atto of Vercelli (885–961) (see below), understands their duties as "preaching, ordering, and instructing," adding, "practices today not at all in use."

In Thera in Greece was found the inscription: "*Angel of the Presbyter Epikto,*" one of about forty-five inscriptions in the region, each introduced by the word *angelos*. The angelology of these inscriptions is taken as Christian as it contains no Jewish characteristics. A central argument for Christian provenance is the title "Presbyter" given to Epikto. She was likely the presbyter of a community of Christians on the island of Thera in the Cylades of the south Aegean sea.

## EVIDENCE OF WOMEN PRESBYTERS

Another inscription, Egyptian, reads: "*[Mummy of] the presbyter Artemidora, daughter of Mikkalos [and] mother Paniskiana. She has fallen asleep in the Lord.*" "Presbyter" is found in the second line, as abbreviated to *pres'b'*. While that could be made to refer to the mother, in the sense of "the elder," abbreviations such as *pres'b'*, as a rule, refer to the title "Presbyter." The placing of *pres'b'* after parents' names, age, and place of origin, moreover, underscores her designation as a presbyter.

Literary support comes from *Testamentum Domini* (TD), a treatise on Orders from the early fifth century, its origins in Syria or Egypt, which twice mentions women presbyters. They are remembered in the community's prayers as follows: *"For the presbyteresses let us beseech that the Lord may hear their supplications and keep their hearts perfectly in the grace of the Spirit and help their work"* (TD 1.35). Later we read of a vigil: *"Let the presbyteresses stay with the bishop until dawn, praying and resting"* (TD 2.19). That means that by the fifth century, women presbyters had not been completely suppressed, even if there is some uncertainty as to their duties. Importantly, these texts indicate that women presbyters were not simply restricted to heretical groups such as the Montanists, but were active in many places in the East until a growing abolition from the fourth century on.

In the West an inscription was found in Centuripae in Sicily: *"Here lies the presbyter Kale who lived fifty years without reproach. She ended her life on 14 September."* From the abbreviation πρεσβ, it may be uncertain if that means *presbytis* or *presbytera*, a false dilemma, however, since both terms are attested as official titles. As mentioned, the letter of Pope Gelasius sheds light on this epigraph, as it does on those of Leta of Tropea and Flavia of Salona in Dalmatia, as already discussed, of whom the abbreviation *prb* (πρβ), is also used.

Yet another epigraph from Salona cryptically reads: *sace[rdotae]+*. The cross attests that this fragment comes from a Christian tomb and does not refer to a pagan *sacerdota*. *Sacerdos* was certainly used as a term for bishops and occasionally for presbyters, from the fourth to the sixth century. That women ministered as presbyters in Salona, makes it possible, while not evident, that here *sacerdotae* refers to bishops.

## FURTHER ARCHEOLOGICAL EVIDENCE

Further archeological evidence continues to be unearthed showing instances of official, liturgical, ministry of women in the church of the first millennium.[20] It is reasonable to suppose that in the future, there may well be many more such discoveries. Among important findings presented by Ally Kateusz in July 2019 to the International Society of Biblical Literature, meeting at the Gregorian University, are three of the earliest surviving images of Christians worshipping at important church altars, showing women in official liturgical roles.

The first is a stone sarcophagus front from Hagia Sophia in Constantinople, c. 430 (CE), now at the Istanbul Archaeological Museum,

---

20. MacDonald, "Artifacts Show That Early Church Women Served as Clergy."

showing a male and a female figure standing on either side of the altar, their arms raised in the *orans* pose. The second, an ivory reliquary box from the same period, depicts a man and a woman standing on either side of the altar of Old Saint Peter's Basilica in Rome, each raising a chalice—clearly recognizable as a liturgical act. The third is a sixth-century ivory pyx from Jerusalem, featuring two women carrying censers of incense at the altar in the Church of the Holy Sepulcher in Jerusalem.

Interpreting depiction of the lifting of the chalice during the Eucharist, as exemplifying priesthood, is not incontrovertible. A woman raising a chalice could be consistent with the female deacon's role in the Eucharist. Moreover, there are no extant ordination ceremonies for women as priests, but there are many for women as deacons. Nonetheless, the most obvious interpretation of these artefacts is that women held ordained, liturgical ministries in the early church.

## WOMEN OVERSEERS— BISHOPS IN THE NEW TESTAMENT

Women acted as patronesses and benefactresses in the social hierarchy of the Roman Empire. For several generations, Luke's reading community would have read Luke 8:1–3 and Acts 16:11–15 as indicating women who were important and influential members of the very early Church. The concluding phrase of Luke 8:3, "out of their own resources" (*ek tōn hyparchontōn*), was such an established benefaction formula that it was often abbreviated with its initials. Certainly, Luke in his challenge to imperial, socio-cultural boundaries, blunts the imperialist understanding of client-recipient and patron-benefactrix characterized in an exchange of loyalty for political support. Paul's description of Phoebe illustrates this.

Luke's readers would never have seen these women as background players or uninvolved donors. The case of Joanna, wife of Herod's steward, suggests that at least some if not all of these were women of means. She and the others mentioned would have been understood as wielding influence on the disciples. They would, to that extent, have been part of the emerging early governance structure of the primitive Church, soon to be referred to as *episkopoi*.[21]

In Luke's post-resurrection narrative, at least some of these women who accompanied Jesus are actually apostles to the apostles (and are

---

21. Miller, *Cut from the Same Cloth*, 203–10.

disbelieved by the apostles). Such *tendenzlös* writing indisputably points to a factual historical core. A comparison with Rhoda, a female servant dismissed as "out of her mind" in Acts 12:12–17, is instructive. When that text is read in parallel with Luke 24:1–11, its closely similar vocabulary reinforces the memory of a primitive tradition of female, apostolic witness meeting male resistance. Some women, Martha as we have already seen, being an outstanding example, were therefore important, formative confessors of the faith: real leaders or overseers of communities. If Luke generally uses *diakonein* to speak of such ministry, he does so when the *diakonos-episcopos* distinction, not to mention its as-yet-unclarified relationship to the initially distinct *presbyteros* line of ministerial development, is still being clarified. A homogeneous structure of church ministry was still far from being calcified.

Paul, himself an apostle, would have understood and referred to his ministry as *diakonia*. He speaks frequently of the *diakonia* with which he has been entrusted and associates it with his apostolic mission. It is the *diakonia* of bringing people to faith (1 Cor 3:5), the *diakonia* of reconciliation (2 Cor 3:6; 5:18), the *diakonia* of the gospel of the glory of Christ and of his lordship (2 Cor 4:1–6). For Paul, *diakonia* stands for his fundamental commissioning as a minister of the gospel of Christ— but that does not mean he was not also an apostle, a title and office he repeatedly claims and the one most markedly celebrated in the tradition of the Church. One can surmise that in the beginning, before a process of domestication and gradual displacement changed things, there were significant women who ministered as importantly and formatively as significant men. Both exercised the ministry of overseeing that would come to be termed episcopacy: women were *episkopoi*.[22]

## WOMEN BISHOPS

At Interamna in Umbria a seven-line inscription from around 500 AD includes the words: *"If you will traveller, recognize this inscription: here rests the venerable lady Bishop Q[. . .]" (venerabilis fem[ina] episcopa Q[. . .])*. The name of this *episcopa* is lost. Interpretation as the wife of a bishop is problematic, since the inscription contains no reference to a husband. The adjective *venerabililis*, found in another *episcopos* inscription from

---

22. The masculine form rather than a putative use of *episkopai* is used by analogy with the occurrence of *diakonos* rather than *diakonissa* for female deacons (see above).

Umbria, was a term usually applied to the clergy, though not limited to them. Some light is shed by canon 14 of the Council of Tours (567): "*A bishop* [male] *who has no bishop* [female] *may have no women in his entourage.*" Against the assumption that *episcop(i)a* refers to wives, the *Historiae* of Gregory of Tours (538–594), frequently mentioning bishops' wives, never refers to one of them as *episcopa,* but as *coniux.*[23]

Yet another acknowledged *episcopa* was demonstrably not a bishop's wife: Theodora the mother of Pascal I, Pope from 817–824, whose father Nonosus is also mentioned without any ecclesiastical title. Paschal I restored many churches, notably Santa Cecilia in Trastevere. In another of his restorations, Santa Prassade, he built the chapel of Saint Zeno, where there are two inscriptions attesting to *"Episcopa* Theodora," one a mosaic and one on a reliquary. In the mosaic, Theodora is depicted with a rectangular halo—indicating a living person of high rank. The last two letters of her name are illegible, yet there are no traces of restoration. The reliquary inscription is fifty-six lines long and includes the following: "*Therefore the aforementioned Praesul has placed at the very entrance of the basilica, on the right side, where the body of his gracious mother, the lady Theodora the bishop, rests . . .*" (benignissime suae genetricis scililcet domnae theodorae episcopae corpus quiescit . . .).

Is the title "bishop" honorific or does placement of the word *episcopa* after Theodora's name indicate episcopal office? In turn, what is the reason the title *episcopa* is omitted in some reproductions of the inscription? Conservative commentators constantly interpret *episcopa* as an honorific for a bishop's wife. But Nonosus, Theodora's husband, was *not* a bishop. Interpretations vary: for some, *episcopa* is an honorific derived from her generous support of the church; for others, it connotes being the overseer of a group of virgins and widows, many of whom are named but are not connected to Theodora, as they surely would have been, were she actually their head; or in another understanding of overseer, she is an abbess; still others see a later interpolation, but even if so, which cannot be established, that does not answer our question, because Theodora is commemorated in two distinct ways. While an element of uncertainty remains, official ministry as a bishop in Rome many not be simply excluded *a priori.*

---

23. Eisen, *Women Officeholders in Early Christianity,* 199–216.

## WOMEN OVERSEERS BEFORE MONARCHIC EPISCOPY

*Episkopoi*, bishops, were originally a group or community of overseers or administrators. The plural usage in Philippians 1:1 clearly conveys that early meaning. House churches were, at least in some cases, overseen and administered by women. Not only the Pauline letters, but later ones from Ignatius, give evidence of this. Priscilla has been frequently mentioned in this regard, others may well include Nympha of Colossians 4:15, who *prima facie* was the overseer (*episcopa*) of a house church, as were Tania (Ign. *Smyrn.* 13.2) and the widow of Strops (Ign. *Pol.* 8.2). When Ignatius writes to the church at Rome, we find, astonishingly perhaps, that he, like Paul before him, makes not a single mention of a bishop there. The word occurs only twice in the letter, both times of himself as a bishop in Syria. Since the office of bishop was a high priority for him, it is scarcely conceivable that if there were a monarchical bishop in Rome at that time, Ignatius would have completely ignored him. He would surely have addressed him personally. It may be considered evidence that such an office did not exist there at that time.[24]

*Shepherd of Hermas* (Rome c. 140 CE), "hovered for a long time on the fringe of the canon, but in the end failed to secure admission,"[25] even though it is included in the Codex Sinaiticus. It mentions a woman called Grapte who may have been an overseer-bishop in Rome, around the first half of the second century, when a monarchic episcopacy was neither a fact nor even an aspiration there.[26] Contemporary sources provide no evidence for a monarchical episcopate at the end of the first century, except in Asia Minor and Syria, and even in that region monarchical episcopate was a still-developing phenomenon. Promoted by Ignatius (c. 115), by the time of Irenaeus (c. 189) it was widely established in the West, but probably not yet in Rome at the time of *Shepherd of Hermas*, where the omission of any mention of a monarchical episcopate is noteworthy. A

---

24. Strand, *The Rise of the Monarchical Episcopate*, 65–88; Burke, *Monarchical Episcopate at the End of the First Century*, 499–518 and 507–8.

25. Kelly, *Early Christian Doctrines*, 59–60.

26. This without prejudice to the ministry and office of Saint Peter in Rome. The Petrine office was Peter's calling and ministry before his coming to Rome and subsequent martyrdom there under Nero c. 64 CE. On the implications of the location and veneration of Peter's tomb, cf. Guarducci, *The Tomb of St. Peter*, 60–93.

community of *episkopoi*, not a single, monarchic *episkopos*, as the primitive practice, is certainly indicated by Philippians 1:1.

Given Grapte's textually acknowledged responsibility for widows, she was probably at least a deaconess, but may have been more, given her obvious importance alongside Clement and the presbyters. It is difficult to find evidence explicitly and unquestionably attesting to women bishops, but in the early stage of the development of the episcopal office, when it was more clearly a ministry of overseeing, administration, and supervision, women apparently exercised that ministry, not only in house churches, but in a wider sphere too.[27]

With the uniform establishment of a monarchic episcopacy, such influential women were installed as deacons, but that at a time when the bishop was frequently chosen from among the deacons. One such deaconess was Olympias of Constantinople, *anamchara* of John Chrysostom, widowed in her twenties and immensely wealthy, with some 250 dependents in the convent by the church in Constantinople and she herself living an ascetic life and ordained by dispensation at the age of thirty.[28]

## ATTO OF VERCELLI (885–961)

Attestation to the historical reality of women priests is also provided by Atto II, a Lombard who became bishop of Vercelli, in modern Piedmont, in 924. A priest named Ambrose asked Atto how the terms *"presbytera"* and *"diacona"* of the ancient canon ought to be understood—a question many ask today. Bishop Atto begins his answer by underlining that since in the ancient Church: "The harvest was great but the labourers were few" (Matt 9:37; Luke 10:2), women too received the Sacred Orders for the helping of men, as is attested in Romans 16:1: "I commend you to my sister Phoebe, who is in the ministry of the church which is in Cenchrae"

---

27. The 'woman' of the early revelations of *Shepherd of Hermes*, an authoritative agent of revelation there, represents a version of a feminine understanding of church that pre-dates later institutional developments. This older woman's reception and transmission of revelation is not reducible to the instruction of leaders who here do not speak for the church, and functions as a strategy for critiquing church leadership. Walsh, *Ecclesia Reconsidered: Two Pre-modern Encounters with the Feminine Church*, 73–91.

28. Brown, *The Body and Society*, 282–84.

(*Commendo vobis Phaebem sororem meam, quae est in ministerio Ecclesiae, quae est Cenchris*).[29]

Expanding on the status of the deaconess, Atto stresses that in the ancient Christian Church not only men, but also women were ordained (*ordinabantur*) and were the leaders of church communities (*praeerant ecclesiis*); they were called *presbyterae* and they assumed the duty of preaching, directing, and teaching *(quae presbyterae dicebantur, praedicandi, iubendi, vel edocendi . . . officium sumpserant)*—the three duties that define the priestly ministry. Atto's statement seems a striking testimony to female, Catholic priesthood in antiquity. For him, it was the Council of Laodicea that prohibited the presbyteral ordination of women.[30] The term he uses, *postmodum*, indicates that the prohibition came "later" or "afterwards" and therefore was not something in place from the beginning. It further indicates that the prohibition was a matter of *synodal law* and *not of Christian doctrine*.

His testimony is strikingly relevant to the present-day debate. He is historically informed, theologically perceptive, and canonically observant. He knows the rules and he keeps them, but he also knows that things were not always exactly so and, by implication, need not always remain so.

## MINIMIZING THE EVIDENCE

The International Theological Commission (ITC) in 2002, did not seem to accept that what is sauce for the gander is sauce for the goose. It consistently minimized the available evidence. Thus, in its view, Phoebe was not a deacon "because the word *servant*"—a somewhat tendentious translation—"is not given a feminine suffix but preceded by a feminine article"; "exegetes are divided on the subject of First Timothy 3:11"; "*women* may suggest women deacons or deacons' wives"; Pliny the Younger—who wrote in Latin and used the term *ministrae*—"does not refer to women deacons because it was not until the third century that the *diaconissa* or *diacona* appeared."

---

29. "*quae est in ministerio Ecclesiae*," seemingly minimizes: "οὖσαν διάκονον τῆς ἐκκλησίας."

30. "Quod Laodicense *postmodum* (italics ours) prohibet concilium cap. 11, cum dicitur: quod non oportet eas quae dicuntur presbyterae vel praesidentes in Ecclesiis ordinari."

Acknowledging the fact that deaconesses are mentioned in the *Didascalia Apostolorum*, it dismisses *Didascalia Apostolorum* as "not official" and insists there was no strict parallel between the two branches of the diaconate with regard to their functions. Neither were *Constitutiones Apostolorum* (Syria 380) ever considered to be a "canonical collection." *Constitutiones Apostolorum* envisaged the imposition of hands with the epiklesis of the Holy Spirit for the deaconesses, sub-deacons, and lectors (cf. *Constitutiones Apostolorum* 8.16–23). The concept of *kleros* was broadened to all those who exercised a liturgical ministry, to include deaconesses, while the widows were excluded. *Constitutiones Apostolorum* insists that the deaconesses should have no liturgical function (3.9.1–2). Obviously, a text does not need to be canonically official to be historically accurate.

It accepts that canon 15 of the Council of Chalcedon (451) seems to confirm the fact that deaconesses really were "ordained" by the imposition of hands (*cheirotonia*); their ministry was called "*leitourgia*" and after ordination they were not allowed to marry. In eighth-century Byzantium, the bishop still imposed hands on a deaconess, conferred on her the stole, gave her the chalice, which she placed on the altar without giving communion to anyone. Deaconesses were ordained in the course of the Eucharistic liturgy, in the sanctuary, like deacons. Still the ITC concludes that despite the similarities between the rites of ordination, deaconesses did not have access to the altar or to any liturgical ministry. These ordinations, it anachronistically suggests, were intended mainly for the superiors of women's monasteries. It references how in the West, councils of the fourth and fifth centuries forbid any ordination of deaconesses.

Deaconesses did indeed exist, their ministry developing unevenly in different parts of the Church. The ITC maintains this ministry was not perceived as simply the feminine equivalent of the masculine diaconate. It concluded[31] that the women deacons of history were not identical to male deacons, as "evidenced by the rite of institution and the functions

---

31. International Theological Commission, *From the Diakonia of Christ to the Diakonia of the Apostles* (2002). The foreword states: "The work was carried out by a subcommission ... presided over by Mgr. Max Thurian. ... [T]his subcommission was not able to extend its work as far as the production of a text [a euphemism for inability to agree]. ... A new subcommission was formed in order to carry out the work, presided over by Rev. Henrique de Noronha Galvão, former student of Joseph Ratzinger and Portugese editor of *Communio*." [Replacements of personnel were not insignificant.] It was then submitted to its president, Cardinal J. Ratzinger, Prefect of the Congregation for the Doctrine of Faith, who authorized its publication.

they exercised."[32] That would imply that eighth-century ordination liturgies such as in the Barbarini codex, virtually identical for men and women deacons, did not incorporate women into the order of deacon, but were mainly for monastic women; whereby the women so ordained, were judged to exercise no liturgical ministry.

Nonetheless that commission has left open the door to the reintroduction of ordained women deacons. Its penultimate paragraph reads:

> In the light of these elements which have been set out in the present historico-theological research document, it pertains to the ministry of discernment which the Lord established in his Church to pronounce authoritatively on this question.

## POPE FRANCIS' COMMISSION ON FEMALE DEACONS

Pope Francis created a study commission on diaconal ordination for women, in 2016, at the request of the International Union of Women Superiors General (UISG). In July 2019, he acknowledged, to disenchantment in some quarters,[33] that the commission had been unable to find consensus and had yet to give a "definitive response." He made it clear however, that while the commission was no longer operative, its members were continuing with their research. The report: "could serve as the launching point for going ahead and studying, and giving a definitive response"; adding: "I am not afraid of studies."[34]

For Pope Francis, the main unresolved issue regarding women deacons of the past was that "there is not certainty that it was an ordination with the same formula and the same finality of men's ordination." In surmising that such ordinations "looked more like those for what would today be the blessing of an abbess," he discloses his basic quandary: "Was it a sacramental ordination, or not? It's what they are discussing and are

---

32. "Le Diaconat: Évolution et perspectives," http://www.vatican.va/roman_curia/congregations/cfaith/cti_documents/rc_con_cfaith_pro_05072004_diaconate_fr.html.

33. Intensified by Francis' ironical description of variant opinions among the commission members as "toads from different wells." By contrast, he also described these differences as a *"varietas delectas"* (joyful variety).

34. Accessible at https://zh-cn.facebook.com/.../posts/2350141635006497; cf. O'Connell, "Pope Francis Says Commission on Women Deacons Did Not Reach Agreement."

not seeing clearly." Consequently, he states, "I cannot make a sacramental decree without a theological, historical foundation."

Posing the question in that manner risks disregarding how the Catholic understanding of "sacrament" has undergone development, especially after the twelfth century. Such development amplifies but does not negate earlier understandings.[35] The problem, moreover, does not seem to be the evidence of ordination of women deacons, but how it is interpreted. Scholars point to manuscripts from the fourth to the sixteenth centuries, in many libraries, including the Vatican Library, which *prima facie* indicate that the consecration rite of women deacons included all elements of sacramental, diaconal ordination (see below): the bishop's laying on of hands; an epiclesis; being vested in a stole; presentation of the chalice to her that she may self-communicate; after which the bishop addressed her as deacon. Why would he do so if that was not what he considered her to be?

Importantly, Pope Francis did not consider the matter closed. It was still an open question for him. In an audience with members of UISG, he made clear that the issue needed further study—though without saying who would do this work.

## SYNOD OF THE AMAZON

The Synod of Bishops from the Amazon, meeting at Rome during October 2019, declared in its final document that the issue of ordaining women as deacons had been "very present" during its discussions. In voting on the synodal document, all of its 120 paragraphs were adopted with the required two-thirds majority. The paragraph dealing with the discussion on women deacons, received 137 "yes" votes to thirty "no" votes. The final text states that the synod bishops recognize the "ministeriality" that Jesus entrusted to women. In a section prior to that, the bishops say they consider it "urgent" for the Church to "promote and confer ministries for men and women in an equitable manner."

In his remarks closing the synod's business, Francis said he was hoping to follow the bishops' text with his own document, likely to take the form of an apostolic exhortation—which unlike an apostolic constitution, a papal encyclical, or a *motu proprio*, neither clarifies doctrine nor enacts law.

---

35. To be discussed in detail in the following chapter.

## QUERIDA AMAZONIA

That Apostolic Exhortation, *Querida Amazonia*, 20 February 2020, was met with disappointment in some North Atlantic circles apparently more focused on the question of the female diaconate than on the synod's primary concerns—the degradation of the Amazonian biosphere and that of the planet itself, as well as the cruelty to its human population—correctly prioritized by Francis. The exhortation equally communicated how little would be achieved in clericalizing women's ministry, if ordained ministry cannot be liberated from clericalism—an insight shared by several feminist theologians.

Nonetheless, the section on "The strength and gift of women" (paragraphs 99–103) somewhat overextends the authentic complementarity of the genders in stressing: "the kind of power that is typically theirs [i.e., women's]" (101); "forms of service and charisms that are proper to women" (102); and "a way that reflects their womanhood" (103). That women are understood to do this "by making present the tender strength of Mary, the Mother" (101) could too easily be restrictively interpreted. Christ's compassion, including its mediation by male presbyters, is no less tender.

The document's orientation in giving this construction a theological basis—"The Lord chose to reveal his power and his love through two human faces: the face of his divine Son made man and the face of a creature, a woman, Mary" (101)—is likewise potentially problematic. The duality of God's self-communication is one of Word-Spirit rather than of gender difference. Mary's *fiat*, empowered by the Spirit, is intrinsic to the mystery of the incarnation of the Word. That *fiat* is no less a paradigm of obedience in faith for male disciples, including presbyters, than is Jesus' priestly ministry and sacrifice an exemplar for the ministry of faithful women in the Church, led by the Holy Spirit.

For all that, this pivotal exercise of synodality may prove seminal not only in relation to coming decisions but as to how decisions will be made. As is quite clear from paragraphs 2, 3, and 4 of *Querida Amazonia*, the issue of the female diaconate is by no means closed. Francis, in an explicit exercise of synodality, spells out that here he wishes "to offer [his] own response to this process of dialogue and discernment." He does not supersede the synod's final document. He is not overruling it: "Nor do I claim to replace that text or to duplicate it." He "proposes a brief framework for reflection . . . that can help guide us to a harmonious, creative and fruitful reception of the entire synodal process" (2). He makes clear that he "would like officially to present the Final Document" and specifies that he has "preferred not to cite the Final Document in this Exhortation, because I would encourage everyone to read it in full" (3). Positive about the synod and its document, he prays that "it may inspire in some way, every person of good will" (4).

*Querida Amazonia* initiates a test case in the exercise of a re-emphasized collegiality. Proposing deeper change, it moves away from a monarchic model of decision-making and proposes to episcopal conferences, a synodal process *cum Petro* rather than a *Roma locuta*-like verdict to be received *sub Petro*, to engage the whole Church in the process of discernment. The Bishops of the Amazon have proposed an orientation; the Pope wants everyone to reflect deeply on all they have said—just as he has himself. The exhortation does not replace the synodal document, but rather assumes it in an invitation to "read and apply it" (2–4). We observe the emergence of a new, creative hermeneutic, dialectically incorporating both the synod's final document and Francis' apostolic exhortation. The very fact that the Church is on a learning curve in advancing such processes is an indication of this newness. The synodal document, while advancing the case for women's diaconal ordination, is not the formal request of a bishop or bishops' conference.[36] It is an open invitation for other episcopal conferences, especially in Latin America, to respond, to advance what was proposed in the Amazon synod in light of that hermeneutic.

References in *Querida Amazonia* to *Evangelii Gaudium*[37] (paragraphs 226–28) at this point, provide an orientation as to how this synodal journey may continue. The overall principle is that *"Unity prevails over conflict."* While "[c]onflict cannot be ignored or concealed[, it] has to be faced. . . . [T]he best way to deal with conflict . . . is the willingness to face conflict head on, to resolve it and to make it a link in the chain of a new process. . . . [I]t becomes possible to build communion amid disagreement, . . . a way of making history in a life setting where conflicts,

---

36. Cardinal Gracias (Mumbai), president of the Indian bishops' conference, in a Vatican interview on 21 February 2020, that followed the February 17-19 meeting of the Council of Cardinals, pointed out that prelates from the nine-nation Amazonian region could still petition the Vatican on a case-by-case basis for the diaconal ministry of women through ordination. They must ask formally. That path was still open.

37. Apostolic Exhortation *Evangelii Gaudium* (24 November 2013), 228: AAS 105 (2013), 1112–13.

tensions and oppositions can achieve a diversified and life-giving unity[;] ... a resolution which takes place on a higher plane and preserves what is valid and useful on both sides ..." (229). "The message of peace is not about a negotiated settlement but rather the conviction that the unity brought by the Spirit can harmonize every diversity" (230).

That interpretative background suggests an ecclesiology and a construction of ministry surpassing simplistic binaries, but allowing for diversity, according to the deep pastoral needs of particular churches, coupled with the spiritual capacity to live with difference. Discernment continues. The issue is not closed.

## MEANING IN CONTEXT

Understanding the titles *episcopa, presbiterissa, diaconissa* should not be reduced to a decontextualized binary: *either* wives *or* ordained. Episcopal epitaphs written by Venantius Fortunatus in early medieval Gaul illustrate episcopacy as a kind of family inheritance with *episcopae*, women who administered church property, ruling that inheritance for the good of the Church. Under these circumstances, *episcopa* could also often mean wife of the bishop. Such co-adjudication of property undermined the hierarchical model of Church proposed by contemporary reformers. But if *presbyterae* were similarly the wives of priests, does that mean that these women were merely the wives of priests and bishops, or did they have their own ministries? Women certainly did distribute Holy Communion up to the twelfth century, as attested in two manuscripts from that period, a practice that persisted long after it had been forbidden.

No ordination rites for *presbyterae* survive, but there is a reference to the blessing of *presbyterae* in the Romano-Germanic Pontifical from the tenth century. Moreover, absence of any extant, separate ritual for the ordination of *presbyterae* does not necessarily rule out ordination. The same rite might have been used for both men and women, as illustrated in the twelfth-century Roman Sacramentary for the blessing of an abbot or an abbess, whose prayers are, grammatically speaking, only in the masculine gender.

At times the texts seem to distinguish different kinds of deaconesses: (i) women, especially widows, called deaconesses; (ii) the wives of deacons; and (iii) ordained deaconesses. Gennadius of Marseilles (480) refers to "widows or holy women chosen for the ministry of baptizing women, ... able clearly and wisely to teach ignorant and rustic women ...." If wives of deacons still played an important role in administering Church property with their husbands, that did not exclude them from joining with the husbands in liturgical ministry as well. Ordained deaconesses are implied—apart from various liturgical texts—by the decree of the Council of Tours (567) that deaconesses would relinquish sexual intercourse with their husbands after they were ordained. That was repeated by Leo VII (938) and the pseudo-Isodorian decretals that forbade the marriage of deaconesses.

While many ordination rites for deaconesses are substantially the same as for male deacons, that of Egbert of York (d. 766) displays differences. While they receive the same consecration, they are to live as virgins and their role is not altogether clear. Overall it seems undeniable that deaconess assisted at the altar and did so with episcopal approval. Women were not designated *episcopae, presbyterae*, or deaconesses simply because they were wives of the ordained, but rather because they exercised such ministry in the Church. When abbesses came to be considered deaconesses, that was also because they performed the ministries of deaconesses. Key to understanding ordination in this period is to focus on it as to ministry in the Church and not to a personal state, much less one understood metaphysically.

All this unfolded in a socio-cultural context that in early feudal Europe was often that of estate churches corresponding to domains where both bishops and estate owners understood the church as an extended household. Here many priests and deacons married and passed their ministry on to daughters and sons. It was a Church far less monolithic than it was to become. The reforming model of Church aimed at being more centralized, more hierarchical, and more independent of the politico-economic powers. It pursued those aims primarily through enacting and enforcing canon law. If it aimed to promote its independence through clerical celibacy, that should not be seen too strictly. There were married clergy in both models up to the twelfth century.

Earlier contours of the ministry of deaconess may be glimpsed when those ministries were subsumed into that of an abbess exercising many ministerial functions later reserved to the presbyterate. One of the most important of these was hearing her nuns' confessions. In many cases—those of Saint Ita and Saint Bertilla are well documented—they heard confessions of the surrounding population as well. Abbesses were recognized as the ordinary ministers of penance in their environment. They read the Gospel, distributed Holy Communion, and instructed the young in the faith. To argue that their ordinations, of which rites are extant, were not "true" ordinations, on grounds such as not including laying on of hands or not leading to the priesthood, is anachronistic. Historically, there can be little doubt. The evidence seems overwhelming.

One simply should not assume in the first millennium the degree of centralism and uniformity such as we have known in recent centuries, as if decrees of Popes and local councils were immediately and universally followed. Most of the Merovingian decrees simply failed. The Church of the first millennium was one where women were ordained to ministries that they exercised with the approval of their local bishops.

## ORDINATION RITE FOR WOMEN DEACONS

The Barbarini codex was copied around 780 AD from a Constantinopolitan model. One part of it reflects Eastern liturgical practice for the ordination of both male and female deacons from the third to the eighth century. Place the full text of the codex for the ordination of male and female deacons in parallel and the substantial equivalence will be evident.[38] There are only tiny differences. The male ordinand kneels to receive the anointing, the female ordinand bows her head. The prayer for the ordination of the woman deacon is indeed somewhat different in secondary details, but not in any substantive, theological sense as regards the fact and meaning of the ordination, but rather in a manner that recognizes and blesses what is female:

> Holy omnipotent Lord, through the birth of your only Son, our God, from a Virgin according to the flesh, you have sanctified the female sex. You grant not only to men, but also to women, the grace and coming of the Holy Spirit. Please Lord, look on this your maidservant and dedicate her to the task of your diaconate, and pour into her the rich and abundant giving of your Holy Spirit, and preserve her that she may always perform her ministry—*leitourgia*—with orthodox faith and irreproachable conduct according to what is pleasing to you. For to You is due all glory and honour.

---

38. This has been done by John Wijngaards and is accessible at www.womendeacons.org/rite-manuscript-barberini-gr-336.

After the "Amen" to this first prayer of ordination, the prayer of thanks made by another deacon is exactly the same, irrespective of whether it is a female or male deacon who is being ordained. During that prayer, the bishop imposes his hand on the head of the ordinand, whether male or female. The prayer he prays is, as above, slightly different for male and female deacons but again, not so in any substantive, theological sense regarding the reality of ordination, apart from how it recognizes, esteems, and blesses the female in ordained ministry.

> Lord, Master, you do not reject women who dedicate themselves to you and who are willing in a becoming way, to serve your Holy House, but admit them to the order of your ministers—*leitourgón*. Grant the gift of your Holy Spirit to this your maidservant who wishes to dedicate herself to you and fulfil in her the grace of the ministry of the deaconate, as you have granted to Phoebe the grace of your deaconate, whom you had called to the work of the ministry—*leitourgia*. Grant her Lord, that she may preserve without guilt in your Holy Temple, that she may carefully guard her behaviour, especially her modesty and temperance. Moreover, make your maidservant perfect, so that, when she will stand before the judgement seat of your Christ, she may obtain the worthy fruit of her excellent conduct through the mercy and humanity of your Only Son.

Taken individually and *a fortiori* together, many of the phrases in those prayers unmistakably point towards a real and true ordination:

(1) You do not reject women who dedicate themselves;

(2) but admit them to the order of your ministers;

(3) fulfil in her the grace of the deaconate;

(4) as you granted to Phoebe the grace of your deaconate;

(5) whom you had called to the work of the liturgy;

(6) you have sanctified the female sex;

(7) You grant not only to men, but also to women the grace and coming of the Holy Spirit;

(8) dedicate her to the task of your deaconate;

(9) pour into her . . . your Holy Spirit . . . that she may always perform her ministry—*leitourgia*—with orthodox faith.

These theologically dense phrases strongly indicate that in this ordination rite, women ordinands were truly ordained.

## MANUSCRIPTS OF WOMEN'S DIACONAL ORDINATION

The ordination rite, *rituale, euchologion*, of women deacons is preserved in ten MSS.[39]

The extant rites are:

(1) the Codex Barberini—Vatican Library gr. 336 (780 AD);

(2) the Bessarion Codex—Grottaferrata Γ ß 1 (ninth/tenth cent.);

(3) the Sinai Codex—gr. 956 (tenth cent.);

(4) the Paris Codex—Coislinus gr. 213 (1027 AD);

(5) the Messina Codex—Oxford, Bodleyan auct. E. 5.13 (1130 AD);

(6) Codex Vaticanus gr. 1872 (twelfth cent.);

(7) Codex Vaticanus gr. 1970 (twelfth cent.);

(8) the Athens Codex—National Library of Greece ms. 662 (twelfth to fourteenth cent.);

(9) the Cairo Codex—library of the Patriarchate of Alexandria ms. 104 (fourteenth cent.);

(10) the Mont Athos Codex—St. Xenophon monastery ms. 163 (fourteenth cent.).

Their interrelatedness reflects Church practice back to at least 550 AD. Barberini gr. 336 codex is in the Vatican Library since 1902, when Pope Leo XIII acquired the MSS of Cardinal Francis Barberini. The Barberinis had acquired the collection of the library of the Dominican Convent of St. Mark through the Florentine Senator Carlo Strozzi (1587–1670). That our codex was part of that collection for centuries is clear from notes written on it by monastic librarians.

It was used by successive Greek-Byzantine bishops in Italy, who celebrated the Byzantine rite until the end of the sixteenth century—and still celebrated in the Byzantine monastery of Grottaferrata. General use

---

39. For references to historical research as well as to where these MSS are held, I am indebted to J. Wijngaards, *The Ordained Women Deacons of the Church's First Millennium*, pp. 18–25, esp., p. 19 notes 38–47.

fell into decline in the tenth/eleventh century when uncial characters were no longer easily read. That script allowed Jean Morin, who examined the codex in the Barberini library in 1655, to date it to before 850. Scholars read the intercession: "for the most trustworthy kings, and for the queen beloved by Christ" (§ 37.4) in the Anaphora of Chrysostom as referring to Irene, the wife of Leo IV (775–80), thereby dating the codex to c. 780 AD. The rites contained there are earlier. The various versions are remarkably uniform, suggestive of an ancient tradition, faithfully preserved. Consider again the first invocation of the Holy Spirit over the woman deaconal ordinands:

> Holy and Omnipotent Lord, through the birth of your Only Son our God from a Virgin according to the flesh, you have sanctified the female sex. You grant not only to men, but also to women the grace and coming of the Holy Spirit . . . . (see above)

This is the text of Barberini gr. 336, (see above), from Byzantine communities in Italy ca.780 AD. A virtually identical text is found in the Bessarion Codex; copied in Constantinople around 1020 AD and in the Codex Coislinus gr. 213: "euchologion of the Great Church in Constantinople," 1027 AD. This applies especially to the prayer parts of the rite—considered its most unalterable element. Rubrics show only minor variations, indicating how the rite was no dead text. Minor changes demonstrating that the rite was celebrated in a variety of contexts, also help to reconstruct its original form.

Wijngaards convincingly builds a "family tree" showing the relationship between the various MSS. Barberini gr. 336, Xenophon gr. 163 and Bodleyan E.5.13 are almost identical, copied from a "master," termed "family A." Grottaferrata Γ β 1 codex, Sinai gr. 956 and Vatican gr. 1872, showing matching variations; indicate what he terms "family B." Codex Coislin gr. 213 and Cairo gr. 104 have the same initial paragraph emphasizing that the ordinand should: "have lived as a chaste virgin . . . ," both derived from "family C."

Thus already in the sixth/seventh century, models of the ordination text existed which go back to a more ancient parent. All the later MSS reflect that early model. While the ordination of women declined in the Graeco-Byzantine churches from the eleventh century onwards, that the rite was still faithfully copied in later MSS, proves its antiquity, and the unwillingness of Church authorities to discard sections of the euchologion handed on, even if no longer in use. That rite for the ordination of women deacons, as exemplified in these ten codices, represents a well-established practice dating from c. 500 AD that covered all the lands where the Byzantine liturgy was celebrated.

Scholarship supports the argument that female deacons were considered as belonging to the same order as male deacons.[40] Whatever ministry they exercised was sufficiently "diaconal" in nature for them to be called by what had become the technical, ecclesial term: namely, "deacon." Ordination ceremonies for women deacons are known from the early third century. Literary and epigraphic evidence of women deacons is preserved in many regions, often against pressure to end the practice of their ordination. That detail is significant. The memory of women deacons was preserved in the face of opposition, which implies that the ministry of at least some of them was so much appreciated, venerated indeed, that it could not be allowed to be forgotten.

## WOMEN'S MONASTIC RITUALS AND THE DIACONATE

While cognizant of the distinct question of how women deacons actually ministered, Phyllis Zagano highlights the question of how women deacons were ritually acknowledged. In an attempt to recover something of the tradition of women deacons whose ordination ceremonies are known from the third century, she evaluates historical and current ceremonies for Cistercian and Carthusian nuns as compared with known, diaconal ordination ceremonies from earlier times.

Literary and epigraphical evidence of women deacons survives in many regions, often against pressure to end the practice. Radegund (520–586), wife of Frankish King Clothar, was ordained deacon and women deacons existed in various regions up to the twelfth century. As late as the eleventh century, Popes allowed bishops to ordain women as deacons.

Zagano's hypothesis is that the tradition of ordaining women to the order and office of deacon was connected to or subsumed within other monastic rituals, beginning with the sixth-century Rule of Caesarius of Arles, which argued strongly for the claustration of women religious. Thus, where a bishop is needed for a contemporary ceremony, the ceremony historically relates to ordination as it developed over the centuries.

40. Zagano, "Remembering Tradition; Women's Monastic Rituals and the Diaconate," 787–811.

Where a bishop is not necessary to the ritual, that ritual more clearly relates to permanent, monastic profession, made at the hands of the abbess or prioress.

Cistercian and Carthusian women's religious orders were founded in the reformist wave of the eleventh century. Yet they preserve the memory of women's diaconal ordination in surprisingly illuminating ways. When a Carthusian nun makes her consecration as a virgin (four years after solemn profession), she receives the stole, maniple, and cross from the presiding bishop, along with certain liturgical rights—an aspect of the ceremony stemming from a time when such liturgical rights and privileges were clearly delineated. Whereas the woman superior, usually the abbess, presides over the monastic profession, the Carthusian consecration of a virgin is usually presided over by a bishop.[41] Vestiges of the ceremony of ordination as deacon—most especially reception of the stole, which marks the reception of Holy Orders—were incorporated into monastic ceremonies, where solemn profession and consecration of a virgin had subsumed or displaced diaconal ordination, which remains a well-remembered part of women's monastic life in the Orthodox churches, now being slowly rediscovered in the Western Church.

Women deacons faded as church structures developed in the West. Evidence of their existence diminishes beyond the sixth century, though they are known to have existed long beyond that, even as late as the twelfth century. As women deacons faded into history, in the emerging socio-cultural milieu, one dominated by feudalism, monastic life became the only approved means of women's self-donation to God and ministry. Active, non-cloistered women religious (with the rise of the apostolic orders under different socioeconomic conditions) would appear much later, not to mention various secular institutes of women and, most importantly, active committed lay women, today the very backbone of service in the Church. Extant diaconal ordination ceremonies followed women into monasteries. These monastic women, initially at least, knew whose ministerial descendents they were. Nonetheless, even to this day, monastic women may be ordained to the diaconate in a few Eastern churches, which are recovering these traditions.

The earliest significant manuscript evidence of the ordination of women as deacons in early liturgical practice is from the fourth-century

---

41. That is nowadays often extended to final profession ceremonies in religious congregations of women of various congregations, whether of Pontifical or Diocesan right. That is a matter of honor and does not imply ordination.

*Apostolic Constitutions*. The prayer for the ordination of a woman as deacon from the *Apostolic Constitutions*, like the later ritual from the Barbarini codex, is nearly identical to that for a male deacon.[42] There are other minor differences, but they are of a secondary nature. In the East the male ordinand touches the altar with his forehead; the woman stands upright; the man receives the Rhipidion—a sacred fan—as symbol of his office, but the woman does not.

As anyone who has presided at or participated in the Holy Eucharist in warmer climes immediately recognizes, the Rhipidion was probably originally an ordinary fan to keep insects away from the consecrated species and came to be considered "liturgical," even though merely rubrical, because of this function, before being constructed as "sacred" and intrinsic to the ordination, even being used to argue for an essential distinction between male and female deacons. Also in the East, the male distributes communion, and the woman does not, although she self-communicates from the chalice. It was a duty of the woman deacon to bring communion and otherwise minister to sick women. That such distinctions do not refer to the ordination as such is evident from the fact that today, once again, there are women "ministers of the Eucharist" in the Church who bring Holy Communion to the sick and distribute it to both men and women—even during the Sacred Liturgy.

## A TRUE ORDINATION

Evidence for ordained female deacons in the early Christian period seems undeniable.[43] Eastern rituals for ordaining men and women deacons are both termed "ordinations" (*cheirotonia*) and are performed in the ecclesial assembly during the sacred liturgy, by the local bishop through the imposition of hands. The bishop declares his intent by asking for "divine grace"; the ordinands are led to the altar; the ordinations, of both men and of women, take place within the sanctuary during the Eucharist. Further, the bishop invokes the Holy Spirit, recites two prayers—proper to major orders—and presents stoles—also proper to major orders—to both male and female ordinands, each of whom self-communicates from the chalice. It is difficult to understand how substantially identical liturgies can be considered sacramental for men but not for women.

42. As discussed in detail by Karras, *Female Deacons in the Byzantine Church*, 272–316.

43. Karras, *Female Deacons in the Byzantine Church*, 273.

The tradition of deacon-abbesses was reflected in Benedictine and Cistercian abbeys of Catalonia, whose abbesses wore the stole at liturgy. The abbess presides at the Liturgy of the Hours, and imparts a formal blessing at the conclusion of Vespers. These practices may help us to recover some of the lost tradition of women deacons. Even though the Second Council of Orleans (533) had ruled that henceforth no women would "receive diaconal benediction due to the frailty of her sex"—then a new form of argumentation—it has long been believed that the tradition of diaconal ordination was brought to Prébayon, an ancient woman's monastery (ca. 616) and first to join the Carthusian order (1245). The ceremony of giving the stole, maniple, and cross to the Carthusian nun during her consecration as a virgin may derive from the practices there.

As recently as 1942, the *Dictionnaire de Droit Canonique*[44] stated that Carthusian nuns' ritual could be called a *consecration virginali-diaconissale*, related to the ritual for women deacons of the early church. Roger Gryson concluded: "From a doctrinal point of view, since for several centuries, a large portion of the church followed this practice [of ordaining women as deacons] without raising a theoretical problem, it is perfectly conceivable to confer on women a diaconal type of ministry. Women deacons then receive a true ordination, with nothing distinguishing it formally from the ordination of their male colleagues."[45] It need hardly be clarified that being ordained deacon is to receive Holy Orders.

## IMPENDING CHANGE IN THINKING AND LAW

The evidence overwhelmingly points toward the reality of women's ordination in the first millennium. Even then, from the fifth century onwards, there was increasing opposition to it. In the high Middle Ages, that opposition won out, but did so by confusing a socially constructed anthropology of the sexes with theological truth as well as by narrowing the understanding of ordination. We now turn to examine those developments, their precisions, their limitations, and their enduring influence—now being slowly eroded.

---

44. These massive tomes may be accessed at www.theologica.fr/Pg_Dictionnaires-DroitCanonique.htm.

45. *Le ministère des femmes dans L'Église ancienne*, 113. Reading this book over forty years ago sparked the present writer's interest in studying this question.

CHAPTER 5

# Women's Ordination in the Middle Ages

IN THE HIGH MIDDLE Ages a new form of argumentation developed regarding Holy Orders. Its reflections on women's ordination were contextualized by the feudal structures of society as well as a superior-inferior anthropology of the sexes and were acculturated to that power structure. Confusing the dominant social construction of the relationship between men and women with divine ordinance, it confused the consequent Church discipline with immutable, theological truth. That way of thinking, never quite exiting from the false assumption of female inferiority, has shaped the theology of Holy Orders down to our own day, not least regarding the question of women's ordination.

## EARLY MEDIEVAL DOCUMENTS

Several medieval ordinals referred to commissioning rites for women as "ordination," as did Popes and bishops. Early medieval documents demonstrate widespread use of the terms *ordinatio*, *ordinare*, and *ordo* in regard to the commissioning of women's ministries. None of these sources, covering Christian history from the fifth through the twelfth century, distinguished such an ordination, when considered precisely as ordination, from that of priests or deacons.[1] In 1018, Pope Benedict VIII conferred on the cardinal bishop of Porto the right to ordain bishops, priests, deacons, deaconesses, and subdeacons.

---

1. Macy, *The Ordination of Women in the Early Middle Ages*, 481–507.

In similar vein Bishop Gilbert of Limerick[2] wrote in his *De statu ecclesiae*[3] (c. 1135): "The bishop ordains abbots, abbesses, priests, and the six other grades."[4] The latter are deacon, subdeacon, acolyte, exorcist, lector, and porter. Gilbert was not Norman; his name was *Gille*, or more likely *Giolla*. Seathrún Céitinn refers to him as *Giolla Easpuig*. The *Chronicon Scotorum* gives *Gilli escop Luimnig*.[5] Giolla Easpuig is being very specific regarding ordinations, distinguishing himself explicitly from Almarius, whom he accurately cites as positing nine grades, including psalmists, an order Giolla explicitly excludes: "*in numero gradum Ecclesiae, psalmistos non ponimus*"; whereas he explicitly includes abbesses. These are the words of one who was, after Saint Malachy, the leading Church reformer in twelfth-century Ireland.

Sometime after his appointment as Papal Legate, he wrote *De statu ecclesiae*,[6] and sent it to "the bishops and priests of the whole of Ireland." In the accompanying letter, he proposed that a Church structure was required in which all members would find their place and placed a sketch of this structure at the start of his tract. Giolla was preparing them for the changes that were being contemplated and which would be revealed at the Synod of Raith Breasail (1111 CE) where he presided as papal legate;[7]

2. There was a "bewildering diversity of offices and Masses at the time," D'Alton, *Limerick*, 9.262. Schmitt, "Gilbert v. Limerick," *Lexikon für Theologie und Kirche*, 4.890, writes how Gilbert "*arbeitete für die Veneinheitlichung der irischen Liturgie.*"

3. *Pace* Gwynn, *The Irish Church in the 11th and 12th Centuries*, 125, who concludes that *De usu ecclesiastico* and *De Statu ecclesiae* refer to the same document, *De uso ecclesiastico* is a letter *ad episcopos Hiberniae*. It begins: *Episcopi [et] presbyteri totius Hiberniae* and ends a half page later with *Amen*. It presents *De Statu Ecclesiae*, which is given in PL as *Liber de Statu Ecclesiae*, where it occupies three-and-a-half pages of close print. In col. 2 of p. 1002 it is made clear that this, including its teaching on ordination, is a blueprint for comprehensive Church reform. *De usu ecclesiatico*, Migne, PL 159, 995 and Liber de Statu ecclesiae PL 159, 997–1004.

4. "*Ordinat Episcopus Abbatem, Abbatissam, Sacerdotum et caeteros sex gradus*" Migne, *Patrologia Latina*, 159.1002d.

5. Letters exchanged with Anselm after August 1107, reveal that Giolla was not consecrated by the archbishop of Canterbury. He was chosen as bishop of Limerick, by Muircheartach Ua Briain, then *Ardrí*, to reform the Church within an Irish context, separate from Canterbury.

6. *De statu ecclesiae* (sic), is printed in *The Whole Works of the Most Rev. James Ussher*, Dublin, 1847–64.

7. "Is ré linn an Mhuircheartaigh fós do horduigheadh seanad nó comhdháil choitcheann in nÉirinn i Raith Breasail an tan fá haois an Tiarna 1100, do réir sheinleabhair annálach eaglaise Chluana hEidhneach Fionntain in Laoighis, mar a gcuirthear síos na neithe prinnsiopálta do rinneadh san treanadh soin; agus fá hé Giolla

the first, according to Saint Bernard, "to function as legate of the apostolic see throughout the whole of Ireland."[8] The enactments of the synod itself were revolutionary: a whole new Church structure, similar to the one he had outlined in his tract. When Cellach, the bishop of Armagh, died in 1129, Giolla strongly urged Malachy, the successor chosen by reformers, to take on reactionary forces. He died in 1145.

When he wrote of ordaining abbesses, he almost certainly saw that in continuity with the ordination of women deacons, as discussed in the previous chapter, but nonetheless, as a real ordination. The church structure he succeeded in having adopted for Ireland included regulations for such ordinations. One can reasonably conclude that in twelfth-century Ireland, at least one bishop who was also the Papal Legate who presided at a groundbreaking synod, considered the Church capable of conferring ordination on women and instructed his fellow-bishops accordingly.[9]

## TERMINOLOGICAL DELINEATION

References to ordination in the Middle Ages, however, in the manner that term was used, were about to acquire new delineations. *Ordo, ordinatio,* and *ordinare* would come to carry different and narrower precisions in meaning from earlier usage. But those differences do not negate the belief and practice according to which ordinands, including women, had previously been validly ordained. If there was a legitimate development of doctrine in relation to how ordination was understood, that does not contradict the fact that those ordained previous to that development were truly ordained to ministry. Just as if in the first millennium presbyters neither used the term "transubstantiation" nor even knew what the word meant, and may never have even encountered it,[10] that would

---

Easpuig easpog Luimnigh fá leagáid ón Phápa an tan soin do n'arduachtarán ar an gcomhairle sin." Céitinn, "Foras Feasa ar Éirinn: An Treas Leabhair" (1634), 298, 306.

8. Holland, "Gille (Gilbert of Limerick)," in Duffy (ed.), *Medieval Ireland: An Encyclopedia,* 333.

9. There is no direct evidence that he did so. The nuns' monastery at Ballynagalliagh was founded in 1283 and was, moreover, in the Diocese of Emly. That in Limerick itself was founded around 1171; that of Saint Catherine O'Conyl in 1261. But records of medieval women's religious houses in Ireland are meagre. Most of the ancient Celtic women's monasteries, many with independent traditions, had died out before 1111 (cf. n.21 infra). Gwynn and Hadcock, *Medieval Religious Houses in Ireland,* 307–26.

10. While comparable terms were in use from the fourth century, the earliest known use of the actual term "transubstantiation" was by Hildebert of Lavardin in the

not mean that they did not truly call down the Holy Spirit to transform the species of bread and wine into the living self-gift of the risen Christ. After the twelfth century, the theology of ordination acquired a new level of intelligibility but that does not mean that those ordained before that, according to a supposedly, less developed, but ecclesially approved, theology, were not truly ordained.

Before the thirteenth century, considerable diversity existed both over what constitutes an *ordinatio* and which states or *ordines* should be considered "clerical." Ordination, moreover, was not seen as irreversible until the thirteenth century. Everyday usage of the terms *ordo, ordinatio* and *ordinare* continued throughout the Middle Ages to describe not only the creation-installation of bishops, priests, deacons, and subdeacons but also of porters, lectors, exorcists, acolytes, canons, abbots, abbesses, kings and queens. In 1199, Innocent III described canon lawyers as a separate *ordo*. As late as the 14th century, *ordo* was used to designate the sacrament of extreme unction. Marriage was referred to as an *ordo* as late as the fifteenth century. For some medieval canonists, *ordinatio* did not necessarily have the kind of sacramental meaning, it would later assume.

If early sources discussing ordination, cannot be read with the assumption that they are treating the matter in the manner of Lateran IV or Trent, neither may such ordinations be dismissed simply because they not appraisable in neo-Trindentine terms. Yves Congar wrote that: "*ordinare, ordinari, ordinatio* signified the fact of being designated and consecrated to take up a certain place, or better a certain function, *ordo*, in the community and at its service."[11] Ordination was a process through which a Christian was introduced into the episcopal or presbyteral or some other order. To ordain was wider than to consecrate or bless or designate; more than the prayer of ordination-consecration: it was the entire, ecclesial process of which these are part. Election and designation are already the first moments of the ordination.

There are many witnesses to this.[12] For Peter Damien, ordination is the act of establishing a Pope or bishop in the office he is charged to do. Often *ordinare* and *eligere* were used as synonyms and for the liturgical rite, the traditional term was "consecration"; thus ordination was

---

eleventh century. Lateran IV in 1215 spoke of the elements being "transubstantiated."

11. Congar, *Note sur une valeur des termes ordinare, ordinatio*, 7–14.

12. From *Vigilantia Universalis* of Nicholas II, 1059, one may infer that being ordained was being assigned to a charge or an office; paragraph (4): "And we ordain that those of the aforesaid Orders who . . . in the churches to which they have been ordained . . . shall above all things be zealous."

perfected only by consecration. From Gregory VII on, ordination designates the liturgical ceremony, but *ordinare, ordinatio* still retained the sense of institution into charge and responsibility. After the Gregorian reform and in the *Decretals* of Gratian 1140, *ordinare* comes to refer to the sacrament of Order.[13]

For early medieval canonists, *ordinatio-ordinare* does not necessarily have the sacramental sense *as that was later understood*. Ordination was the process of election, nomination, and canonical institution. In the view of many scholars, the *Decretals* of Gratian have both senses. The link between presbyteral ordination and the service of a Christian community, as later elaborated by the scholastics, was dominated by reference to the power to consecrate the Eucharist and to absolve sins as well as to its permanent, indelible character, personally possessed, in a construction of ordination that was almost solely vertical and non-communitarian. Twelfth-century theology shifted understanding of priesthood from the service of the Christian community to the *potestas conficiendi*—the power to confect the Eucharist as well as that to absolve sin. Exegesis shifted to justify this position. Henceforth, "Do this in memory of me" would be interpreted accordingly.

Historically, connection to a community over which the priest presides is the condition for presiding over the Eucharist. In a magisterial study, H-M. Legrand argued convincingly that in the early Church, priests presided at the Eucharist because they presided over the Christian community. He demonstrates this from Didache, Clement, Justin, Irenaeus, Hippolytus, Tertullian, and Cyprian, and concludes that we do not take sufficiently seriously the link between Eucharist and the community of the Church.[14]

Chalcedon (451 CE) had declared as *akyron, irritum* (i.e., null or non-existent) the act of imposing hands [ordination] without a title of ministry—there was no absolute ordination. Integral ordination comprised several moments and acts, including induction into presidency of

---

13. "Note sur une valeur des termes *ordinare, ordinatio*," 11 n.23 and 12 nn.25 & 13, for references.

14. Legrand, *La Présidence de l'Eucharistie selon la Tradition Ancienne*, 409–31. He wrote this study because he was: "Frappé de trouver cette idée exprimé par deux fois, au détour d'une phrase dans la Relation de la Commission Théologique centrale de Vatican II sur le n.28 de Lumen Gentium, il nous a paru interessant de la vérifier." The phrase in question was "Cum iam in Novo Testamento et in aevo post-apostolico . . . presbyteri ut rectores communitatis, sint rectores eucharistiae . . . ." *Schema Constitutionis De Ecclesia* 1964, relation de pp. 101–2 n.28, cited by Legrand, *La Présidence de l'Eucharistie*, 410 n.1.

a community as a basis for presidency at its Eucharist. It would be reductionist to dismiss first millennial ordination, including that of women, as a merely functionalist notion of ordination, as if it did not imply a true consecration to the exercise of the corresponding ministry. The substantive issue is whether or not women and men ordained as deacon or presbyter with that understanding, truly *ministered* as deacons or priests as those ministries and offices were then understood in the Church. It would be anachronistic to dismiss first-millennial Church practice because it was not interpreted according to a second-millennial theological vocabulary.

In the early centuries, women were commissioned for several different *ordines*, including those of widow, virgin, and deaconess. The early Middle Ages also bore witness to the ministries of *episcopae, presbyterae*, canonesses, abbesses, and nuns. *Episcopae* and *presbyterae*, one may repeat, were not simply spouses of bishops or priests. Bishops' wives are usually referred to in sixth-century literature as *coniux*, not *episcopa*. Even if they were wives of the ordained that did not necessarily preclude ordination to ministry. A list of forbidden marriages ascribed to Pope Gregory II, found in the ninth-century Pseudo-Isidorian *Decretals*, includes injunctions against marrying *presbyterae*, deaconesses, and nuns. This may be seen as a canonical demand for celibacy, equivalent to that ascribed to male priests, deacons, and monks.

Importantly, that demonstrates that women priests, *presbyterae*, and deaconesses existed and that church authorities expected them to be celibate. In that case, the women involved could not have been simply presbyters' wives, *uxores*, much less *mulieres subintroductae*. Whatever the details of the ministry of these women, and however the understanding of that ministry related to later theologies, they were clearly considered during this period to hold an "ordained" office and ministry in the Church just as male bishops, priests, or deacons did.

## ORDER OF CONSECRATED WIDOWS

Consecrated widows, if considered an order, were most likely of a different kind. In the deutero-Pauline letters, *domus* had emerged as a preferred model for Church, one where the private life of the patriarchal household idealized the subordination of respectable women as *matronae*. Closure of teaching roles to women began, later canonized by episcopal synods. Consecrated widows—developed almost as an alternative to ordination, portraying selected, idealized women as "model laity"[15]—represented new norms of social relations within the Church-*domus*: the template of a well-functioning Christian public sphere. That Order, which began as a ministry to poor women, is not a modified, monastic coenobitism under bishops, but a re-alignment of the earlier ministry. A select group of exemplary, lay women become showpieces of their bishop-patron, sanctioning the patronage and supervision by which bishops promoted Church as *domus* and episcopy as patriarchate.

During persecutions, some wealthy women had provided alternatives to confiscated spaces. The ninth-century *Liber Pontificalis* recounts the ministry of several: Lucina, Priscilla, Vestina, Flavia Domitilla, and Juliana. Bishops relied on women patrons long past that period, but undertook to control their involvement, not least by distancing them from the service of the altar. Nonetheless, spectacularly generous gestures conveyed the personal prestige of aristocratic women into the public, Church space, representing them at the altar through personal relics[16] rather than through their bishops. Such displays demonstrated limits to the pre-eminence of episcopal *oikonomia*.

Bishops responded by regulating wealthier widows, re-assimilating autonomous women within the *domus*-Church. The Order of Widows occupies the space between increasingly restricted, female ordination and autonomous, female patronage. Bishops became heads of the Order. It becomes an antitype of aristocratic woman patrons; an ideal of submission for the Christian community as a whole. Between the second and fourth century, when their office was "professionalized," we find bishops preoccupied with defining roles for women. As aristocrats became bishops, they assumed the trappings of civic authority. Women's authority was contracted as the status of bishops rose.

In earliest Christianity, widows were cared for as part of the Church's duty of charity. By the second century, a Consecrated Order of Widows appears as a regular feature of Church, growing in size and significance, but increasingly subordinated to episcopal control. Later manuals specify

---

15. Irene San Pietro, *Modeling the Church Household: Widows as Idealized Laity*, accessed at www.academia.edu.

16. The oft-quoted example is of Melania the Younger (b. 383), who "gave her silk dresses to the altars. This the holy Olympias (b. 361) had done." Pope Silvester (314–335) had decreed: "that the sacrifice of the altar should not be celebrated on silk, ... but only on naturally produced linen, just as the body of our Lord Jesus Christ was buried in a linen shroud."

entry requirements, in a code for successful applicants that hardly reflects the social reality of poor widowhood. Instead, a few are selected to be served by the Church in a constructed status of "ecclesiastical widowhood," intended to model an ideal exemplary order.

The *Apostolic Constitutions* (3.1, 2) read: "Choose your widows not under sixty years of age, that in some measure the suspicion of a second marriage may be prevented by their age. . . . But let not the younger widows be placed in the Order of Widows . . . ."[17] If the Order were a charity, destitution might be an expected criterion, but something else is at work: selected widows are displayed as symbolic capital in a stylized form of social reality where episcopal administration of charity legitimates authority. Poor widows needing the Order merely to escape poverty jeopardized that symbolic project. The proposed Church model of *domus*, in both its power and insecurity, rests on the *paterfamilias* role. The Order of Widows endorsed the bishop's aptitude in distributive justice, his *oikonomia*, validating episcopal status and discretion over the "Church household."

A transitional form in the evolution of hierarchy is disclosed: ordained clergy are distinct from laity; widows, nuns, abbesses, and *matronae* are distinct categories, suggesting that consecration is distinct from ordination. The example of the widow-matron upholds an orderly Christian public life based on patriarchal domesticity. In that construction of Church order predicated on the bishop as *paterfamilias* and the Church as *domus*, idealizing the subordination of respectable women as *matronae*, the members of an Order are not considered consecrated for ministry, but exist to showcase the *oikonomia* of the *paterfamilias*.

In a post-patriarchal understanding of social relations, however, stressing mutuality, equality, and responsibility, and insisting how "to each has been given a manifestation of the Spirit for the common good" (1 Cor 12:7), that *paterfamilias-domus*, ecclesial construction cannot be said to decide whether today women may or may not be ordained.

## WOMEN'S MINISTRIES LATER RESERVED TO THE PRESBYTERATE

A letter of Pope Benedict IX in 1033 proclaiming that all clerics were free of lay duties, included the "orders" of religious woman and deaconesses, who were thereby clearly distinguished from "the laity." As early medieval

---

17. Accessible at www.thenazareneway.com "Apostolic Constitutions" book_I-VI.

writers would probably have understood the term, these women were in fact "ordained clerics." At that period, abbesses exercised functions later reserved to the presbyterate, such as hearing their nuns' confessions, as evidenced in four monastic Rules,[18] those of Columban, Donatus, Basil, and the *Regula Cuiusdam ad virgines*.[19] It is also implied by *Capitularium regum Francorum* (476–987), where it is declared an abuse that some abbesses gave benediction to men by the imposition of hands.[20] There are several references to Saint Ita (d. c. 570) hearing confessions and imposing penances.[21] In 1210, Innocent III withdrew the right of the abbess of Las Huelgas to hear confessions.[22] Given such prohibitions, it would

   18. Morris, *The Lady was a Bishop*, cf. Appendix 6, "Abbesses with Powers of Confession," 140–43.
   19. *Patrologia Latina*, vol. 88, col. 1053–70; chapter 6, *De assidue danda confessione*, and chapter 7, *De non manifestandis sororum confessionibus*; which also mentions senior sisters to whom the abbess has confided this ministry.
   20. *The Lady was a Bishop*, 142.
   21. *Codex Killkenniensis*, aka *Codex Ardmachanus*, was written in the fifteenth century by more than one scribe. There may originally have been 160 or 168 leaves, but in its present state, the manuscript has lost folios 1–32, 36–38, with individual leaves removed elsewhere, such as folios 100, 137, 153. *Vita Sanctae Itae Virginis* was edited by Plummer, in *Vitae Sanctorum Hiberniae*, 116–30. In paragraph XVI, 121 concerning a nun who had sinned, we find: "*confessa est veritatem rei. Et sanata est, agens penitentiam secundum iussionem Sanctae Itae.*" Again in para. XVII, another case: "*Alia quoque virgo . . . audiens suam iniquitatem ex ore Dei formulae dignam egit penitentiam . . . .*" Again, (para. XXV): "*quidem vir occidit fratrem suum; et tactus penitentia, venit ad sanctam Itam et egit penitudinem secundum iussionem eius.*" In para. XXXI on p. 127, there is the interesting case of a young man who came with two others who do penance after Ita's ministry, but doubts why they should come to a female. In para. XXXIV a penitent returns from as far as Connaught: "*Et ipsa agens dignem penitentiam.*" Ita is traditionally spoken of as the "foster-mother of many saints" (C.E. vol. 8, 201). Burns judiciously understates her ministry in writing how: "the Celtic Church at the time encouraged women to become leaders of men as well as of women." She was reported to be a fearless confessor to both, handing out tough penances though forgiving and compassionate to both (ibid., 102–3).
   22. Elected pope on January 8, 1198, Innocent III's papacy was marked by efforts to establish papal, monarchical authority within the Church. He reformed the Roman Curia, shaped a powerful doctrine of papal power within the Church and in secular affairs, and in 1215 presided over Lateran Council IV, which cemented fundamental change in clerical and lay practices within the Church. His pontificate, hugely important for the development of the medieval Church, represented the apogee of the medieval papacy. Law was the key element in achieving this. While Pennington, *The Legal Education of Pope Innocent III*, 70–77, argues that evidence of Innocent being a Bologna-educated canonist is slight, he is nonetheless regarded as one of the great lawyer Popes of the Middle Ages. An enormous collection of decretal letters were written

seem unconvincing to suggest that this practice was merely one of sisterly correction.

"Ordination" is used for the consecration of an abbess in several sacramentals. In the *Mozarabic Liber Ordinum* (fifth-eleventh centuries), chap 23, *Ordo ad ordinationem Abbatissum*, she is clothed in sacred vestments and crowned with a mitre. The ordination prayer begins: *"Omnipotens Domine Deus, apud quem non est discretio sexuum."* There is wide evidence of Abbesses' crosiers—more than ceremonial, where *traditio instrumentorum* was considered integral to ordination. Several twelfth-century canonists argued that the reading of the Gospel in church by abbesses was proof that they were the successors of the earlier deaconesses. That such diaconal functions continued into the thirteenth century seems evident from the fact that it was precisely these diaconal functions of abbesses that Pope Innocent III disallowed in his letter of 1210: "Abbesses . . . bless their own nuns, hear their confessions of sin and, reading the Gospel, presume to preach publicly."

Pope Innocent's ruling followed a half-century of canonical debate concerning women's ministries. Several scholars, including the doyen of canonists, Rolando Bandinelli of Bologna (1105–81), the future Pope Alexander III (1159–81), granted that women had once been ordained deacons but that the Church later disallowed that practice. These canonists present no intrinsically theological reason, nor even an argument from tradition, why deaconesses could not once again be ordained if Church law should so decide. Their argumentation is *canonical, not theological*. It concerns *discipline, not doctrine*. Most canonists agreed with Atto of Vercelli that the former ministry of deaconess had been replaced by the contemporary ministry of abbess.

Others, starting with Rufinus in twelfth-century Bologna, the first to produce a Summa of Canon Law, took a dogmatic approach to law that would have enormous influence on Church thinking to this very day, not least in relation to the question being examined here.[23] He sought, as some still do seek, to give theological status to legal rulings, in what was then a novel form of argument, but one that has proved enduring and difficult to dislodge. Its derivative argumentation distinguished between an "ordination" that is a blessing of the granting of a particular function, and

---

during his pontificate, showing keen awareness of the problems involved and which only a trained lawyer or lawyers could have drafted. They reveal a practised administrator employing trained lawyers to promote his vision of the Church.

23. As will be examined in chapter 7.

an "ordination" that is sacramental. For the majority who made that distinction, the "ordination" of deaconesses, or *presbyterae*, was *thenceforth* considered non-sacramental. However, a minority, while employing the new terminology, still held the ordinations of deaconesses in the early Church as valid sacramental ordinations.

## CHANGING CANONICAL CLIMATE

The Apparatus written by Joannes Teutonicus, on the Decretum after the Fourth Lateran Council of 1215, recorded the opinion of some scholars that when nuns are ordained they receive the character of orders. The canonical climate, however, was changing.[24] That abbesses when ordained receive the character of orders was by then a minority opinion, but nonetheless tenable without implication of heresy, demonstrating how the concept of ordination was in flux at that time. For over 1,200 years, therefore, the validity of women's ordination—even as understood by some post-Lateran IV theology—remained, at the very least, an open question. The continuity of practice, belief, and teaching all down the centuries, on which many apologists for the *status quo* today insist, does not tally with the historical facts as smoothly as they might prefer.

The connection between ordination and the ministry of the Eucharist was still under debate in the middle of the twelfth century. Confessions were still being heard by non-ordained religious in the beginning of the thirteenth century.[25] Later, some religious orders removed examples of this practice from their early histories. Theologians in the twelfth century debated the relationship between ordination and the power to absolve sin at the same time as they were debating the relationship between ordination and the Eucharist. In that regard, it is of particular importance to recall that the doctrine of the Church, as taught in Vatican Council II, is that "priests, as co-workers with their bishops, have the primary duty of proclaiming the Gospel of God to all."[26] Too much on both sides of the

---

24. Raming, *A History of Women and Ordination*, vol. 2, 93.

25. Confession to laypeople is permitted, by the greater number of medieval theologians, usually in case of necessity. Albert the Great, arguing from baptism conferred by a layman in case of necessity, ascribes a certain sacramental value to absolution by a layman, as does Aquinas, who even according to his later theology still sees something sacramental (*quodammodo sacramentalis*) in this confession; most add that if the penitent survives he should seek absolution for a priest.

26. *Presbyterorum Ordinis*, Decree on the Ministry and Life of Priests, No. 3.

present debate, by contrast, centres virtually exclusively on priesthood as the power to celebrate Mass, usually understood in the restricted sense of the power to confect the Eucharist.

Lists of Christian rituals later considered "sacraments" differed until the *Sentences* of *Peter the Lombard* (ca. 1150) became a standard theological text and his list of seven major liturgical rites considered "sacraments" in the richer sense was adopted into Church doctrine. That is certainly Catholic teaching, but the heart of what it teaches was always taught, even if differently conceptualized. Therefore, in earlier—but from a Catholic point of view, quite legitimate—conceptualizations, women were quite clearly capable of being ordained to diaconate and presbyterate, even if eventually, canonically disbarred from those ministries.

Just as doctrine legitimately developed in the Lombardian direction, so it could legitimately develop beyond it. Just as any such legitimate development would never negate the ecclesial doctrine of seven sacraments, neither does that doctrine negate what preceded it. Pius XII (1947) in arguing that *traditio instrumentorum* is not required for the substance and validity of ordination, guardedly but significantly added: "If it was at one time necessary even for validity by the will and command of the Church, everyone knows that the Church has the power to change and abrogate what she herself has established." The same hermeneutic of continuity that holds fast to the doctrine of seven sacraments holds equally fast to the validity of liturgical practice and theology in the first millennium.

The twelfth century was a watershed. Ordination came to be considered intrinsically—indeed, almost exclusively—linked to power to confect the Eucharist and to give absolution in ritual-sacramental penance. Scholasticism, in the thirteenth century, laid out the underlying reasoning and its arguments and conclusions passed into the definitions of general councils, notably Trent. But at the level of popular preaching and common understanding, these were then read back into the writings, debates, and practices of earlier centuries and sometimes even the knowledge of earlier ordinations of women was lost, resulting in the opinion that held sway prior to the emergence of the present debate.

Yet as late as the early thirteenth century, there were still bishops and theologians who considered women to have been validly ordained. Thus, the answer to the historical question of whether the Church ever considered women as ordained clergy, does in fact, appear to be in the affirmative. Women were considered to have been ordained, at the very least in some ecclesial circles, for over half of Christian history.

## SACRAMENTAL ORDINATION

The question of whether women were ever ordained—nowadays often phrased, "ever sacramentally ordained"—implies a shared and fixed understanding of something that developed and changed over Church history. To elevate one definition of ordination as normative is moreover, a theological judgement, one that must be convincingly argued and not merely stated. From a historical point of view, one can determine only that women were considered ordained by the contemporary Church according to the definition-understanding of ordination at that time.

Most scholars did not consider such historical contextualization and adopted the criteria of Jean Morin (1655): that the ritual be called ordination; be to "major orders"; be celebrated at the altar by the bishop through the laying on of hands; and vesting in the stole; with the ordinand communicating under both species. Some saw no substantive difference between ordination rites for female and male deacons; others claimed a substantive difference based on the canonical bar on the female deacon to proceed to priesthood, something hardly determinative, given the conventional rather than doctrinal nature of sequential ordination. More precisely, others insisted that historically speaking, one cannot answer the question of whether or not women received a true sacramental ordination, because that concept emerged only much later.

The "form" of the sacrament was not always a fixed matter. Traditionally, after the fifth century, the handing over of certain ritual objects—*traditio instrumentorum*—was considered essential for ordination. In 1947, Pius XII ruled that the laying on of hands was the only "matter" necessary for the ordination of a priest. To apply that to the past, however, would be anachronistic, as Pius XII very precisely acknowledged.[27]

---

27. *Sacramentum Ordinis*, 1947: (2) "the humble petition has again and again been addressed to the Holy See that the supreme Authority of the Church might at last decide what is required for validity in conferring of Sacred Orders." (3) "Now the effects which must be produced and hence also signified by Sacred Ordination . . . are found to be sufficiently signified by the imposition of hands and the words which determine it. . . . [T]he *traditio instrumentorum* is not required for the substance and validity of this Sacrament. . . . If it was at one time necessary even for validity by the will and command of the Church, everyone knows that the Church has the power to change and abrogate what she herself has established." A.A.S. 1948, 5–7. In the original, that final sentence reads: "Quod si ex Ecclesiae voluntate et praescripto eadem aliquando fuerit necessaria ad valorem quoque, omnes norunt Ecclesiam quod statuit etiam mutare et abrogare valere." Contrast that with the recurring phrase in recent Roman documents: "The church has no power/authority to . . . ."

Until the eleventh century, there was no necessary progression from deacon to priest. Ten Popes from 715–974 were deacons when ordained bishop, without ever being ordained presbyter. Since the "fixed sequence" appeared only in the second millennium, it could hardly be used as a criterion for valid ordination before that. Similarly, only in the twelfth century, would ordination become an anointing for spiritual service not tied to any particular community and so its subsequent understanding could scarcely be used as a criterion for determining the validity of ordination before that.

At the beginning of the thirteenth century, terminology regarding Holy Orders begins to acquire new distinctions. Pope Urban II at the Council of Benevento 1091, limits ordination to priesthood and diaconate. Peter Lombard seeks to define ordination by linking it directly with a spiritual power and office given to the one ordained. This is modified by Alexander of Hales, who limits Orders to those offices linked to the Eucharist, thus cementing something quite different to the earlier understanding of ordination, when it was linked not to an irrevocable power, but to a particular mission in a particular community. These shifts mirrored the feudal society where they emerged. Priesthood was now seen as a personal state of life, a status, more than a ministry to a given community. It was personalized. Ordination had acquired a new and narrower definition.

The criteria for ordination emphasized thereafter simply would not have been applied during the first twelve centuries. Ordination was not even the sole term used before these changes. Rituals that comprised ordination varied over the centuries and theology had not yet been sidetracked into a legalist mindset which delineated precisely what ceremonies constitute a "valid" ordination. Before that, conferring the *power to perform* the rituals of the Church was not the essential purpose of ordination. Hardly surprisingly, the shift in understanding also resulted in the power of the priesthood expanding to take over almost all ritual roles in the Church, whereby ministries formerly performed by, for example, abbesses—such as baptizing, preaching, and hearing confessions—were reserved to the priest.

By contrast, in the first millennium there was no *general* understanding that only a priest was truly ordained. If from Peter Lombard onwards, regarding what would come to be called the "form" of the Eucharist, there was growing agreement in the West that the words of institution consecrated the bread and wine, there was not yet unanimous agreement on that at least until the Fourth Lateran Council (1215). That council may be seen as a benchmark in the understanding of ordination, which excluded from Orders all those who did not or later would not celebrate Mass. Previously, ordination meant the *process* by which a man or woman was chosen, installed, and consecrated for a particular ministry in the Church. To that understanding, women were certainly considered to have been ordained to ministry.

These developments may be illustrated by considering ministries performed by women later reserved to male clergy. Extant sources, one may note, may be somewhat misleading, in that after the twelfth century, there was no reason to reproduce liturgical texts for ordinations of women. References were simply dropped if not removed in collections reflecting the views of those selecting and preserving them. On the other hand, one may well ask why past legislation forbids women from carrying out liturgical ministries they were now assumed never to have exercised. Many of these prohibitions, moreover, were aspirations more than implemented decrees.

## INJUSTICE TO WOMEN

If medieval theologians were possessed of a socio-culturally constructed mindset different to ours, that does not mean that they did not explore deep questions with great finesse. They discussed the ordination of women in detail, in a serious theological attempt to understand what had become the accepted practice of their non-ordination, as witnessed in canonical legislation. In doing so, they seem to have mostly operated on the contemporary assumption that women had never been sacramentally ordained at any time in the Church's history. But whether they understood that practice to be ecclesiastical convention or of divine institution was less evident. Some realized full well and argued accordingly that if only the former, it would be an act of injustice to exclude women from Holy Orders.[28]

The earliest medieval treatment of the sacrament of Orders appears among the canonists and that canonical approach still shapes the official discourse. Their case was based on an appeal to ancient, mostly provincial, Church synods. But as serious theologians realized, a canonical argument was—as it still is—insufficient to demonstrate that this was the only possible theology or policy. Something more would be necessary.

---

28. Martin, *The Injustice Of Not Ordaining Women*, 303-16.

Theologians, in commentaries on the *Sentences* of Peter Lombard, began to develop arguments based on symbolism. To Bonaventure's thinking, the roles of man and woman are complementary: the woman affords rest and a sense of fulfilment to man, while man provides for and supports the woman. In a parallel way, the Church, also seen as feminine, becomes the place where God finds rest. God guides and directs the Church through Christ, a masculine mediator, and God's activity is expressed in each of the sacraments; it is declared appropriate that the minister of the sacraments be masculine rather than feminine.[29]

Thomas Aquinas asked if the feminine sex was a deficiency of nature, which prevented ordination.[30] His approach looked to a socio-political

29. Bonaventure appears to be talking about idealized relations between man and woman, the symbolic value of masculine and feminine, not actual experience. Modern developments of this speculation are found in the work of Louis Bouyer, Hans Urs von Balthasar, and Desmond Connell, Archbishop of Dublin (1988–2004). Bouyer constructs a phenomenology of men and women based on their sexuality, which situates them in the world in an essentially different manner. Male sexual activity occurs outside of self and intermittently. Man's sole function in the world is that of representing, a representation found also in the priesthood. Hans Urs von Balthasar finds this "difference so profound that to the woman is assigned not representation, but being, and to the man, the task to represent." This seems arbitrary, with little methodological foundation. These authors never seem to take into consideration the existing relationships shaped by the social differentiation of the sexes and cultural considerations. Theology enjoys no particular competence to decide typically masculine or feminine qualities: this is better determined by social life and by the human sciences, not necessarily excluding biology. For Connell, "[The priest acts] not just as minister, but in a representational role" and "It is important to distinguish between acting as a representative and acting as a representation" ("Women Priests: Why Not?" 6–8, 10). This seems to make an unverified shift in meaning; passing from the sacrament of orders to an implied sacrament of the priest.

30. Despite its frequent assertion, and despite his surpassed, mistaken views on female inferiority, Aquinas does not hold that the female is a deficient male. Aristotle's "the female is, as it were, a defective male" came to the scholastics in the translation *femina est mas occasionatus*—something caused unintentionally or accidentally, implying something deficient. Aquinas, *Summa Theologiae* (1.92.1), replies: "the female may not be intended by the male semen, but it is most certainly intended by nature. Since God is the author of nature, the female is intended by God. Being intended, it is not defective." His arcane wording, reflecting a biology long surpassed, requires interpretation. "With respect to the particular nature, the female is something defective (*occasionatum*), for the active force in the male semen intends to produce a perfect likeness of itself in the male sex. . . . But with respect to universal nature, the female is not something *occasionatum*, but is by nature's intention ordained for the work of generation." Here in recondite, scholastic usage, and building on a now-defunct biology, "particular nature" means the power or force in a particular thing; here the particular nature is the male semen, an argument Aquinas repeats in *Summa Contra Gentiles*

rather than liturgical model of constructing the question, and focused on the relationship between being-in-authority and being-a-subject-of-authority. The feminine was characterized as having the status of being a subject; the masculine represented the role of authority. Accordingly, women were considered as not naturally in a position of "eminence," while men were. Aquinas read 1 Timothy 2, 1 Corinthians 11, and the first chapters of Genesis as suggesting that the status of being-a-subject was the symbolism of the feminine. That reading, in fact, *assumed* its conclusions, it did not establish them.

Thomas' starting point, rather than examining ministry, discusses authority. It is political rather than liturgical. Fundamental to his thinking is the assumption that the recipient of Holy Orders must be by nature in a position of authority. This becomes Aquinas' precise theological reason why he considered it inappropriate to ordain women. But that social-psychological line of argument was not theological; and moreover, contradicted common experience. Theologians were obliged to acknowledge that some women at least, were brighter and more competent than many men and sometimes faced difficulties with greater courage. Would it not be a mark of prejudice, even an injustice, to deny Holy Orders to those women who had demonstrated marked ability?

It seemed inconceivable to Duns Scotus (1265–1308) that the Church could deprive even a single person, let alone an entire sex, of this "status"—note the feudal-hierarchical construction—unless under Christ's direction. He wrote:

> This is not something held just because the church decided it so, but this is something received from Christ. For the church would never have presumed that the entire female sex through no fault of its own, was deprived of an action ordained for the salvation of the woman herself and of others in the church through her, since this would seem to be the greatest of injustices, not only to the sex as a whole but even to a few persons. If, however, it were at present licit by divine law for women to have an ecclesiastical

---

(3.94). He argues explicitly that for both woman and man, the primary task is more than procreation, but to know and understand the world. On Genesis' statement that the first woman was formed from the side of the first man (*Summa Theologiae* 1.92.3), he writes that woman was not formed from man's head, because she should not dominate him. Neither was she formed from his feet, for she should not be despised by man, as though she was subject to him as a servant. Rather she was made from his side so as to signify that man and woman should be conjoined as allies (*socialis coniunctio*). Nolan, *What Aquinas Never Said about Women*, 11–12.

Order, it could well redound to their salvation and that of others through their ministry. And the Apostle was not establishing just a statute when, referring to public teaching in the church, he said (1 Tim. 2): "I do not permit a woman to act as teacher...," it was because Christ has not allowed it.[31]

## A NEW LINE OF ARGUMENTATION

This introduces a new line of argumentation. In its present-day form, with the dominant force attributed to it by *Inter Insigniores* and *Ordinatio Sacerdotalis*, a force previously absent, it will be eventually but mistakenly vaunted as ancient and continuous. Scotus was so struck by the prospective injustice of the situation that a command of Christ could be the only possible basis for it. Key to resolving the issue from that perspective, therefore, is the need to locate a clear and relatively unambiguous statement that demonstrates that Christ actually prohibited women's ordination—something impossible to locate. Under those conditions, however, conferring Orders would depend less upon the Christian community than upon the seemingly arbitrary will of Christ.

The early Church's developing theology of ministry, however, had focused not on powers conferred but on the ecclesial relationship into which the ordinand was configured. *Eucharistic presidency followed from pastoral leadership over a community.* The choice of a candidate for Holy Orders was never seen as coming directly from Christ almost without reference to or as if from outside a worshipping church community. But God, to an increasingly nominalist way of thinking, is free to be arbitrary. In explanation, Scotus initially attempts theologically plausible lines of argument, but invariably ends up falling back on earlier medieval theologians: women are excluded from Orders because their status is one of being-subject and not one of eminence.

Clearly, such argumentation does not and cannot demonstrate Christ's intention—establishing which, as we have seen in chapter 2, may prove an all but impossible task. To sustain his argument, Scotus examines the figure of the Blessed Virgin Mary. She is most worthy of all possible graces, yet the grace of Orders was apparently not given to her. He is aware that the tradition calls Saint Mary Magdalene *apostola* and a great teacher in the early Church. He acknowledges this, but argues, somewhat

---

31. Duns Scotus, "Ordinatio" 4, d. 25, q. 2, cited by Shannon, "A Scotist Aside to the Ordination of Women," 353–54.

arbitrarily, that it represents a special privilege given by Christ to Magdalene as an individual; one that does not generate a precedent and ceases with the death of the person possessing the favor, as in canon law.

Scotus' thinking on the question was followed by Antonio Andreas (Franciscan), Bishop Durandus (Dominican), and William of Rubio (Franciscan). Each of these held that the Church would be unjust if she unilaterally deprived a whole sex of access to Holy Orders. No statute resting simply on the authority of the Church could bar a woman from Orders, if she were in fact capable of receiving them. The statute, they concluded, rests on a divine law. Under nominalist influence the issue was sidelined: justice was hidden in the unfathomable mind of God, argument was no more based on sacramental symbolism. Emphasis was focused on the practice of the Church, considered infallible and indefectible. Theologians turned their attention to justifying that practice.

## PROPOSED AS DEFINITIVELY HELD

Contemporary attempts at justifying that practice, argue that the non-ordainability of women has been "received from the Lord" and is the constant and universal practice of the Church.

*Ordinatio Sacerdotalis* (1994) of Pope John Paul II was an "Apostolic Letter," *On Reserving Priestly Ordination to Men Alone*. In the first paragraph, we read:

> When the question of the ordination of women arose in the Anglican Communion, Pope Paul VI . . . reminded Anglicans of the position of the Catholic Church: "She holds that it is not admissible to ordain women to the priesthood, for very fundamental reasons. These reasons include: the example recorded in the Sacred Scriptures of Christ choosing his Apostles only from among men; the constant practice of the church, which has imitated Christ in choosing only men; and her living teaching authority which has consistently held that the exclusion of women from the priesthood is in accordance with God's plan for his church."[32] . . . Paul VI directed the Congregation for the Doctrine of the Faith to set forth and expound the teaching of the church on this matter. This was done through the Declaration

---

32. This is a direct quotation from Paul VI, *Response to the Letter of His Grace the Most Reverend Dr. F. D. Coggan, Archbishop of Canterbury, concerning the Ordination of Women to the Priesthood*, 599.

*Inter Insigniores*, which the Supreme Pontiff approved and ordered to be published.

*Ordinatio Sacerdotalis* concludes:

> Wherefore, in order that all doubt may be removed regarding a matter of great importance, a matter which pertains to the church's divine constitution itself, in virtue of my ministry of confirming the brethren (cf. Lk 22:32), I declare that the church has no authority whatsoever to confer priestly ordination on women and that this judgment is to be definitively held by all the church's faithful.

Joseph Cardinal Ratzinger, then Prefect of Congregation for the Doctrine of the Faith (CDF), and later Pope Benedict XVI, in a Letter of October 28, 1995, regarding *Ordinatio Sacerdotalis*, wrote:

> The Pope's intervention was necessary not simply to reiterate the validity of a discipline observed in the church from the beginning, but to confirm a doctrine "preserved by the constant and universal Tradition of the church and firmly taught by the Magisterium in its more recent documents," which "pertains to the church's divine constitution itself. In this way, the Holy Father intended to make clear that the teaching that priestly ordination is to be reserved solely to men could not be considered "open to debate" and neither could one attribute to the decision of the church "a merely disciplinary force."[33]

He continued:

> Certainly, the understanding of the reasons for which the church does not have the power to confer priestly ordination on women can be deepened further. Such reasons, for example, have been set out already in the Declaration *Inter Insigniores* (October 15, 1976), issued by the Congregation for the Doctrine of the Faith and approved by Pope Paul VI, and in a number of the documents of John Paul II (for example, *Christifideles Laici*, 51; *Mulieris Dignitatem*, 26), as well as in the *Catechism of the Catholic Church*, No. 1577).[34]

---

33. Joseph Cardinal Ratzinger, Prefect, CDF, *Letter Concerning the CDF Reply Regarding Ordinatio Sacerdotalis: Reply of the Congregation for the Doctrine of the Faith to a Dubium*. See our earlier discussion on this point in chapter 1.

34. "Only a baptized man (*vir*) validly receives sacred ordination." The Lord Jesus chose men (*viri*) to form the college of the twelve apostles, and the apostles did the same when they chose collaborators to succeed them in their ministry. The college of bishops, with whom the priests are united in the priesthood, makes the college of the

A crucial point to be considered is that the CDF stated that in the Apostolic Letter *Ordinatio Sacerdotalis*, the non-ordainability of women "has been set forth infallibly by the ordinary and universal magisterium." Arguing somewhat loosely from a non-consequential reference to *Lumen Gentium* 25.2, which as already referenced, does indeed affirm the infallibility of the ordinary and universal *magisteria*, but certainly does not apply that to the question of women's ordination, it continued:

> the Roman Pontiff, exercising his proper office of confirming the brethren (cf. Lk 22:32), has handed on this same teaching by a formal declaration, explicitly stating what is to be held always, everywhere and by all, as belonging to the deposit of faith.[35]

Importantly, the CDF neither claimed its own statement to be infallible, nor did it attach infallibility to Pope John Paul II's Apostolic Letter of May 1994. Rather, it appealed to what it constructed as the constant, universal teaching of the Church's magisterium as teaching this opinion infallibly while offering no conclusive evidence in support of that construction. Cardinal Ratzinger, as Prefect of CDF, suggested that that evidence had been set out *already* in the declaration *Inter Insigniores*. These important distinctions are frequently blurred in conservative, populist treatment of the issue.[36]

## PATRISTIC WITNESS

In arguing for the continuity of this teaching, *Inter Insigniores* presented five supporting patristic authorities.[37] The first is Irenaeus in *Adversus Haereses* 1.13.2, a passage, however, that describes a gnostic religious service with overtones of magic. The second is Tertullian in *De praescriptione haereticorum* 41.5, who is also speaking of heretical sects. The third citation is from Firmilian of Caesarea (d. c. 268), who opposed Pope Stephen I in the matter of the rebaptism of heretics. Writing against the Pope,

---

twelve an ever-present and ever-active reality until Christ's return. The Church recognizes herself to be bound by this choice made by the Lord himself. For this reason the ordination of women is not possible. This quotes CJC 1024 : "A baptized male alone receives sacred ordination validly."

35. AAS 87, (1995), 1114.

36. *Ordinatio Sacerdotalis: An Exercise of Infallibility*, "Ordinatio Sacerdotalis . . . is a textbook case of infallibility in action." https://www.ewtn.com/library/ISSUES/ORDIN.TXT revised June 3, 1994. That statement simply misses the point.

37. AAS 69 (1977), 98–116.

he describes a woman who was "so deeply under the sway of the principal demons that she managed to disturb and deceive the brethren for a long time by performing astonishing and preternatural feats. . . . [S]he would pretend to sanctify the bread and celebrate the Eucharist . . . ."[38] She was therefore unfit to be a presbyter, but *not because she was a woman*, rather because she was considered demonically possessed.

The fourth patristic citation is found in fragments of Origen's commentary on 1 Corinthians 14:34-35: "Women should be silent in the churches[;] . . . it is shameful for a woman to speak in church." Apart from faulty exegesis, whereby Origen wrongly assumes these to be the thoughts and words of Paul,[39] the basis of Origen's argument is not admitted today, so the argument does not hold. Women do legitimately preach in church on many occasions.[40]

The fifth citation is from Epiphanius in *Panarion* 49.2-3, 78.23, and 79.2-4.9. Epiphanius, as we have seen, always diminishes the ministry of women. His underlying thinking is exhibited in 79.2.1.

> Now then, servants of God, let us adopt a manly (*sic*) frame of mind and dispel the madness of these women. The speculation is entirely feminine, and the malady of the deluded Eve all over again. Or rather, it is the malady of the snake, the seducing beast, and the false promise of the one who spoke in it.

His misogynist mindset scarcely makes him a credible witness. Neither singly nor together then, can these references be constructed as witnessing to the constant universal teaching of the Church.

The second proposition of *Inter Insigniores* named "the central reason for this opposition to the ordination of women: the intention of the Church to remain faithful to the type of ordained ministry willed by Christ." Three authorities were adduced in support of this claim. The first is *Didascalia Apostolorum* c. 230:[41]

---

38. For the patristic references, see Wright, "Patristic Testimony on Women's Ordination in *Inter Insigniores*," 516-26.

39. Cf. chapter 3 n.23.

40. CJC 766 reads: "Lay persons can be admitted to preach in a church or oratory . . . ." This reverses a long trend and follows from Vatican Council II's teaching that all the baptized must concern themselves with the proclamation of the gospel (LG 12,31,33,35; AA 3,6,10,25). There is no hint of any distinction between women and men in the canon.

41. Incongruously, another Vatican document, downplaying the ordination of deaconesses, writes disparagingly of the same source: "Towards 240 there appeared

> That a woman should baptize, or that one should be baptized by a woman, we do not counsel, for it is a transgression of the commandment, and a great peril to her who baptizes and to him who is baptized.

But one cannot reasonably argue from that to an inability of women to receive ordination. The church today certainly does not regard women as incapable of teaching or baptizing. Further, if one may argue the inability of a woman to receive Holy Orders from an assumed inability to baptize, may one not argue for the capacity of a woman to be ordained from her capacity to baptize, a capacity frequently exercised today in places where there are no priests.

The second reference is the *Apostolic Constitutions* c. 375. In Book III, c.6:

> We do not permit women to teach in Church . . . for our Master and Lord himself Jesus Christ . . . nowhere sent out women to preach although he did not lack them. For . . . if it had been necessary for women to teach, he himself would first have commanded these also to instruct the people with us. For: "if the man is the head of his wife" (1 Cor 11:3), it is not right that the rest of the body should govern the head.

Here a gratuitous assumption is made about how Jesus acted and what is more, Jesus' assumed way of acting is purportedly explained by an untenable, supposed, natural inferiority of women.

The third authority quoted is John Chrysostom in his *Six Books on the Priesthood* 2.2.20: "when someone has to preside over the Church and be entrusted with the care of so many souls, then let all womankind give way before the magnitude of the task—and indeed most men."

Notably, Chrysostom makes no appeal here to the example of Christ and the desire to remain faithful to it. "Priesthood" in this passage moreover, refers to the office of bishop, not the presbyterate. John is encouraging a man named Basil to accept ordination as a bishop by explaining what a noble task it is: those called to be bishops should be superior to the rest of Christians; and in his view, all women and most men fail here. Chrysostom denies the possibility of ordaining women because he considers them to be fundamentally inferior, and unequal to the task.

---

a singular canonico-liturgical compilation, the Didascalia Apostolorum (DA), which was not official in character." International Theological Commission, *From the Diakonia of Christ to the Diakonia of the Apostles*, 4.4.

The fundamental equality of women and men is now unambiguously the teaching of the Church.[42] It may or may not always be acted on in a consistent manner but it is nonetheless Catholic doctrine and thereby a norm of Christian praxis. The early Fathers were voicing a contemporary prejudice. If they were mistaken, as they were, and as were the medievals also, regarding the supposed inferiority of women, then they were mistaken regarding the inability of women to be ordained priests, at least to the extent that such supposed inferiority was an intrinsic reason for their stance—as it inevitably was. *Inter Insigniores*' citing of patristic testimony offers scant support for the claim that not ordaining women is motivated primarily by the intention to remain faithful to the will of Christ.

## THE SCHOLASTICS

According to Thomas Aquinas, theology, *fides in statu scientiae*, has as its proper aim the understanding of revealed truth. However opaque our intellect, it remains true that God is truth and that our search aims at the understanding of that truth, even if never reaching it fully. This also obtains in regard to the ordination of women. The human intellect—oriented as it is to unrestricted understanding—must of necessity inquire as to whether the proposition of the non-ordainability of women is an intelligible one, and secondly, how such an assumed intelligibility might be grasped or established. Those questions concern constitutive elements of the natural order: the division of the sexes, and how that relates to divine wisdom.[43]

Priesthood as a sacrament involves a natural sign, one that pertains directly to the Church's public nature. The assumption that the priest must be male ties this sacramental sign to the biological-natural differentiation of the sexes and posits an intelligible link between the two in terms of theological anthropology. Such a supposedly intelligible link, however, since it impacts directly upon the daily service and sanctification of the people of God, would represent an intelligibility to be understood; it would hardly pertain to "God's inscrutable will." *If* God willed to exclude women from priesthood, there would have to be a meaningful reason for such an exclusion.

---

42. *Gaudium & Spes* 12, 9, 29, 60.
43. Ferrara, *The Ordination of Women*, 706–19.

Pope John Paul II emphasized Christ's sovereign freedom in calling the Twelve, stressing the historical Jesus' transcendence of cultural conditioning. But the question remains: *if* Jesus willed to restrict the apostolic ministry to males—something as we have seen, all but impossible to establish—then what was his *reason* for doing so? An appeal to merely factual tradition (written with a miniscule *t* rather than a majuscule *T*), an actual *modus operandi* of the Church under given circumstances, as distinct from the Tradition handed on by Christ and the apostles, cannot be decisive, because if it were, that would collapse the distinction between authoritatively binding Tradition and purely historical and changeable practices—traditions with a miniscule *t*. The latter refer to customs and habits, some relatively new and others relatively old, that illustrate how elements in the Church think and act in the concrete, in a given time and place. Tradition (majuscule *T*) properly so called, concerns nothing less than the transmission and reception of the gospel.[44]

According to *Inter Insigniores*, the scholastic doctors' refusal to admit the ordination of women was inspired by the "same conviction" of fidelity to Christ as was that of the apostles. Four scholastics are cited in support: Bonaventure, Duns Scotus, Richard of Middleton, and Durandus of Saint-Pourgain. Conspicuously absent is Thomas Aquinas. The other four are cited as affirming the extrinsic argument from tradition, an appeal to the will of Christ, continually upheld by the Church. Ironically, even when they do so, they propose its intelligibility by way of what the declaration elsewhere calls a "faulty" argument—a reference to woman's traditionally alleged, inferior status—in an argument based on the priest's hierarchical role as leader, his *eminentia gradus*, and not on his sacramental role.

## A "FAULTY" ARGUMENT

Thus, Bonaventure (1221–74):

> He who rules bears the type of Christ the Head; thus, since a woman cannot be the head of a man, she cannot be ordained. ... Such is the perfection of Order, in which there is a conferral of power, which on multiple grounds can be evidently shown not to befit women.

Scotus presents a similar argument:

---

44. As magisterially elaborated by Congar, in *La Tradition et les traditions*.

> Order ... is a certain grade of eminence over others in the Church and is for a certain act of superiority which must somehow be signified by natural eminence of condition and rank. But woman is naturally in a state of subjection in relation to man, and therefore cannot possess a rank of eminence over any man. ... If then she could receive Order in the Church, she could preside and rule, which is against her condition.

Richard of Middleton (1249–1308), asserting that "Christ instituted this sacrament for conferral on men only, not women," argues for the "reasonableness" of this. It is, he writes, because:

> public teaching does not befit women on account of the weakness of their intellect; and woman's state of subjection and natural inferiority make her by nature incapable of representing the eminence of rank in which one is constituted by Order.

Durandus, a fourteenth-century Dominican of nominalist tendencies, who opposed Aquinas, holds that women are barred from priestly ordination by the institution and precept of Christ. But, anachronistically, Christ's will is purportedly based on a "sound reason": that order places one in a rank of superiority over the non-ordained, a rank that it does not befit women to have over men, since women are in a state of subjection on account of their bodily weakness and intellectual imperfection.

Crucially, all four, even when making an "external" argument from a supposedly universal tradition, defend that argument from tradition of attributing women's non-ordainability to the supposed will of Christ by asserting *women's natural "state of subordination"*: an argument labelled "faulty" by *Inter Insigniores* itself.

Like Scotus, Thomas argues that the male sex is so required for the validity of orders that a woman's "reception" of the sacrament would be invalid. The sacrament is a sign and hence requires not only the reality signified (*res*), but also the signification of that reality (*significatio rei*). Since woman's alleged state of subjection makes it impossible for the female sex to signify any eminence of rank, women are incapable of receiving the sacrament of Order.

Significantly, despite his recognition of the importance of Christ's institution of the sacraments, in regard to this issue, Thomas foregoes any appeal to Christ's intention and relies solely on an attempted, intrinsic theological argument. Likewise Bonaventure, who—in the very text cited by *Inter Insigniores*—makes no appeal to Christ's institution. *Inter Insigniores* claimed the appeal to the will of Christ was normative for the entire scholastic period. But Thomas and Bonaventure, usually considered the greatest of the scholastics, make no such appeal and rely solely on the intrinsic argument. Scotus, Richard of Middleton, and Durandus employ both intrinsic and extrinsic arguments.

All these five scholastics defend the "reasonableness" of the refusal to ordain women with the same "faulty" intrinsic argument from women's "natural inferiority." They so argue, *pace* the Declaration, not merely "often," but *always*. Appeal to Christ's intention is a late phenomenon within scholasticism, unknown to its two greatest exponents and probably a consequence of the anti-intellectual milieu obtaining after 1277. Thus, the Declaration's interpretation emphasizes the argument of a tradition continually appealing to the assumed will of Christ, very far beyond what is historically warranted, and proposes it in a de-contextualized historical and intellectual vacuum.

## EXCLUDING THOMAS AQUINAS

Conspicuous by his absence in the declaration's list of scholastic precedents for an argument against the ordainability of women, precisely because of Christ's teaching, is Saint Thomas Aquinas. He makes no such appeal to the will of Christ in discussing the ordainability of women and relies on an attempted, intrinsic theological argument. *Inter Insigniores* argued that scholastic refusal to admit the ordination of women was inspired by the "same conviction" of fidelity to Christ as was that of the apostles. Yet the greatest of the scholastics is absent from this list because he does not argue as that list claims the scholastics do, in an unbroken chain from the apostles. Aquinas' absence here merits further consideration.

Pope Leo XIII, in August 1879, issued an encyclical letter *Aeterni Patris*, subtitled "On the Restoration of Christian Philosophy in Catholic Schools in the Spirit of the Angelic Doctor, St. Thomas Aquinas."[45] Leo wrote that:

> Among the Scholastic Doctors, the chief and master of all towers Thomas Aquinas ... because ... in a certain way he seems to have inherited the intellect of all.[46] The doctrines of those illustrious men, like the scattered members of a body, Thomas collected together and cemented, distributed in wonderful

---

45. A.S.S., vol. XII (1879), 97–115.
46. "Aeterni Patris," n.17.

order, and so increased with important additions that he is rightly and deservedly esteemed the special bulwark and glory of the Catholic faith.

This achievement was:

> celebrated by Popes . . . and by Councils. In the Councils of Lyons, Vienna, Florence, and the Vatican . . . one might almost say that Thomas took part and presided over the deliberations and decrees of the Fathers, contending against errors . . . with invincible force and with the happiest results. But the chief and special glory of Thomas, one which he has shared with none of the Catholic Doctors, is that the Fathers of Trent made it part of the order of conclave to lay upon the altar, together with sacred Scripture and the decrees of the supreme Pontiffs, the Summa of Thomas Aquinas, whence to seek counsel, reason, and inspiration.[47]

He aimed: "at restoring the renowned teaching of Thomas Aquinas and winning it back to its ancient beauty."[48] He exhorted his:

> venerable brethren, in all earnestness to restore the golden wisdom of St. Thomas, and to spread it far and wide for the defence and beauty of the Catholic faith to . . . implant the doctrine of Thomas Aquinas in the minds of students, and set forth clearly his solidity and excellence over others.[49]

Pope Leo presented Aquinas not only as the foremost scholastic but also as the scholar who collected and cemented the theologies of all others to produce an enduring work, considered the glory and bulwark of the Church. Pope Leo set forth clearly Aquinas' solidity and excellence over others, and called on bishops and theologians to restore this renowned teaching.[50] So in seeking to argue that the scholastic doctors' refusal to admit the ordination of women was inspired by the "same conviction" of fidelity to Christ as was that of the apostles, how can Thomas be omitted? The reason is that on this question the scholastic *par excellence* did

---

47. "Aeterni Patris," 21 & 22.
48. "Aeterni Patris," 25.
49. "Aeterni Patris," 31.
50. Transcendental Thomism, placing epistemology prior to ontology, and prioritizing the philosophical method of Aquinas over repetition of the content of his corpus, took its point of departure from Pope Leo's *quam vetera novis augere et perficere maluerunt*, "Augment and complete the old with the new." Lonergan, *Verbum: Word and Idea in Aquinas*, 220.

not argue as the CDF insists the scholastics did. *Inter Insigniores* disingenuously excludes Thomas from its scholastic witnesses to the argument from tradition, because here Aquinas makes *no argument* from tradition.

The declaration's interpretation emphasizes the "extrinsic" argument from tradition far beyond what is historically warranted. If there were such a "tradition," as continually and firmly held as the declaration insists, Aquinas would surely have known about it. But he employs only the "faulty" intrinsic argument. His method, consistent with theology as *fides quaerens intellectum*, seeks to give a rational, reasonable explanation for something his faith seeks to understand, but from the point of view of modern epistemology, does so without factoring in the interpretative nature of all understanding as well as the social construction of all interpretation.

## SUBJECTION IS NOT NATURAL

In doing so, what Thomas meant by "natural resemblance" is disappointingly clear. Responding to the objection that slaves, being in a state of subjection, are like women barred from orders, he gloomily writes: "The sacramental signs are representative by reason of natural resemblance. Now woman is in a state of subjection by nature, which is not the case with a slave. Hence the two cases differ." Both are in a "state of subjection," but differently: woman is in a state of subjection *by nature* and hence *irreparably*.

Here Thomas risks contradicting his own understanding of "nature." The "state of subjection," to which he uncritically appeals, is socially constructed; and that social construction, incorporating, as we now understand it to do, systematic subjugation, does not correspond to "right reason": hence it is *not* "natural." The scholastics' reasoning legitimated politico-cultural prejudices that they could have critiqued philosophically, but for the most part did not. Ibn Rushd (Averroes) (d. 1198) argued that since women have a similar nature to men, then they are essentially on the same level with men in respect of civic activities. Women can be philosophers and rulers, if they have been properly trained. He holds that women can lead worship, and is not averse to women becoming judges.[51]

---

51. Belo, *Some Considerations on Averroes' Views Regarding Women and Their Role in Society*, 1–20.

The contemporary magisterium rejects the possibility of ordaining women on two bases: tradition and theology, external fact and intrinsic meaning, and as we shall explore in the next chapter, does so in a new way unknown to the earlier tradition, at least in the dominant force it is now given. Appeal to tradition, moreover, is primary and normative only insofar as it reflects the will of Christ, even though thereby reducing the arguments from theological meaning to secondary importance, a reduction reaching its apogee in *Ordinatio Sacerdotalis* and repeated ever since. That approach seems incommensurate with the nature of the doctrine under discussion, with the traditional practice of Catholic theology, and with the historical facts.

The theological tradition prior to Vatican II knows only one intrinsic argument against the ordination of women: the "faulty" argument from women's assumed inferior status, an argument linked to the priest's hierarchical rather than ministerial role. Such linkage *prima facie* seemingly contradicts the obvious signification of Luke 22:24–27 (cf. Matt 20:25–27; Mark 10:42–45; cf. also John 13:4–15). The placing of this text by Luke as a frame to his Eucharistic institution narrative, away from its more original context as illustrated in Mark 10:42–45, represents a direct rejection of the illusion that "grades of power" or "eminence" have anything to do with Eucharistic presidency.

Moreover, attempts as in both *Inter Insigniores* and *Mulieris Dignitatem* to justify the maleness of the priest *via* the notion of "representation" of Christ, by way of nuptial imagery or by invoking the *in persona Christi* axiom in that context, are effectively unknown prior to Vatican II.[52] Such argumentation, far from restating ancient theological tradition, strives to inaugurate a new one. Traditionally, the ministry of the priesthood is summed up as the threefold "office entrusted by Christ to his apostles of teaching, sanctifying, and governing the faithful." Based on an assumption derived not from Christ, but from socio-cultural structures promoting male pre-eminence, traditionalist theology balks at governance by women and on that ground debars them from ordination.

---

52. It may be said to be partially anticipated in Pius XII's *Mediator Dei*, 40: "Only to the apostles, and thenceforth to those on whom their successors have imposed hands, is granted the power of the priesthood, in virtue of which they represent the person of Jesus Christ before their people, acting at the same time as representatives of their people before God . . ." 20 November 1947.

## WOMEN EXERCISING QUASI-EPISCOPAL JURISDICTION

The assertion that a woman cannot exercise ecclesiastical jurisdiction and governance, especially over the ordained, is not however, borne out in Church history. In 1187, King Alfonso built an abbey for Cistercian nuns at Las Huelgas, in Spain, to serve as a retreat for the *infantas* of Castile and members of the nobility who wished to "serve God in religion." The following year, Pope Clement III placed the monastery under the Apostolic See, exempted from the authority of the local Ordinary. The Abbess-Prelate of Las Huelgas was subordinate only to the Pope, with a similar jurisdiction to that exercised by bishops in their dioceses and styled herself "prelate" in correspondence with the Pope.

She became Lady of towns and villages, exercising full temporal and spiritual powers. She exercised authority over the secular population, but also over the entire religious estate: nuns, friars, priests and pastors of all the parishes in 54 villages, with their convents, churches and hermitages. She, not the bishop of Toledo, granted faculties to the ordained, signed in her own hand, to confess, to preach and to celebrate Mass and the sacraments. She attended and approved the election of prioresses in another twelve Cistercian monasteries under her jurisdiction. It may be plausibly argued that such governance was feudal and ill-suited to modern conditions. But that does not distinguish it from countless other canonically sanctioned, diocesan structures of those different times, not to mention the Papal States.

Far from being an abuse, as sometimes asserted,[53] for seven centuries her authority was endorsed by Clement III, Honorius III, Innocent IV, Alexander IV, Pius V, Sixtus V, Urban VIII, Leo X, Innocent VIII and Clement XII. Her privileges remained intact until *Quae Diversa* of Pope Pius IX (14 July 1874), reformed all exempt, ecclesial territories, placing Las Huelgas under the authority of the archbishop of Burgos.

Thus the Abbess of Las Huelgas, with *quasi-episcopal* powers, was a female church leader who for over 700 years, up to modern times and with papal approval, ruled an extensive territory effectively like a bishop. The abbesses of Monteviliers in Normandy, of Wadstena in Sweden, of Luca and of Conversano in Italy, exercised similar authority. The latter had a vicar general who was a bishop; she wore pontifical gloves, sandals,

---

53. For references to such misunderstandings, see Morris, 'Women and Episcopal Power', 205–10.

ring and pectoral, mitre and staff to receive the obedience of the clergy in her territory. The last such abbess of Conversano, who died in 1809, was buried with mitre, crosier and full Episcopal regalia.

## PETER LOMBARD (1096-1160)

The scholastics often enquired into what may appear to be surprisingly modern questions. Around 1155, Peter Lombard asked whether God could have assumed humanity in the female sex.[54] He initially attempted an answer with some contemporary, catechetical coherence: Christ could indeed have chosen to assume human nature as a woman, but it was better not to have done so. Arguing initially that it was more appropriate that Christ was born of a woman and assumed a male body in order to show his liberation of both sexes from sin, his argumentation then fell back on assumed male superiority: Christ ought to take on the male sex since it is the more honourable.

Albert the Great (1200–1280) gives the question definitive direction for the Middle Ages. He asks: "Whether Christ ought to have assumed humanity in the female sex?" Albert then advances, for the first time, an injurious interpretation of Aristotle's argument that a woman is a defective man,[55] arguing that since Christ ought to represent perfection, not an imperfection of nature, he should be incarnate as a man.

Bonaventure rephrases the question as: "whether it would have been fitting for God to assume the female sex for the restoration of the human race?" He asserts the principle that reparation corresponds to ruin, but addresses several new arguments. One is drawn from Chrysostom, to the effect that God should choose the weaker sex, since His power is better displayed by a woman's victory over the devil. Bonaventure's reply first repeats the then-common interpretation, without nuance, of Aristotle's presumed view that a woman is a defective man and then elaborates an

---

54. Gibson, "Could Christ Have Been Born a Woman?" 65–82.

55. For a more nuanced discussion of this issue, cf. Sparstot, "Aristotle on Women," 8. Aristotle considers the home as the prototype of all political relationships. Here the wife has full policy-making capacity but is said to be *akyron*, not in control. The patriarch decides. The difference in authority derives from different functions they perform in the household, the essential difference relating to the different ways they contribute to generating offspring. But these differences do not add up to saying that males are more reasonable or virtuous or better in any clear sense. Women as such are not inferior to men as such. Aristotle's thinking is incompatible with the assumption that women are too emotional to be left to their own devices.

objection based on the supposed Pauline view that a woman ought not to be head of the Church. It would be a perversion of order, since according to the apostle, the head of a woman is man (1 Cor 11:3). God, therefore, ought not to do something that would be destructive of the order He came to restore. Bonaventure supports this by citing Aristotle's view that the male is active, the female passive.[56] His response is based on the assumed greater dignity of the male sex, which renders it the more fitting.

Aquinas addresses these questions in terms of appropriateness. He counters the argument that the victory of a weak woman gives praise to God, with the view that glory comes not only from the infirmity of the victor, but also from the magnitude of the victory and the congruence of the fighters. Peter of Tarantaise (1224–76)—future Innocent V, for five months in 1276—sees the incarnation of the Word in a female as not impossible, but nonetheless not ordained: "it is not possible *de potentia ordinata*, however much it is possible *de potentia absoluta*. Or it would be better said that if God did do it, it would not be unsuitable." Denis the Carthusian frames the issue strongly in terms of propriety: "The Son of God ought not to assume human nature except in the more excellent sex, namely, the male," stating "it was more fitting for the Son of God to assume human nature in the male sex than in the womanly."

Words denoting suitability, propriety, or congruence abound in Sentence literature. A different understanding arises after 1277.[57] Things are as they are because it is more suitable, and in the last analysis, because God wills it. It becomes less important to know that God could have willed it otherwise, than to learn from what He has in fact ordained.

## UNKNOWABLE DIVINE VOLITION

Such reasoning, appealing to an unknowable divine volition, as expressed in the assumed (but not established) will of Christ, enshrined in a claim that it has been unswervingly upheld by the Church, one that too often all too silkily glides over history and liturgical practice, still seeks to hold sway.

---

56. This line of argumentation, with uncritical reference to its Aristotelian underpinnings and used to legitimate female subjugation, repeatedly recurs in contemporary Islamic writing, drawing especially on Maulana Mawdudi's still widely influential, *Purdah and the Status of Women in Islam*, 135–37, 141–48.

57. Wippel, "Thomas Aquinas and the Condemnation of 1277," 233–72.

CHAPTER 6

# New Answers to a New Question

SINCE THERE WERE WOMEN consecrated for ministry during the first millennium; since the medieval argument as to their putative non-ordainability was predicated upon a false anthropology of the sexes; since the fundamental equality of women and men is now unequivocal Catholic teaching; since there is not, in fact, a clear and universal adherence to the teaching of non-ordainability of women that through the ages has continually appealed in a coherent way to the established will of Christ and the apostles; and since *de facto* many women have excelled in serving, teaching, and guiding the people of God, it would seem, from the point of view of centuries-long practice, that here the Church is dealing with a new question that requires a new answer.

## TRADITION AND TRADITIONS

*Inter Insigniores* dismisses 1 Corinthians 11:2–16—historically speaking, interpreted in terms of women in church being obliged to cover their heads—as expressing a non-obligatory, disciplinary prescription: "considered time bound and antiquated [*caduca*] . . . concern[ing] practical disciplinary questions of only minor importance. . . . These prescriptions are no longer obligatory [*quae praescripta iam non urgent*]." John Meier compares this with Paul's use of technical, rabbinical terminology for tradition in that passage.[1] Paul has "handed on" (*paredoka*) sacred traditions (*paradoseis*) that must be held fast (*katechete*). Paul will use comparable *paradosis-traditio* terminology for the narrative of the institution of the

---

1. Meier, *On the Veiling of Hermeneutics (1 Cor 11:2–16)*, 212–22.

Eucharist (11:23) and for the primitive creed concerning Christ's death and resurrection (15:1-5). In 1 Corinthians 11:2-16, did Paul, unlike *Inter Insigniores*, consider the question of the veiling of women, a problem that touches the substance of the apostolic tradition? The declaration judges Paul's problem of veiling women as one of "practical disciplinary questions of only minor importance."

For both Paul and *Inter Insigniores*, the only definitive argument is fidelity to apostolic tradition. Paul, albeit for culturally conditioned notions of decorum, identifies the veiling of women as something to be upheld. The declaration sets aside as minor discipline, a Pauline regulation observed by the Church for close on two millennia, even if for cultural reasons mistaken for apostolic tradition, because of longevity. Indeed, its continued observance in many places outside North Atlantic territories poses the question of the socio-cultural rather than theological basis for many secondary Church customs. For Meier, the declaration makes a negative judgment on women's ordination based on inability to change an assumed, apostolic regulation-tradition, while its own treatment of an apostolic discipline in 1 Corinthians 11:2-16, illustrates the opposite.

Moreover, it anachronistically imports later, developed theology, ritual, and practice of the priesthood into earlier decades. It *presumes* that Jesus and the New Testament writers were concerned about the ordained priesthood *as it is understood today in the Church*, a reality that despite its embryonic presence from the beginning of the Christian community, appears for the first time *in this developed form* in Clement (ca. 96) and Ignatius (ca. 113). The New Testament has little to say about women becoming Catholic priests *in the sense that this is discussed today*, because it does not operate with today's concept of the ordained priesthood.

The priesthood *as we know it now* was fully established no earlier than the end of the first century—even if embryonically, multifariously, and dynamically present beforehand. Up to that, while charisms were clearly distinguished, ministries were complex, in flux, and developing. Different services of a substantive kind, later incorporated into the priestly ministry, were carried out by various members of the community. From what we have sought to examine in this study, it seems evident that in the primitive Church, many such ministries, which would ultimately become associated with the priestly ministry, were never restricted to men.

The assertion that the attitude of Jesus and the apostles provides a permanent norm excluding women from ordained, priestly ministry, presents both a logical and a methodological difficulty in the claim that the source for such a norm is the intention, or even the words, of Jesus. Only a conscious, theologically coherent, decision on the part of Jesus or the apostles could provide such a clear imperative. Such a decision, however, cannot be demonstrated.[2]

Certainly, presidency of the Eucharist was never arbitrary, but always by election-designation-prayer-installation. The charismatic structure of the primitive Pauline churches clearly distinguished charisms. Presbyters were chosen from those who were gifted with the charism of leadership of the community: apostles, prophets, teachers, and *episkopoi*. In the primitive Church, these quite evidently included both men *and women*. The people of God as a whole were indeed designated as a priestly people, but not as an assemblage of individual priests. Moreover, the presbyteral ministry, as distinct from the episcopacy-diaconate structure to which it was already united by the end of the first century, had clear links with structures of Jewish liturgy, where it was strictly regulated. It is all but certain that designation as a presbyter was not something simply appropriated individually nor exercised in a casual fashion.[3]

Relatively little is known, however, as to who presided at the Eucharist in the primitive Church. Less still is known about how prospective Eucharistic presidents, women or men, were actually "set apart" for that ministry. Our only evidence is that prophets and teachers fulfilled this ministry (Did. 10:7; cf. 13:3; Acts 13:1–2),[4] and prophecy is a charism that Scripture attests as given to women (1 Cor 11:5; Acts 21:9).[5] Other ministries, apparently more significant in the earliest period, such as missionary preaching, teaching of new converts, and notably, administration and service of local churches, were quite evidently exercised by both men and women.

---

2. Catholic Biblical Association of America Task Force, *Women and Priestly Ministry*, 608–11.

3. Legrand, *La Présidence de l'Eucharistie selon la Tradition Ancienne*, 410–11.

4. The word λειτουργούντων (Acts:13:2) indicates Eucharistic worship. Didache 10:7 reads: "But suffer the prophets to hold Eucharist as they will." In Did. 13:3, "prophets" are equated with "High Priests."

5. The New Testament, in this passage, recognizes female prophets. According to Eusebius, Philip's daughters lived and ministered at Hierapolis after his death (*Hist. eccl.* 3.39.9). In all probability, that ministry included presidency of the Eucharist (cf. Acts 13:2; Did. 10:7).

## THE CHOICE OF THE TWELVE

The non-ordination of women could be correctly considered as part of the Tradition—as distinct from custom or practice, however long-standing—only if such a principle could be shown to have a scriptural or apostolic foundation and thereby linked to the will of Christ as known by these two means. The fact that no women are included in Jesus' call of the Twelve is frequently invoked as an argument that restricting the priesthood to males is the will of Christ. Focusing on the conspicuous contrast between Jesus' "voluntary and courageous" attitude toward women and that of his milieu, *Inter Insigniores* holds that Jesus' not calling any woman to be a part of the Twelve has nothing whatever to do with cultural conformity.

The composition of the Twelve, however, as far as that can be known historically, could neither govern nor be governed by the place of women in the subsequent ministry of the historical Church.[6] The choice and composition of the Twelve may not properly be viewed from the perspective of later Church law and practice. The Twelve are to be interpreted, from their symbolic importance, as an eschatological warning. In the time of Jesus, there were only two and a half tribes; in the eschatological time, the fullness of unity would be restored. Consequently, by choosing twelve men, Jesus announces that the eschatological time is approaching; that he comes to gather together the twelve tribes of Israel—and ultimately all humanity—who will be judged by his word. Thus the Twelve will act as eschatological judges, symbolically as the twelve sons of Jacob (cf. Matt 19:28). The horizon of interpretation is imminent eschatology, not historical ecclesiology. Imminent eschatology quite obviously offers little detail about the presumed structures of a Church subsequently understood to continue for millennia.

The Last Supper, passion, death, and resurrection of Jesus can be historically understood only in terms of expectation of an imminent *eschaton*. That alone makes linkage between the historical Jesus and the ministerial practice of the later Church problematic, even if still feasible in its fundament, though not in all its details, many of which developed—albeit in most cases, legitimately—in response to historical conditions scarcely envisaged during the time of the apostles. The symbolism of the Twelve would have been severely compromised if Jesus had included women, or for that matter, a Samaritan, Greek, or Celt, and similarly so, if

---

6. Legrand, *Traditio perpetuo servata? The Non-ordination of Women: Tradition or Simply an Historical Fact?* 482–508.

those gathered in the upper room (Acts 1:15–26) made Mary part of the Twelve. The presence of a woman in the Twelve would simply have made no sense in those historically and eschatologically conditioned, symbolic terms.

When Luke historicizes the eschatological and symbolic function of the Twelve, he limits their mission to Israel, as the trustees of a mandate received from Jesus. As soon as pagans begin entering the church, the Twelve disappear from history. The members of the Twelve are not replaced in *that symbolic role* after their death. The legitimacy of popular catechesis notwithstanding, the elders and the bishops are not understood in the Pastoral Letters as having succeeded the Twelve.[7] The absence of women among the Twelve implies no valid conclusions about Jesus' intentions concerning the presence or absence of women in the exercise of ministries in the historical church. Similarly the absence of gentiles among the Twelve cannot be constructed as indicating that Jesus intended to exclude gentiles from ordained ministries in the church

Any appeal to continuity with Jesus' intentions concerning ministry must verify whether the apostolic communities referred back and conformed to his historical example when conferring or denying the exercise of ministries to women. There is no evidence that they did so. They seem to have acted for reasons of decorum, as dictated by cultural adaptation. The example of Jesus in choosing the Twelve, and likewise the absence of Mary from the Twelve, provide *no* conclusive basis as to whether or not women should be either admitted to or excluded from Holy Orders in the Church of today.

In Judaism, circumcision of the male is the sign of the covenant with God. In the church, it is achieved by baptism, for both men and women. Paul, in Galatians 3:27–28, proclaims the end of the divisions found in the old order. His gender-inclusive understanding of vocation, responsibility, charism, and ministry was effectively practised in the proto-Pauline communities, even if less so in the deutero-Pauline ones.

## CULTURAL ADAPTATION

Adoption and adaptation of the "household codes," *Haustafeln*, by the post-apostolic Church was a significant factor in initiating the downplaying of the status of women in the Church. These were ethical traditions

---

7. Brown, *Priest and Bishop*, 51–69.

found both in Stoicism and in Jewish Hellenism, a version of which was promoted in the reforms of Roman civic life enacted by Augustus, at the time Rome changed from a republic to an empire. They enjoined submission of the wife to the husband, children to their parents, slaves to their masters. Christianized household codes are proposed in Colossians 3:18–4:1; Ephesians 5:21–6:9; 1 Peter 2:13–3:7; Titus 2:3–5; 1 Timothy 2:9–15, and 5:9–15. The everyday, practical nature of an individual's household duties was related less to the principles of a religious belief system than to socially demanded, specific actions and duties. Their patriarchal style, notable for the absence of Paul's teaching against gender discrimination (Gal 3:28), represents a departure from the more egalitarian organization of the earliest churches. The apostolic communities first permitted and then subsequently sought to restrict the ministerial activity of women. Adaptation to the demands of the surrounding culture, apologetics, and missionary activity led to a gradual exclusion of women from the ministry of the word and from governance.

It is ironically relevant to the present debate in the Church about the ordainability of women, that this restriction and progressive exclusion of women came about from *cultural adaptation, not from theological principles*, still less from an appeal to the expressed will of Christ. In contemporary missiological terms, it was an acculturation but not an inculturation of the gospel. It does not at all seem to have resulted from the conscious duty of being faithful "to the example of the Lord." Just as the absence of women from the Twelve is not a conclusive argument regarding the ordainability of women; the growing restriction of women from ministry during the post-apostolic period is clearly explicable by factors other than that of trying to be faithful to the will of Christ.

## SACRAMENTAL REPRESENTATION BY NATURAL RESEMBLANCE

The argument of the magisterium is not without its defenders.[8] Their defence stresses Aquinas' belief that only a priest has the power of consecrating *in persona Christi*,[9] but their arguments seemingly seek more to justify that rather than establish it. Thomas states that "the consecrating

---

8. Butler, *Quaestio Disputata: In Persona Christi*, 61–80.
9. Aquinas, *Summa Theologiae*, 3, q. 82, a. 1.

virtue is not only in the words of consecration, but also in the power delivered to the priest when he is dedicated and ordained." For him, the:

> priest also bears Christ's image—*sacerdos gerit imaginem Christi*—in whose person and by whose power he pronounces the words of consecration. . . . Just as this sacrament in a certain way (*quodammodo*) represents Christ's passion, so the priest in a certain way represents Christ.

When *Inter Insigniores* defends the fittingness of symbolic correspondence of gender, it appeals to Thomas' principle that sacraments represent what they signify by way of natural resemblance. Thus, Thomas judges that only someone in grave need of physical healing is competent to receive Extreme Unction. That example is invoked to argue against the ordination of women, an argument that turns on the relation of gender symbolism to sacramental reality. It proposes that persons enter into sacramental signification and that their bodily condition may be a relevant factor.

Yet Thomas answers the question "whether a woman can baptize?" in the affirmative, citing Pope Urban II, Pope 1088–99 (Decree XXX)—a woman is permitted to baptize in case of necessity. He argues against the seemingly obvious implication, by stating that because Christ is the chief baptizer, and because "in Christ there is neither male nor female," a woman can baptize in an emergency. The principle of instrumentality is invoked in the case of emergency, because baptism is necessary for salvation. He argues that there is no need for a symbolic correspondence of gender between Christ and the minister of baptism, because the minister functions only as an instrument—not a representative—of Christ.

It is important to note that there has been profound reinterpretation and nuanced understanding of "baptism as necessary for salvation" in the Church since the time of Thomas. As we read in *Gaudium et Spes*:

> For by His incarnation the Son of God has united Himself in some fashion with every human being. . . . Christians, conformed to the likeness of that Son Who is the firstborn of many brothers, received "the first-fruits of the Spirit" (Rom. 8:23) by which they become capable of discharging the new law of love. Through this Spirit, who is "the pledge of our inheritance" (Eph. 1:14), the whole person is renewed from within, even to the achievement of "the redemption of the body" (Rom. 8:23). . . . All this holds true not only for Christians, but for all people of good will in whose hearts grace works in an unseen way. For, since Christ died for

all people, and since the ultimate vocation of humankind is in fact one, and divine, we ought to believe that the Holy Spirit in a manner known only to God, offers to every person the possibility of being associated with this paschal mystery.[10]

In this ground-breaking, purple passage from Vatican II, the Catholic Church teaches a universal soteriology whereby the Holy Spirit, *in a manner known only to God*, and therefore in a manner wider than that of baptism and membership of visible Christianity, offers to every human being the possibility of being saved through being incorporated into Christ's redemptive death and resurrection.

Consequently, baptism is not necessary for salvation in the narrow, precise, but mistaken sense, that the unbaptized cannot be saved. Baptism incorporates the baptized into the community of worship, service, and witness that embodies and historically mediates and celebrates God's endless offer of salvation to all people. Baptism is thus a more basic and originating vocation to ministry than Holy Orders. Baptism, and not Holy Orders, is the seal of Christian identity. That baptismal seal of Christian identity may be both received and administered by a woman. It is not obvious why someone capable of receiving baptism, a more fundamental incorporation into Christ, is in principle incapable of receiving Orders, a substantially distinct and hugely important but nonetheless derivative share in Christ's life and ministry.

Aquinas invokes the principle of instrumentality to allow for women administering baptism in the case of emergency because baptism was considered necessary for salvation. The Eucharist, however, is no less necessary for salvation when that term is understood more amply (cf. John 6:53–58), and moreover, forms part of Christian initiation as historically and theologically understood. Today very many concerned Catholics note a quasi-permanent emergency whereby huge numbers of believers are denied participation in the Holy Eucharist because of a more or less permanent shortage of presbyters, due not least to the present canonical arrangements.[11]

---

10. "... cum omni homine quodammodo Se univit... Quod non tantum pro christifidelibus valet, sed et pro omnibus hominibus bonae voluntatis in quorum corde gratia invisibili modo operatur. Cum enim pro omnibus, mortuus sit Christus cumque vocatio hominis ultima revera una sit, scilicet divina, tenere debemus Spiritum Sanctum cunctis possibilitatem offerre ut, modo Deo cognito, huic paschali mysterio consocientur." *Gaudium et Spes* 22.

11. This was a key issue at the synod entitled "The Amazon: New Paths for the

## "BEING HEAD" AND "BEING SUBJECT"

In discussing Holy Orders, Thomas explicitly relates what he considers the masculine symbolism of "being head" and the feminine symbolism of "being subject" to the question of sacramental realism. Whatever use is made of his theology to argue for a solely male presbyterate, an evaluation of that theology can scarcely simply jettison this constitutive aspect of his thought on this matter. The rather whimsical notion that although Thomas interprets the "natural gender symbolism" inherent in the sacramental sign hierarchically, it is nevertheless possible to interpret this natural symbolism non-hierarchically, in order to argue the reasonableness of refusing ordination to women, neglects a constitutive element intrinsic to his argument in this area. It also ignores the fundamental relation between nature and grace that governs his conception of sacrament.[12]

For Thomas, the natural sign, the matter of a sacrament, bears a natural likeness to the effect of that sacrament in sanctifying its recipient: "water cleanses"; "baptism cleanses spiritually." "In regard to the whole community, a person is perfected in two ways: firstly, by receiving power to rule the community, and exercise public acts, the spiritual counterpart to which is the sacrament of order . . . ; and secondly, in regard to natural propagation This is accomplished by Matrimony . . . ."[13]

Thomas explains sacraments neither on the basis of historical origin nor alleged "direct reference to the mysteries of Christ," but on the basis of the human nature that they elevate and sanctify—the very opposite of an imaging of grace by nature. Far from imaging an already existing,

---

Church and for Integral Ecology," that held its first business session on October 7, 2019, according to Cardinal Claudio Hummes, the synod's *relator* general, who pointed to the serious implications of Catholics without access to the sacraments, given that up to 80 percent of people in the Amazon region have "a limited sacramental life." Voting on the Synodal document took place October 26, 2019. All of the 120 paragraphs of the document were adopted by the assembly with the required two-thirds majority. The priestly ordination of *viri probati* received 128 yes votes and forty-one no votes. The ordination of women deacons received 137 yes votes and thirty no votes. Before bringing up the issue of married priests, the synod's final text makes a number of references to the importance of the Eucharist in Catholic life. It cites Second Vatican Council documents as well as John Paul II's 2003 encyclical *Ecclesia de Eucharistia*, which states: "The church draws her life from the Eucharist." "There is a right of the community to the celebration, which derives from the essence of the Eucharist and its place in the economy of salvation."

12. Ferrara, *A Reply to Sara Butler*, 61–91.
13. Aquinas, *Summa Theologiae*, 3, q. 65, a. 1.

quasi-Platonic, Christian world, as for example, one according to which male gender, juxtaposed with the female, was imagined somehow to image the divine, natural signs in fact represent the structure and dynamism of human existence, which Christ's grace redeems and elevates. Far from positing an alienating superstructure, they incarnate grace in human existence. Thus, according to Thomas, the sacrament of Holy Orders perfects "natural" "eminence" in the public order of society, by granting the recipient pre-eminence in the ecclesial community.

Under these circumstances and to that way of thinking, it is solely and precisely women's alleged inability to signify public eminence in the natural order that makes them incapable of receiving Holy Orders. Quite obviously, that socio-culturally constructed "alleged inability" is not admitted by the Church today. Insisting on its corollary, however, even while seeking to disavow the assumption from which the corollary is drawn, constitutes an ecclesially incoherent disempowerment of women.

On the other hand, the argument that just as women may acquire eminence and power in politics, so may they acquire eminence in the church, may simply, even if unwittingly, intensify the false construction of the presbyterate as "power," whether exercised by women or men. Without reimagining and reconstituting the presbyterate as *service*, and that as ministry within a servant church, ordaining women will of itself do little to effect renewal of the Church. But that does not mean that it should not happen. We may not excuse ourselves from doing what is just, simply on the grounds that it might be abused.[14] Otherwise, abuse of the office of priesthood by some men should debar men from ordination.

## WHAT IS SIGNIFIED BY ONE'S GENDER?

Realizing the now untenable assumption of female inferiority in such argumentation, some supporters of an appeal to Thomas to justify the present canonical arrangements, regarding a solely male presbyterate, seek to investigate whether an understanding of the proposed symbolic

---

14. *Abusus non tollit usum*. Nonetheless, reintroduction of women's ordination will open up several other considerations. Will it increase clericalism? Will it make the Church more just? In the case of the female deaconate, it will pose the question of the character of diaconal ordination, in particular that of its being an order in its own right and not merely a step to the presbyterate. We might well also ask at this historical juncture—not least in the aftermath of CSA scandals—what are the (culturally variant) distinctive gifts of women currently being denied to pastoral ministry?

value of gender difference is limited to this hierarchical, superior-inferior consideration. To the counter-argument that women are eligible for the office of prophet, one greater than the priesthood, they reply that prophecy is not a sacrament; there is no signification involved, only the reality. "In matters pertaining to the soul woman does not differ from man as to the thing [*res*], for sometimes a woman is found to be better than many men as regards the soul."

For Thomas, this argument might go: what is in question is not one's potential for spiritual pre-eminence, but what is signified by one's gender. To the objection that since the power of orders resides in the soul, and "sex is not in the soul," so that sexual difference should be irrelevant to the reception of the sacrament, those appealing to Thomas for support would reply that the impediment to ordination lies in an incapacity rooted in the bodily nature of being a woman, for symbolizing ordination. The female sex is thus constructed as an impediment to Orders at the level of bodily sacramental signification. One may well ask whether this is a truly theological argument or one that follows from first internalizing and then seeking to justify the contemporary law.

That line of argumentation, wishing to reject the hierarchical understanding of sexual differentiation to which Thomas appealed, strives to imagine another, non-hierarchical, way of understanding the complementarity of the sexes that may illuminate the reasonableness of this determination. Along such lines, *Inter Insigniores* itself foregoes as "faulty," "subordinationist" explanations of masculine-feminine symbolism. It draws on Thomas' general principle that sacramental signs must be perceptible and represent what they signify by way of natural resemblance. Yet when Thomas calls the priest the "image" of Christ, he refers to the fact that the priest is configured to Christ, in ordination, by means of a sacerdotal character, an invisible, spiritual sign (*res et sacramentum*); something "in the soul," one might say, and not merely symbolic correspondence between the priest and Christ on the level of gender.

*Inter Insigniores* specifies that symbolic correspondence of gender is required of the priest: "in actions which demand the character of ordination and in which Christ himself, the author of the Covenant, the Bridegroom and Head of the church, is represented, exercising the ministry of salvation." It locates the putative, "natural resemblance" to Christ, effected by the priest's maleness, not at the level of dramatic representation, but at the level of sacramental signification. Maleness, to this way of arguing, links the priest to Christ at the level of the sign, a sign considered to have been established by the fact of the incarnation and thereby bound up with the mystery of God's covenantal love.

## CHRIST AS BRIDEGROOM

This is attempted through elaboration of the metaphor of Christ as bridegroom. Attested in Scripture and celebrated in the Liturgy, that metaphor is solidly established.[15] Less convincing is its extension to make the argument that only a male can be ordained a priest. If the priest is a sacramental sign of Christ the bridegroom, of which the gender of the priest is seen as intrinsic to the symbol, then the grace of the sacrament of Orders would make Christ's masculinity as bridegroom present in the priest.[16] That tends to construct the bridegroom symbol into something far too comprehensive and primordial as if it undergirded and included many, if not all, other Christic metaphors. Moreover, it assumes rather than explains that a presumed natural-biological symbolism of gender enters into the question of who may be a sacramental sign of Christ in his role as priest and head of his body the Church.

Bridegroom/bride is not an all-embracing metaphor/symbol. The oft-quoted text from Ephesians 5:25-27, speaks not within a context of gender complementarities, but of married fidelity. Married partners model themselves on Christ's fidelity to the Church, not the other way around. Christ is not like a bridegroom; bridegrooms rather, are exhorted to love faithfully like Christ. Sexuality-marriage is not the referent, it is the metaphor. The covenant is the fundament. The bridegroom-bride "nuptial" relationship is a metaphor rather than the core meaning of covenant, whose root meaning is the bond of fidelity, within a many-faceted divine-human relationship. While there certainly are positive references comparing the covenant to loving fidelity between God and Israel (Is. 62:5), that fidelity invites and demands, as intrinsic to and constitutive of it, a new, interior covenant of the heart (Jer 31:32-33), something scarcely gender specific.

The *maleness* of Christ hardly takes on overriding symbolic significance in the exercise of the ministerial priesthood when considered in terms of the great variety within the people of God. Complementarity

---

15. The allusions are widespread if mostly indirect: Matt 9:14-15; Luke 5:33-35; John 2:9; 3:29; 2 Cor 11:2; Rev 19:7; 21:2; 22:17.

16. Picken, "If Christ is Bridegroom, the Priest Must Be Male?" 269-78.

of the sexes, and thereby the metaphor of bridegroom, hardly stretches in a fixed way, across all generations and conditions: women and men, young and old, multicultural, single and married, any more adequately, than would "shepherd" and perhaps less so than "vine" (John 15:1–10), of which all Christians, irrespective of gender, are organically united branches. While the Church as a whole is the beloved called to the marriage feast of the Lamb, not all Christians singularly and principally return spousal love to Christ. Each is a beloved disciple in different ways as friend, servant, disciple, sister or brother, companion—and especially as forgiven sinner. If the Church is the manifold household of God (Eph 2:19), with a variety of gifts, then dominant or singular reference to the image of bride-bridegroom may well be too narrow to describe it fully. "A metaphor is a metaphor. God is not married to Israel any more than God is a shepherd of sheep."[17] Christ is not any more or any less a "bridegroom" than he is a "shepherd," a "vine," or a "door."

The metaphor of bridegroom is, moreover, socially constructed. It is not universally understood as implying equality, mutuality, and complementarity, as purportedly so in North Atlantic countries. In many cultures, not least in places where Christianity is flourishing, close behind this metaphor lurks all that the medievals inappropriately supposed about male superiority and, with it, female inferiority.[18] Contextually speaking, the nuptial image, far from transcending the subordinationist framework, is frequently disclosed as simply a variant of it. Metaphors can also function to "naturalize" ideological constructions. The metaphor of Christ the bridegroom can in several contexts actually reinforce this inequality, as even our faith understands that Christ-bridegroom is "greater." This is no less the case for all metaphors with a culturally constructed referent. What is at stake is the core meaning they communicate in Scripture and apostolic tradition, in this case, covenant fidelity: hardly something that a male can signify by greater "natural resemblance" than a female.

## IN PERSONA CHRISTI

The theology of *in persona Christi*, as well as the somewhat restrictive theology of priesthood that appeals to it, as a corroboration of why the priest must be male, is, overall, strongly Christomonist and lacks Trinitarian

---

17. Picken, "If Christ is Bridegroom, the Priest Must Be Male?" 274.
18. O'Brien, *The Construction of Pakistani Christian Identity*, 535–39.

breadth. That resulted in an impoverished pneumatology in commonly understood teaching of the recent past on both Eucharist and priesthood. The history of Christianity displays a difference in emphasis, if not to say understanding, concerning the agent and moment of consecration during the Eucharist. Western thinking stresses the priest as representative of Christ in the sacramental action in which Christ's words are recited with all that will later be made to imply regarding the question of who may or may not represent Christ. The East, by contrast, stresses the invocation of the Holy Spirit in the epiclesis.

One way to broaden this discussion, so as to preclude a dichotomization of these tendencies, is to stress that the "invocation" or "epiclesis" applies to the whole of the anaphora.[19] The Eucharistic prayer forms a single whole and it is not even possible to contrast an epiclesis for the consecration of the gifts and an epiclesis asking for those present to be sanctified, even if both occur. That reciprocated understanding is wonderfully expressed in the response of the deacon to the priest at the end of the "great entrance" in the Byzantine liturgy: "The Holy Spirit himself will concelebrate with us all the days of our life."[20]

Western Eucharistic theology in the first millennium was not without a rich pneumatology. Pope Gelasius, whom we have already encountered in chapter 3, wrote of "the way in which the heavenly Spirit whom we invoke must come to consecrate the divine mystery." It must equally be noted that most early Eucharistic prayers either contain the words of institution or refer to them.[21] In this way, there developed the idea that the consecration is intimately connected with the repetition of the account of the institution, including the words of that institution. The scholastics, seeking further precision, built on this, albeit in a somewhat restrictive manner, arguing that Christ gave the Eucharist to the Church to "do this" in memory of him, *using his words*.

The Orthodox, by contrast, believed it was simply a narrative and that it was necessary to add the epiclesis. The scholastics accepted it was a narrative, arguing that it was therefore also necessary for the celebrant to have the intention of speaking in the name of Christ and as in the

---

19. Congar, "The Holy Spirit in the Sacraments" in *I believe in the Holy Spirit*, 228–43.

20. Congar, "The Holy Spirit in the Sacraments," p. 231; for references cf. p. 245 n.18.

21. The classic exception is found in some versions of the *Anaphora of Addai and Mari* in the East Syrian Liturgy.

person of Christ. But emphasis on this, sometimes to the exclusion of consideration of the epiclesis, seeing ordination as conferring the power to consecrate the Eucharist, especially when that was reduced to the instrumental causality of the word spoken by the priest *in persona Christi*, made this way of thinking "somewhat isolated, hardened and material."[22]

## *IN PERSONA ECCLESIAE*

To an instrumentalist reading, it might seem "clear to any onlooker that . . . the priest is ritually enacting Christ's part in relation to the other worshippers, . . . reciting his words, repeating his gestures, serving as host at the sacrificial meal."[23] Such naive parallelism between the Last Supper and the Mass, bypasses the primarily ecclesial form of the Eucharist as an act of the Church outside of which the meaning of *in persona Christi* in this regard cannot be legitimately determined.

> Each sacrament is a personal saving act of the risen Christ himself, but realized in the visible form of an official act of the church as such. . . . Just as Christ through his risen body acts invisibly in the world, he acts visibly in and through his earthly body, the church, in such a way that the sacraments are the personal saving acts of Christ realized as institutional acts of the church.[24]

That, in turn, highlights another, integral aspect of the question being studied here, often overlooked both by proponents and opponents of women's ordination, who neglect the purely sacramental nature of ordained priesthood *vis-à-vis* the one and eternal priesthood of Christ. For the Eucharist is always celebrated by the Eternal High Priest, acting visibly in and through the people of God.

Undue emphasis on the Christological aspect of *in persona Christi* means that priestly, liturgical ministry *in persona Ecclesiae* is constructed as a sub-set of *in persona Christi*. When the pneumatological aspect is emphasized, presbyteral ministry *in persona Christi* is seen as a sub-set of *in persona Ecclesiae*. Both ways of thinking hold that only the priest can consecrate the Eucharist, but one prioritizes a power inherent in the priest through ordination, while the other sees it as possible by virtue of

---

22. Congar, "The Holy Spirit in the Sacraments," 235.
23. *Quaestio Disputata: In Persona Christi*, 74.
24. Schillebeeckx, *Christ, the Sacrament of the Encounter with God*, 59.

the grace of the Holy Spirit, for which priests and indeed people—"And with your spirit"—ask God to be operative through them in the Church. The epiclesis, especially in the East, though also in the Roman canon,[25] is spoken in the plural, indicating how it is the whole priestly people who invoke the Holy Spirit. It is the people of God in liturgy who act in *persona Christi*, the priest ordained to act *in persona Ecclesiae*, thereby, but not as it were in an ontologically prior manner, acts *in persona Christ*.

That has lead some theologians to critique the doctrine of *in persona Christi* as if the pronouncing by the priest *in persona Christi* of the institutional words of Christ bestows on them a value or power that is immediately consecratory. Although many Orthodox invest the phrase *in persona Christi* with meaning, a definition of the priestly action—*in persona Christi*—that identifies the priest with Christ is unknown to that tradition. In the West, virtually exclusive attention to the words of institution—downplaying, if not all but effectively excluding, the work of the Spirit[26]—led to the rest of the anaphora being devalued and endangered the unity of the Eucharistic prayer.

That problem came to a head when scholastic theology sought to define the precise moment of consecration and at least from the time of Innocent III (Pope: 1198–1216) onwards, to the enunciation of the principle that the transubstantiation of the species had to be instantaneous, an interpretation that may have seemed intelligible when applied to *res et sacramentum* thinking, but seems unconvincing when examined in the context of holistic, liturgical celebration. The three new Eucharistic prayers introduced into the Latin rite, post-Vatican II, may be said to have re-balanced the matter, but the implications of a richer pneumatology regarding the action of the priest *in persona Ecclesiae*—and only thereby *in persona Christi*—in the Eucharistic celebration have yet to be adequately appropriated. One aspect of such an appropriation is a rediscovery of the pneumatological element in the Eucharistic liturgy that dents an exclusively *res et sacramentum* approach to ordination and the consequent insistence on a solely male priesthood to represent Christ, to the extent that it appeals to such an approach.

25. The Roman Missal (1962) reads: "Hanc igitur oblationem servitutis *nostrae*, sed et *cunctae* familiae tuae, *quaesumus* Domine, ut placatus accipias: diesque *nostros* in tua pace disponas, atque ab aeterna damnatione *nos* eripi, et in electorum tuorum etc." (Italics ours.)

26. Some argued that a silent epiclesis occurs in the imposition of hands at the *Hanc igitur*.

The resurrected Christ is a pan-cosmic reality, but as confessed and thanked and imitated, he is present in and as the Church, his mystical body, the primordial sacrament of Christ, who is the sacrament of God. This is made sacramentally visible in the sacred Liturgy. It is primarily the whole mystical body and liturgically speaking, the whole assembly, the priestly people, who sacramentally bear a "natural resemblance" to Christ. Together we are the body of Christ. Tradition—it is worth repeating—shows that priests presided at the Eucharist because they presided over a community—not the other way round—as we mostly find today.

The priest acts towards Christ in *persona Ecclesiae* and within that role acts towards the rest of the assembly *in persona Christi*. Only by first acting *in persona Ecclesiae* can priests act *in persona Christi*. To pray the Eucharistic prayer, priests must be ordained within a community and represent this community: there is no absolute ordination.[27] In receiving Holy Communion, priests scarcely act primarily *in persona Christi*; in sharing Holy Communion within the liturgy, they do, as albeit in a derivative way, do the ministers of the Eucharist, male or female.

## LITURGICAL PERSPECTIVES

Common reflection on these issues is essentialist, its underlying conception of Church order seen as determinative of the Church's life and prayer rather than determined by them. Here *lex credendi* holds sway over *lex orandi*. These two ought not be in opposition, but rather serve as mutually corrective—*ut legem credendi lex statuat supplicandi*.[28] Reflection on the *lex orandi* can critique and alter the hitherto supremely dominant *lex credendi*.[29]

In the received, pre-Vatican II tradition, ordination was focused on priestly power: "Receive power to offer sacrifice to God and to celebrate Mass." That interpretation of ordination—now surpassed—is still at least subliminally operative in much of the contemporary debate. The true role

---

27. "Neither presbyter, deacon, nor any of the ecclesiastical order shall be ordained at large, nor unless the person ordained is particularly appointed to a church in a city or village, or to a martyry, or to a monastery. And if any have been ordained without a charge, the holy Synod decrees, to the reproach of the ordainer, that such an ordination shall be inoperative, and that such shall nowhere be suffered to officiate." Council of Chalcedon (451), canon 5.

28. DS 246.

29. Fink, "The Sacrament of Orders," n.3.

of the Church and of the Holy Spirit in this sacrament was somewhat obscured. The Vatican *Declaration on the Admission of Women to the Priesthood* argues: "It is true that the priest represents the church, which is the Body of Christ. But if he does so, it is precisely because he first represents Christ himself, who is the Head and Shepherd of the Church." To this mentality, a priest first seemingly represents Christ, and only then the Church. But nowhere in the revised rite of ordination is there any suggestion of prior, "direct" intervention by Christ bypassing the action of the Church assembled for prayer. Ordination is an act of Christ present in and as the assembled Church, who acts in, when, and as the Church acts liturgically.

The Church assembled is the primary sacrament of Christ, in all its liturgical actions expressing itself as the sacrament of Christ.

> Christ is always present in His church, especially in her liturgical celebrations. He is present in the sacrifice of the Mass, not only in the person of His minister, "the same now offering, through the ministry of priests, who formerly offered himself on the cross,"[30] but especially under the Eucharistic species. By His power He is present in the sacraments, so that when a person baptizes it is really Christ Himself who baptizes. He is present in His word, since it is He Himself who speaks when the holy scriptures are read in the Church. He is present, lastly, when the Church prays and sings, for He promised: "Where two or three are gathered together in my name, there am I in the midst of them" (Matt. 18:20).[31]

A former, one-sided application of "power" to ordained priesthood was corrected. Where once the bishop would have said to the newly ordained priest, "Receive power to offer sacrifice to God," he now says, "Accept from the holy people of God the gifts to be offered to Him." When the Church invokes the Spirit upon deacon, presbyter, or bishop, this invocation is in function of the ministry that is being given. The ordained are assigned ministries: their role is primarily one of service.

The ordained are asked by the Church to embody and manifest the mystery of Christ, so that the assembly may see in someone from among them what they are baptized to become. Because such embodiment involves a transformation and a mission, the assembled Church once again

---

30. Here *Sacrosantum Concilium* is quoting the Council of Trent, Session XXII, *Doctrine on the Holy Sacrifice of the Mass*, c. 2.

31. *Sacrosanctum Concilium* 7.

invokes the Spirit of God. In the life and ministry of the ordained, the Church asks and expects to see a manifestation of its own identity and vocation. Reciprocally, the ministry of the ordained priest is to call forth the priesthood of the people of God. The people of God as a whole, both throughout the world, in a local church, and in a given Eucharistic assembly, are a "priestly people," a "kingdom of priests" (*basileion hierateuma*) (1 Pet 2:9; Rev 1:6; 5:10). The ordained priesthood—priesthood of the order of the presbyterate—exists in the Church as a ministry of service in order to enable the church to be what it is constituted and called to be—a *priestly people*.

## INTERDEPENDENCE OF PRESBYTERATE AND PRIESTLY PEOPLE OF GOD

The fundamental priesthood is that of the people of God, the derivative priesthood, while really distinct in kind, is that of the presbyterate. One may well wonder how gender difference, if irrelevant to what is the fundamental priestly service to God, should be considered central to the derivative, albeit distinct, presbyteral ministry to that priestly service.

Vatican II insisted that the rites clearly signify the reality of faith, which they bring to expression.[32] If the Church at the time of Trent was primarily concerned to insure that the sacraments effect what they signify, this has now been balanced with the concern that sacraments signify what the Church believes and confesses they effect.[33] To lead in worship is to pray publicly with faith, in an atmosphere of faith, where the presence of God makes its claim on the assembled people of God and where the people can respond to God's approach to them. That cannot be realized merely by reciting prayer texts, however splendidly written.

This allows for a more phenomenological understanding of *in persona Christi* as identifying a spiritual depth proper to the baptized, that when sacramentally celebrated, under the gift of the Holy Spirit through ordination, discloses how it is embraced by Christ as his own. This is guaranteed by the Church's faith expressed and sacramentally celebrated, in the

---

32. *Sacrosanctum Concilium* 21.

33. "Rightly, then, the liturgy is considered as an exercise of the priestly office of Jesus Christ. In the liturgy the sanctification of the person is signified by signs perceptible to the senses, and is effected in a way which corresponds with each of these signs; in the liturgy the whole public worship is performed by the Mystical Body of Jesus Christ, that is, by the Head and His members." *Sacrosanctum Concilium* 7.

invocation of the Holy Spirit and the laying on of hands. It demands that priests live in accordance with that faith, placing their lives at the disposal of the Holy Spirit. The fidelity of Jesus to his own human life, as it was revealed by God, is the fidelity to which each human being, and especially each ordinand, is called, and it is the existential space within which the ordained person's "natural resemblance" to Christ may be found.

The ordained are servants of the mystery of Christ, a mystery whose primary manifestation is the Church, especially when it is assembled for liturgical prayer, which, it goes without saying, is not to be imagined as separate from action for social transformation and justice, but rather the source and summit of that action, as the Eucharist is of the whole Christian life.[34] It is always in the context of the priesthood of all believers that the priesthood of the ordained is to be understood, because that ministerial priesthood is established to activate and to illustrate the priesthood that belongs to all the baptized.

The interdependent mutuality of the priesthood of the presbyterate and the priesthood of all the believers, who are not exclusively male; the ordination to that priesthood in the Church by the resurrected Christ, who has transcended gender, present in that gender-inclusive assembly; the orientation of priesthood to service in ministry rather than power; and an enrichment of the notion of *in persona Christi* to include imitation of the fidelity of Jesus to his own human life, as it was revealed by God, in fidelity to the deepest dimensions of one's own humanity and a renewed awareness of the action of the genderless Holy Spirit in the Eucharistic liturgy as well as in the sacrament of Orders; singularly, and *a fortiori* together, severely dent the unproven postulate that women may not be ordained. All the more so when that proposition never exits from the shadow of the presumption of female inferiority.

## NATURE AND GRACE

Arguments for the non-ordainability of women from a Thomistic perspective are based on an assumed "natural resemblance" to Christ effected by the priest's maleness at the level of sacramental signification. The term *natural* in Thomistic philosophy, however, does not mean visible or sensible or biological *tout cour*.[35] Thomas does not propose a naive, empirical

---

34. *Lumen Gentium* 11, *Catechism* 1324.

35. There is a twofold common usage of the word "nature": nature as the natural

understanding of "nature," but one based on "right reason" or correct understanding. Thus the *nature* of something is that which makes it to be what it really is. What makes us to be what we really are, what we are "in Christ," is *baptism*, not gender. The criterion of theological truth is *theological, not empirical*. Biology cannot always be a decisive, theological criterion.[36]

Here we likewise emphasize a theological rather than merely biological "natural resemblance" to Christ; a likeness, indeed a connaturality, according to the order of grace. Paul's claim that "in Christ there is neither male nor female" (Gal 3:28-29) is less a statement about gender roles than about how baptism prefigures and inaugurates the glory of the risen Christ to be revealed in each of us. For Thomas indeed, the priest is configured to Christ, in ordination, by means of a spiritual, sacerdotal character, *res et sacramentum*, and not merely by symbolic correspondence on the level of gender.

The relationship between "nature and grace" is a classic debate in Catholic theology. Karl Rahner (1904-84) sought a "third way" between scholasticism as then commonly taught, and some versions of the *nouvelle théologie*. Neo-scholastic thinking was extrinsicist, constructing an understanding of God's grace as if gifted from "outside" or "above" on nature. The *nouvelle théologie* emphasized an intrinsic orientation of nature to grace: there is no "pure nature" which then accepts grace; but rather a "natural desire," *desiderium naturale*, within human nature for God.

Rahner's *tertium quid*, termed the "supernatural existential,"[37] argued that *desiderium naturale*, positive, unconditional, internal, and utterly gratuitous, while not given "after," from "above," or from "outside," is nonetheless a strictly supernatural orientation to participation in the

---

world, the ensemble of things that have had a genesis; and nature as the essence of something; what is natural for something. In that second usage, it means the source within the growing being: the primary intrinsic source of movement or change belonging to something by virtue of what it is. Giuseppe Tanzella-Nitti, *The Aristotelian-Thomistic Concept of Nature and the Contemporary Debate on the Meaning of Natural Laws*, 240.

36. Catholic theology does not necessarily hold to biological monogenism. Pope Pius XII, in *Humani Generis* (1950), did so, but only insofar as polygenism was constructed as denying original sin. Theological monogenism (i.e., all humankind forms a unity whose origin is God) has replaced biological monogenism, which need not be presupposed. Rahner, "Monogenism" in *Sacramentum Mundi*, 974-77 and "Original Sin," in ibid., 1148-55.

37. Rahner distinguishes *existential* from *existentiell*. The former refers to the ontological dimension of human finitude; the latter to its everyday categorical dimension.

divine life, gifted in grace. Building on Aquinas' *potentia obedientialis*,[38] he posited that human beings, as recipients of God's self-communication in grace, are created as capable of receiving that grace.

He surpassed a long-standing "extrinsicism" whereby supernatural grace appears as a superstructure, imposed by God's free decree, upon human nature, beyond the range of experience. Human persons, that construction suggested, experience themselves as "pure nature"; orientation to a supernatural end seen to consist in external divine decree, and not considered constitutive of human nature as such. Here Rahner also diverged crucially from the *nouvelle théologie*, which he judged as positing that grace is distinguished from other created gifts—all of which arise from God's freedom—only in respect of the greatness of the gift but not in respect of how it is unexacted, *ungeschuldet*.[39] He insisted that if God wills an unexacted, supernatural end for the human person, then God simultaneously, freely gifts the human person a disposition to that end. He rejected a notion of human nature including that supernatural end as intrinsically necessary to its essence, because that would jeopardize the supernaturality and unexacted gratuitousness of that end.

God creates women and men such that they can receive the Love which is God's Self while accepting that for what it is: astounding, unexpected, unexacted gift, not owed to them. To receive this gift however, human persons must have a congeniality for it; making them capable of receiving it precisely as free gift not owed to them. That capacity is the central and abiding existential of all women and men as they really are. Thus human "nature" if and when juxtaposed to the supernatural, is what Rahner terms "a remainder concept"—*Restbegriff*[40]—which continues to have meaning to highlight the giftedness of the supernatural existential. But it is never found in a distillable, "pure" state separated from that supernatural existential; neither as one upon which God's grace is imposed from outside (neo-Scholasicism) nor as a "nature" with an intrinsic *desiderium naturale* for God (*la nouvelle théologie*).

---

38. For Thomas, obediential potency implied passivity and indetermination and following Cajetan, was generally reduced to non-repugnance by neo-Scholasticism.

39. Rahner elaborated this in "Eine Antwort," *Orientierung* 14 (1950) 141–45; published as emended, in English, in "Concerning the Relationship between Nature and Grace," 297–318, cf. 304n.2.

40. Rahner, "Concerning the Relationship between Nature and Grace," 313.

He later[41] summed up this position by writing: "God's self-communication as offer is also the necessary condition which makes its acceptance possible."[42] The goal of God's self-gift in grace, the final vision of God, implies an ontological relationship between God and the human person. Not merely a future, ideal reality, it is the historical experience of the graced person in practice, because through the gift of the Holy Spirit—who fathoms the depths of God—we participate in God's being in the "here and now." It is within these existential parameters, the supernatural existential being a definitive, ontological, determinant of a concrete human nature, and not within those of biology, that one finds "natural" resemblance to Christ. The "natural" is never otherwise than always oriented to, suffused with, elevated and sanctified by grace freely given.

Since all females and males bear that "natural resemblance" to Christ by being created in the image and likeness of God, and further, as Christians, by being reborn as coheirs with Christ through baptism, and by being temples of the Spirit of Christ, and still further, bear "natural resemblance" to Christ the high priest through incorporation into Christ through baptism to become a priestly people, a kingdom of priests, one is still left wondering as to the *theological coherence* of the assertion that the female sex is an impediment to receiving Holy Orders. This is especially so when torturously and somewhat futilely trying to justify that without invoking the false assumption of female inferiority.

## INADEQUATE UNDERSTANDING

It seems unlikely, especially given the paucity of priests, that God, who "has hidden these things from the wise and learned, and revealed them to little children" (cf. Matt 11:25), would *de facto* will the celebration of the Eucharist, the reconciliation of sinners, as well as the teaching and guidance of the people of God to hinge on a dubious, esoteric theory, explicable to them only with great difficulty, on the basis of unexamined assumptions, if indeed at all.

Attempting an abstruse reinterpretation of Aquinas' quite obviously inadequate understanding of the relationship between the genders as

---

41. David Coffey's "object is to establish the thesis that, despite appearances, there is no contradiction between Rahner's late and early statements on the supernatural existential." "The Whole Rahner on the Supernatural Existential," 97.

42. Rahner, *Foundations of Christian Faith*, 120–28, 128.

a means of defending his position on the non-ordainability of women goes beyond the bounds of a disciple's loyalty to the Angelic Doctor. That greatest of theologians—like every human being, a person of his time—had his limitations. Like all medieval theologians, he did not have the advantage of knowing in detail the history of Christian ministry, or of the rites of ordination found in contemporary Pontificals. He operated for the most part by making theological statements based on philosophical principles and on current usage.[43] Reliance on these led Aquinas to teach other things about ordination that Vatican II would surpass, if not indeed, repudiate.

For Aquinas there were only three sacred orders: the priesthood, the diaconate, and the sub-diaconate.[44] He repeats that position when discussing—in a markedly unhistorical fashion that pays little attention to tradition—whether the episcopate is an order: "Episcopal power depends on the priestly power since no one can be a bishop who has not received priestly power."[45] That was factually mistaken.[46] Several Popes, indeed, had been consecrated bishop from the deaconate, without ever having been ordained presbyter. For Aquinas, as for the time he lived in, the sacrament of order is related primarily to the Eucharist.[47] Thus, the presbyterate is the summit of the orders since it is directed to the consecration of the Eucharist.[48] Because the episcopate is not directed to the Eucharist, he argued, it is not an order. The same teaching was held by other contemporary scholastic theologians, according to whom a new order was not conferred in episcopal consecration, but simply a new office with new power.

---

43. Bradshaw, *Anglican Ordinal*, 6.

44. Aquinas, *Summa Theologiae*, Suppl. Q. 37, art. 3. 766. Compare this with the Catechism 1536: "Holy Orders is the sacrament through which the mission entrusted by Christ to his apostles continues to be exercised in the Church until the end of time: thus it is the sacrament of apostolic ministry. It includes three degrees: episcopate, presbyterate, and deaconate."

45. Aquinas, *Summa Theologiae*, Suppl. Q. 40, art. 5, 780.

46. Of the thirty-seven Popes during 432–684, *only three* are known to have been ordained presbyters beforehand. Historically, many Cardinals were deacons. The most recent notable case was Giacomo Antonelli (1806–76), a lay papal functionary, ordained deacon in 1840, to be named Substitute at the Secretariat of State in 1841. Created Cardinal-deacon in 1847, he became Pius IX's Secretary of State in 1848.

47. Aquinas, *Summa Theologiae*, Suppl. Q. 37, art. 2, 765.

48. Aquinas, *Summa Theologiae*, Suppl. Q. 37, art. 5.

That however, is not the doctrine of the Catholic Church, which teaches in Vatican II that:

> *the fullness of the sacrament of Holy Orders* is conferred by episcopal consecration, that fullness namely which, both in the liturgical tradition of the Church and the language of the Fathers of the Church, is called the High Priesthood, the acme (*summa*) of the sacred ministry.

and adds:

> One is constituted a member of the episcopal body in virtue of the sacramental consecration and by the hierarchical communion with the head and members of the college.[49]

## THE ETERNAL HIGH PRIEST

The letter to the Hebrews is the New Testament text dealing most comprehensively with Christ's priesthood. Hebrews 5:8–10 is a key passage:

> Although being a son, he learned obedience from what he suffered (*hemathen aph' hōn epathen tēn hypakoēn*): and having been perfected (*kai teleiōtheis*), he became (*egeneto*) the source of eternal salvation to those obeying him, having been designated by God a High Priest, according to the order of Melchisedek.

Theological reflection in relation to women's ordination, as to many other things, needs to pay as much attention to the ascending Christologies of the New Testament as it does to descending Christology. This is not the case in most scholastic theology, as in much patristic theology.

Christ's designation by God (the Father) as High Priest follows from his having been made perfect (*teleiōtheis*). This perfecting of Christ's human capacity to be the compassionate High Priest, mediating universal salvation (Heb 5:1–7), follows from how he learned (*emathen*) total conformity to the will of the Father in his willingness even to suffer to the end, in the project of being faithful to his mission. Scripturally speaking, his capacity to be the High Priest of God's dispensation follows from the fact that "he learned to obey through the things he suffered." Here the modality is developing and dynamic, not static as in much descending Christology. Certainly, Hebrews stresses Christ's fidelity as the fidelity of a son. But in 5:8, "Son though he was," is the subordinate clause; "he

---

49. *Lumen Gentium* 21.

learned to obey through what he suffered" is the main clause, expressing the central dynamic. It is in this "learning" that we may look for a dynamic expression or an existential unfolding of the "natural resemblance" in the signification of what is granted and celebrated in priesthood of the order of the presbyterate conferred in the sacrament of Holy Orders.

Quite obviously, not all baptized males, merely by being male, bear such a "natural resemblance" to Christ the High Priest who "learned to obey through what he suffered." Women—and men as well—who live and minister in long, fruitful, and purposeful, service—even to the point of suffering in fidelity—bear that baptism-bestowed connaturality that is required for the reception of Holy Orders and manifests itself in the capacity to learn to obey through the things it suffers in order to be faithful to Christ.

This seems all the clearer when one averts to the fact that Christ the eternal High Priest, who forever celebrates the one and eternal sacrifice in and through and as the sacramental memorial of the Eucharist, is, in fact, the resurrected Christ and not the historical Jesus. The remembrance implied by the instruction, "Do this in memory of me," likewise points to his risen presence in the Church until the end of time. Prescinding from how the Last Supper narratives represent a historicization of the liturgies of the very earliest churches, that Last Supper is a prolepsis of the glorified Christ's presence among us, even as it encapsulates and completes the radical meal praxis of the historical Jesus.

The risen Christ who is priest forever (Heb 7:22) and "who lives forever to make intercession" (v. 25) is possessed of a spiritualized body rather than a physical one. "What is sown is a natural body and what is raised is a spiritual body" (*egeiretai sōma pneumatikon*) (1 Cor 15:44–45). The spiritualized, risen body of Christ with which he nourishes us in the Eucharist is the life and love and self-gift of one who in resurrection has transcended both death and gender: "For in the resurrection they neither marry nor are given in marriage but are like the angels in heaven" (Mark 12:24–25; Matt 22:30). The Last Supper was indeed celebrated by the historical Jesus. In it the fundament for what is celebrated in the Holy Eucharist, namely the death of the Lord until he comes, is inaugurated. But that real inauguration is predicated on Jesus' impending murder and resurrection from the dead. The Eucharist is an anamnesis of Christ's death and resurrection, not of the Last Supper. That memorial is eternal because the eternal High Priest is the one who eternally offers himself for the life of the world.

The question then arises as to who has a "natural resemblance" to the eternal High Priest who, in his resurrection from the dead, has transcended gender difference. The only feasible answer must lie along the direction of discerning those who by incorporation into Christ through baptism (cf. Rom 6:3–6) take on their baptismal vocation with such dedication as to be able to confess, however haltingly, yet in an at least sufficiently authentic way: "I live not I but Christ lives in me and that life that I live now . . . is through faith in the Son of God who loved me and delivered himself up for me" (Gal 2:20), and can then guide people to live by that faith. That is surely something as possible as it is demanding for both men and women.

## MOVING FORWARD

For Thomas and for those who follow him, to understand "natural resemblance" to Christ, what was in question was not one's potential for achieving spiritual pre-eminence, but the socio-political "eminence" signified by one's gender. Aquinas did not hold that view in an intellectual vacuum. It was contextualized and grounded in a false, hierarchical anthropology of the sexes and sought to give theological meaning to a socio-culturally constructed interpretation of the respective roles of males and females in the household and in society, a set of views that in turn, was rooted in a pre-scientific biology. That biology and that anthropology have now been surpassed. Not only basing itself on such false assumptions, the overall scholastic schema paid little attention to the ecclesial and liturgical context of presbyteral ministry and certainly in the case of their interpreters, not enough to how the One who communicates himself to us in the Eucharist is the risen Christ.

Under these circumstances, in what way can the various declarations from the Vatican on the assumed non-ordainability of women be considered "definitive" and can it really be established that this is what was transmitted by the apostles? Has our study, on the contrary, marshalled sufficient evidence as to require assent to the proposition that women may indeed be ordained and that the time has come to validate that canonically? We will investigate these issues in our final chapter.

CHAPTER 7

# A Theology Whose Time Has Come

ARE THE INSTRUCTIONS FROM the Roman magisterium regarding women's ordination a matter of discipline or doctrine? Did the apostles demonstrably restrict presbyteral ministry to males and pass that restriction on as being according to the will of Christ? What can be inferred for the Church of today from the ministry of outstanding women in the churches of the New Testament? Is legitimate, informed, prayerful, dissent an aspect of discernment, an element in the development of doctrine? How may one infer that the ordination of women represents a necessary pastoral-theological development whose time has come? We will attempt to answer these questions in this final chapter.

## DEFINITIVE DOCTRINE OR PRESENT DISCIPLINE?

Any adequate answer to the question of whether the current position of the Roman magisterium regarding women's ordination is a matter of present canonical discipline or definitive Catholic doctrine requires clarifying the nature and genesis of that teaching as well as comparing that with the nature and genesis both of canon law and theology.

That teaching finds its genesis in the acculturation to patriarchal norms of a previous, radical, gender equality against the background of imminent eschatology, influenced by the Augustan, imperial reforms, as evidenced in the Pastoral Epistles. Despite widespread first millennial, female ministry, as attested in literary, epigraphic, and liturgical sources, several local synods sought to curtail that. It seems evident that they sought to do so through prohibition, rather than through theological elucidation. When writers of note such as Pope Gelasius or Bishop Atto comment on it, they do so in canonical terms. Where theological arguments were adduced, they were mediated through naïve, if not faulty exegesis.

## CANONISTS DECIDING, THEOLOGY FOLLOWING

In the second half of the twelfth century, teaching on women's ordination was still fluid, but canonists were taking it in a decisively different direction. Heloise and Abelard were probably the last to write a comprehensive defence of women's ordination in medieval Western Christianity. A majority, following Gratian, argued that women could not be ordained. That left a problem: Gratian's *Decretum* (c. 1150) contains five references to *presbyterae* and deaconesses[1]—memory of ordained women had not entirely disappeared. Rolandus recognized that women had been ordained, noting that they were not allowed to marry after ordination. Stephan of Tournai opined that these were simply holy women called deaconesses, permitted to read the Gospel at Matins. Nonetheless, the *Summa Monacensis* (1177) saw both early and contemporary ordinations of deaconesses as valid ordinations, something acknowledged by Johannes Teutonicus in the apparatus on the *Decretum*, written after Lateran IV (1215).

Canonists were relentlessly moving towards holding the position that women could not and had never been ordained. Rufinus airbrushed a thousand years' of women's ordination, arguing that such putative ordinations referred not to valid, sacramental ordination, but to some lesser ministry. Huguccio of Bologna solidified that view in his commentary on the *Decretum* (1188): such putative ordinations were merely ceremonies appointing women to some diaconal role. He went further: arguing that a woman is incapable of receiving Orders. His reasoning is entirely canonical: "What impedes this? The law of the Church and sex, that is the law of the Church made on account of sex." His point is made absurdly clear in ruling that a hermaphrodite: "drawn to the feminine more than to the male could not receive Order. If the reverse, the person is able to receive, though ought not to be ordained."

---

1. Quotations from the original sources drawn on here are impressively marshalled by Macy, *The Hidden History of Women's Ordination*, 210–22.

Church teaching, following canonical verdict, was changing dramatically. Canonists had moved from acknowledging that women *had been* ordained to holding that they *never were* and *never could be* ordained. That became the standard canonical opinion. When Johannes Teutonicus wrote that nuns could and did receive the character of orders, that was already a minority opinion, soon to disappear. Guido de Baysio (1298) not only precludes women from Orders but also extends that even to arguing that a woman is not a perfect member of the Church, whereas a male is.

The existence of *presbyterae* was similarly airbrushed out: they were not presbyters, but simply the wives of priests, taken while the latter were in minor orders. If canonists were, in some instances, correct in so describing them, they now went further; arguing that not only were these women not ordained, but they had received no special blessing of any kind. Within about one century, women lost all standing as ordained clergy, despite vast testimony to the contrary. Even abbesses now were simply laywomen, as Innocent made clear in 1210, denouncing their established practice of hearing confessions.

Canonists commented on and taught these new laws, which circulated in informal collections, until Gregory IX in 1234 promulgated them in *Liber Extra*. That was compiled by Raymond of Penafort, who in his *Summa de Paenitentia* (ca. 1235) wrote: "It should be noted that a female is not able to receive the character of any clerical Order," adding that "a *presbytera* is so named since she was the wife of a priest or perhaps a widow . . . ." Other canonists such as Bernard of Botone, whose *Glossa ordinaria* (ca. 1260), became extremely influential, simply followed Penafort. Standard canonical principles on women's non-ordainability, were now in place, as they would continue to be down to today. Subsequent discourse wrote ordained women out of the history of the Church.

Theologians, by and large, followed the canonists. They developed the discourse, but only *after* the canonists had effectively settled the issue. This was facilitated by Peter Lombard's precision on the sacrament of Orders as a sacred sign by which a spiritual office and power is conferred on the ordained—a decisive break with first-millennial theology. Ordination was now tied to power, rather than to ministry. That was solidified by Rufinus' canonical teaching that the character of Orders, like baptism, was irreversible. For Huguccio (d. 1210) it persisted even after death.

In Alexander of Hales' commentary on the *Sentences* (1227), the coupling of Holy Orders with the Eucharist was fully articulated: the power conferred in Holy Orders was the power to confect the Eucharist. Hence, only an ordination so empowering the ordinand could be considered valid and any putative ordination in the past that conferred no such power was not. Ordination was redefined: focused on one ministry and one power. That process of redefinition coincided with an airbrushing of the ecclesial memory of ordained women. It was denied that Paul had even spoken of deaconesses. Based on that misreading, Gratian denied that women could aspire to ordination. The emergent, prevailing opinion held that women were incapable of receiving the character of ordination. It was then concluded that since women could not be ordained, they had never been ordained. References to *presbyterae* and deaconesses were explained away. At most, they were wives of the ordained, if not auxiliaries who performed unimportant tasks in the Church.

If canonists, followed by theologians, came to define ordination as imparting sacramental powers that only males could receive, they did not do so in a socio-political vacuum. Central to the Gregorian reform's accent on the moral integrity and independence of the clergy, was insistence on the supremacy of the priesthood over the laity and of the papacy over the emperor and secular kings. To effect separation of clergy and lay lords and the independence of the Church, the reformers insisted on clerical celibacy. At the Second Lateran Council (1139), they did so by defining any marriage contracted by clergy to be invalid, providing a disincentive for women to marry priests. The Church practice allowing *presbyterae, episcopae*, and deaconesses, understood even in the narrower sense, disappeared. Encouraging celibacy was often supplemented by denigration of women—most luridly by Peter Damian (1007–72). Generally speaking, the laity were sympathetic to these reforms and responded affirmatively to calls not to attend Masses celebrated by married priests.

A language of misogyny, to justify canonically imposed celibacy, provides a backdrop for excluding women from ordained ministry. But of itself it cannot rule it out since women too were vowing themselves to celibacy. A further element was needed; its aim to convince that women could not be the intellectual and spiritual equals of men. That appealed to earlier forms of Roman law which stressed the control of the *paterfamilias* over spouse and children. As taken on by Gratian, the teaching that a woman could not be ordained was contextualized by a law that forbade women to testify against a priest. Considering women as never the intellectual equals of men also drew on a restrictive reading of Aristotle, which in Aquinas' notes on his lectures on Paul, saw "three things as appropriate to women[:] . . . silence, discipline and subjugation . . . ." Such use, both of Roman law and of Aristotle, was conspicuously selective, even unrepresentative of its sources, chosen to bolster a canonical position. Scripture was then re-read through these somewhat misogynist spectacles.

In the medieval period, the non-ordainability of women was indeed argued theologically, but as mediated by, or on the basis of, an anthropology of gender now considered risibly inadequate. A new form of theological argumentation emerged in recent years seeking to base the putative non-ordainability of women on the sacramental aptitude of a male priest in representing the male Christ, precisely because of his maleness. That reasoning has not been received by the *consensus fidelium* and is still under discussion by theologians and by many bishops too.[2] The theological arguments adduced are declaimed but *not established*. The non-ordainability of women as enjoined by *Codex Iuris Canonici* 1024 and the *Catechism of the Catholic Church* 1577 is a law, a norm of behavior, and not a theologically established truth.

Even when decisions banning the ordination of women came from synods or councils, these decisions were legislative canons. They were framed in a genre derived from the legislative-judicial traditions of discourse developed in the Roman Empire, which continued to be a constitutive element of councils down to Vatican I (1870), a form that clearly manifests the assumption that a council is a legislative-judicial body. Vatican I issued eighteen canons; Trent issued more than 130 for its doctrinal decrees alone and much the same for its disciplinary enactments. These canons generally employ the formula: "If anyone should . . . , let him be anathema." Councils from Nicaea to Vatican I had a characteristic style of discourse, composed of two basic elements. The first was the canon or its equivalent. The second consisted in words of threat and intimidation, surveillance and punishment, words of a superior to inferiors, or to an enemy: power-words.[3]

---

2. Consider the forced retirement in 2011 of Australian Bishop William Morris, who simply raised the *possibility* of ordaining women as a solution to that country's severe priest shortage.

3. O'Malley, "Vatican II: Did Anything Happen?" 3–33. He shifts the focus from *what* the council said to *how* it said it, engaging in form-analysis. The council's texts display a literary genre new to the conciliar tradition, utterly different from the legislative mode of all previous councils and crucially important for understanding what happened at Vatican II.

## THEOLOGY AND CANON LAW

What is the relationship between theology and canon law? Some see it as close, even to the point of identification. Some see it as distant, even to the point of radical separation. Others advocate a relationship of varying closeness between them. To discover the nature of the relationship involves clarifying the nature, genesis, and dynamics of the two disciplines as they relate to each other.[4]

Theology has two elements: firstly, God's self-revelation to which the response is faith and secondly, the human effort to understand that. The authority that governs theology is that of faith and reason. The authority that rules canon law is that of legitimate, ecclesiastical power, divine in its origin, but human in its exercise. Theology explicates how the Church has received God's self-revelation; canon law discloses how the Church uses its authority to organize the community of believers. When the Church engages in theology, it seeks to know and understand. When it promulgates a law it intends to impose decisions. Both are produced by the Church; but they are distinct entities, operating at different levels. Theology is the fruit of faith seeking understanding. Canon law is the fruit of faith seeking just, practicable decisions and actions. Distinct, though organically united, they display sharp differences that may not be simply overlooked.

Theology knows no limiting horizons. It seeks to know all God's mysteries as revealed to us, in so far as graced, human intelligence can do so. Canon law is well-defined and circumscribed with precisions; it contains ordering norms issued by an ecclesiastical authority. Theology and law require diametrically opposed hermeneutics, since one is never-ending and the other, extremely limited in scope. These may not be confused. If the hermeneutics suited to theology were applied to law, the Church would be beset with endless uncertainties. If those suited to law were applied to theology, the result would be a simplistic and one-sided strangulation of the intellectual life of the Church in its search for divine truth, leading to a diminution of its grasp of that truth.

Their common origin creates a relationship of intrinsic interdependence. For canon law to be authentic, it must depend on theology, not only in an external way, as when the teaching authority intervenes, but in its very being. If the understanding of revelation does not govern and control the decisions of the Church as reflected in its laws, there is

---

4. Örsy, *Theology and Canon Law*, 158–91.

ecclesial breakdown with potentially disastrous consequences. Theology judges canon law by forming judgments regarding the fittingness of canonical norms. Canon law has no capacity to judge theology because legal ordinances are not theological judgments. It would, moreover, have no criteria with which to do so. Any hapless attempt to do so would display a defective epistemology, confusing the nature of generating and communicating knowledge with that of issuing a command. It would thereby miss the point of how God reveals God's saving love, not by issuing commands, but in speaking the truth and giving us the Holy Spirit to be able to recognize and assent to it in the Church.

Not only can there be a theology of canon law, there must be. This is made obvious when theologians, as they ought to do, reflect on developments in the Church by examining the evolution of its institutions and norms, much of which is canon law. That corresponds in large part to what is being attempted in this study. It may be objected that historically the Church has reached out for values through legislation without first defining them theologically. In those cases, what seems to be involved is an intuitive perception of a value and the decision to appropriate it before that value has been adequately conceptualized or defined. There is no real reversal of the natural process; theological intuition precedes any decision. But legislation can also be sometimes over-dependent on vested interests and be inappropriate.

Those who see canon law as part of theology, intrinsically part of *fides quaerens intellectum*, are often inclined to transfer the qualities of theological realities onto legal activities and norms of action. For them, the rules supporting the word of God should be as permanent as the word itself and considered just as sacred. Supportive scaffolding is confused with the building, after the building has been confused with the household. That sadly overlooks the difference between preserving the people of God through word and sacraments, and the constant accommodation to necessary developments in human society, in the manner one organizes to do so.

As illustrated in the impasse over women's ordination, that usually results in an instinctive resistance to sensible and necessary changes in the law, by demanding a level of devotion to legalities that is due only to the divine word itself, usually putatively justified solely on the basis that the law was correctly enacted. If in some cases, that may be temporarily justifiable on grounds of prudence, it is hardly legitimate to cloak it in the guise of an irreformable, permanent doctrine.

What we find in *Codex Iuris Canonici* 1024 and the *Catechism of the Catholic Church* 1577 and in the Roman documents congruent with these, is an expression of the legitimate authority of ecclesiastical power, however constrained its exercise. It discloses how the Catholic Church uses its own authority to organize the community of believers. Here the Church does not primarily engage in theology, seeking to know more deeply the mysteries of God, but rather promulgates a law, intending to impose decisions, deeming them to be for the common good. Rather than the fruit of faith seeking understanding, it is the fruit of faith seeking decisions and actions with a view to ordering norms. When theological arguments are adduced, that is seemingly done less to establish theological truth than to legitimate law.

Things cannot *a priori* be assumed so to rest forever. Authentic canon law must depend on theology. Theology forms a judgment of the fittingness or otherwise of present canonical norms, including the ones being studied here. Canon law has no capacity to judge theology because its legal ordinances are not theological judgments. There can be no legitimate, canonical circumscription of faith seeking understanding. The Church's legitimate exercise of authority must resist any temptation to transmute legal activities and norms of action into theological truth. That the present ban on the ordination of women may be canonically binding does not *ipso eo* make it doctrinally definitive.

## INFALLIBLE AND FALLIBLE TEACHING

The appropriate response to a solemn witness to the word of God is surrender in faith. The inner dynamic of this witness and response is the action of the Holy Spirit empowering both the witness and the response. But proper emphasis on how the Holy Spirit guides the magisterium may not be allowed to diminish the Spirit's never-ending guidance of the *supernatural sense of faith* in the body of the believers and the co-constitutive significance of that supernatural *sensus fidei* operative in the *consensus fidelium*, in actively receiving and thereby elaborating the teaching of the Church. Each needs the other and is inoperable without the other.

Organs of the Roman magisterium in teaching the non-ordainability of women have, as already discussed, sometimes attempted to imply that this teaching is infallibly taught by the Church. In syllogistic form, their argument might be constructed as follows. Major premise: infallibility pertains also to the ordinary and universal teaching of bishops throughout the world, when they propose, in communion with each other and with the Pope, the Catholic doctrine to be held; minor premise: that women cannot be ordained has been universally and continually held by the church from the beginning to today; conclusion: it is infallibly taught that the church does not have the authority to ordain women.

The major premise is correct and is set forth in *Lumen Gentium* 25.2. The minor premise, however, seems incorrect. It could, moreover, only be established by historical theology followed by authoritative confession and solemn declaration by a Pope or council, and received as such by the people of God, and not merely by declamation in a document from a Vatican dicastery. A central aim of this book has been to examine whether, in fact, this teaching has been universally and continually held. The evidence points in the opposite direction. Therefore, it would seem that the opinion, however longstanding, that the Church does not have the power to ordain women has not been taught infallibly. Furthermore, in general, theologians take an extremely restrictive view, in any theological reference to Canon 749 of the Code of Canon Law: "No doctrine is understood to be infallibly defined unless it is clearly established as such." That women may not be validly ordained has *not* been infallibly taught.

It would, however, be simplistic to suggest that the legitimacy of dissent can be decided merely by invoking the distinction between infallible and non-infallible teaching. *Lumen Gentium* 25 also insisted that:

> religious submission (*obsequium*) of mind and will must be shown *in a special way* [italics ours] to the authentic magisterium of the Roman Pontiff, even when he is not speaking *ex cathedra*; that is, it must be shown in such a way that his supreme magisterium is acknowledged with reverence, the judgments made by him are sincerely adhered to, according to his manifest mind and will. His mind and will in the matter may be known either from the character of the documents, from his frequent repetition of the same doctrine, or from his manner of speaking.

What is this *special way* to show *obsequium* to the Roman Pontiff, even when he is not speaking *ex cathedra*? How can one accept these documents as authentic declarations of the "Roman authorities, with formal authority that cannot be judged simply as if a statement of other theologians," but nevertheless insist, as Rahner among many others did, that "it is not definitive, that it is in principle reformable and it can (which is not to say *a priori* that it must) be erroneous." From the other end of the spectrum, it would surely be heretical to claim that all teachings of the magisterium are without error, or that there is no practical difference in the assent required of ordinary teachings as distinct from infallible teachings, or that all dissent is sinful and to be prohibited, or that obedience to the teachings of the Church can be based solely on authority, and not on truth.

## DISSENT: DISOBEDIENCE OR DISCERNMENT?

The Theological Commission of Vatican II, in a reply to an emendation proposed by three council fathers, clearly indicated that it was well aware of the possibility of legitimate dissent and simply indicated that approved theological treatises should be consulted. Some of these certainly allow for sober, considered, dissent from non-infallible teaching.[5] It would, therefore, be unjust and lacking in theological acumen to treat *a priori* all dissent from the teaching of the magisterium as disobedience. In 1967, the German bishops referred:

> to the fact that in the exercise of its official function, this teaching authority of the church can, and on occasion actually does, fall into errors. The fact that such a thing is possible is something of which the church has always been aware and which she has actually expressed in her theology.[6]

In 1968, the U.S. bishops wrote that:

> There exist in the church a lawful freedom of inquiry and of thought and also general norms of licit dissent. This is particularly true in the area of legitimate theological speculation and research. When conclusions reached by such professional, theological work prompt a scholar to dissent from non-infallible received teaching, the norms of licit dissent come into play.[7]

Already in the New Testament, especially as illustrated by Paul in Galatians 2:11, we see disagreement and dissent in the Church. The unity of the body of Christ does not demand the absence of such disagreement, but rather the capacity to deal with it in a manner that leads to growth

---

5. *Acta Synodalia Conc. Vat II*, lll/8, 88 n.159, as cited by Sullivan, *Magisterium: Teaching Authority in the Catholic Church*, 166–68 & 229.

6. As cited by Rahner, *The Dispute concerning the Church's Teaching Office*, 85–88.

7. Pastoral Letter of the U.S. bishops, *Human Life in Our Day* (1968).

in faith, hope, and charity.[8] The inclusion in canonical New Testament texts of disagreements, whether in Jerusalem or Antioch, is not simply historical reminiscence, but is inspired, canonical Scripture, "useful for correction and training in righteousness" (2 Tim 3:16). Such canonical, scriptural witness to the reality of disagreement as a path towards more adequate understanding and practice, articulates a "truth for the sake of our salvation."[9]

Dissent is an ambivalent word and may seem unhelpful to the extent that it can be used to suggest an attitude of extreme opposition that is ready to break the bond of unity, as in the dissent of an Arius, a Luther, a Döllinger, or a Lefevre.[10] What is intended here, by contrast, is the informed, considered, prayerful disagreement of those who with full commitment to preserve the bond of unity, have legitimately reached a different, positive conclusion to what is being proposed non-infallibly and have done so through a relentless and courageous quest for understanding and truth. One may recall the various disagreements, in their day, with aspects of commonly presented teachings at that time, on the part of Dorothy Day, Thomas Merton, Teilhard de Chardin, Yves Congar, Louis Massignon, or Karl Rahner, in each case eventually facilitating a deeper and more adequate understanding of the faith.

That is the dissent, if dissent it be, of one who seeks to surrender to God and to live by faith and who accepts the Catholic belief in the authority of the Church in guiding and proclaiming the gospel. It is the prayerful, considered disagreement of those who realize that before a doctrine reaches full maturity of expression and can be affirmed with an act of faith, there is a long process of *fides quaerens intellectum*. Far from breaking the bond of unity, such disagreement, an aspect of discernment, strengthens it, by paving the way for the incorporation of key elements or aspects of a theological truth obscured or ignored for culturally conditioned, non-binding reasons.

This study argues that in the case of the development of any "doctrine" on the ordination of women, that process of defining it still has some way to go and the outcome cannot be decided by canon law alone or by declamation by a Vatican dicastery. Under these circumstances, the standpoint of a theologian—or, as in the present case, of very many

---

8. Meier, "Biblical Reflections: The Conflict at Antioch (Gal 2:11f.)," 471–75, and Just, "The Apostolic Councils of Galatians and Acts," 261–88.

9. Cf. *Dei Verbum* 11.

10. Orsy, *The Church: Learning and Teaching*, 90–100.

theologians and exegetes and an increasing number of bishops—is not at all a matter of dissent, but rather an element in discernment, a necessary contribution to the development of doctrine in assent to revealed truth still in a process of searching for fuller expression.

## SOCIAL CONSTRUCTION OF INTERPRETATION

Every interpretation is socially constructed and contextualized within a matrix of assumptions, beliefs, and practices. A practical rule of action or norm or orientation can be socio-culturally conditioned and open to change as a result of a changed socio-cultural situation. Many concrete rules of action implicitly enshrined contradictions—in this case, the unwarranted assumption of female inferiority—where the contradiction could not be perceived, or at least, was not perceived in earlier socio-cultural situations. Many provisional statements of belief assumed certain parameters that were subsequently shown to be inadequate.

A classic example is found in the monogenism-polygenism debate during the last century. Today Catholic theology does not necessarily hold to biological monogenism. Pius XII, in *Humani Generis* (1950), did so, but only insofar as polygenism was constructed as denying Original Sin[11]—a subject whose adequate theological understanding requires a reading of Genesis 3 in the light of Romans 5, and even then as interpreted by the church fathers (Augustine in particular) and councils, and after that, many fine distinctions. Theologically, all humankind forms a unity whose origin is God—theological monogenism. Biological monogenism need not be presupposed and no longer is. The matrix of assumptions undergirding a provisional postulate of the non-ordainability of women, if and when likewise shown to be inadequate, as many believe it already has been, could no longer be assumed to hold. Another example may be found in Gregory XVI's opposition to democracy and his statement in the encyclical *Mirari Vos* (1832), pronouncing it "false and absurd, or

---

11. "When there is a question of another conjectural opinion, namely, of polygenism so-called, then the sons of the church in no way enjoy such freedom. For the faithful in Christ cannot accept this view . . . for it is by no means apparent how such an opinion can be reconciled with what the sources of revealed truth and the acts of the magisterium of the church teach about original sin, which proceeds from a sin truly committed by one Adam, and which is transmitted to all by generation, and exists in each one as his own." *Humani Generis* (1950), n.37 with references to Romans 5:12-19; and Conc. Trid., session V, can. 1-4.

rather mad, that we must secure and guarantee to each one liberty of conscience."[12] Church historians could produce many more examples.[13]

Theologians and the Roman magisterium need each other for the proclamation of the word to which both are subordinate. In this light, theologians who remain in communion with the magisterium, but propose a different theological answer to a pastoral question to that given by the code of canon law and the Catechism, as well as the Roman documents congruent with that position, far from indulging in a manner of dissent that injures the unity of the body, are making a much-needed contribution to the development of doctrine and are thereby *strengthening* the bond of unity. Here the theologians—who are indeed fallible and can also sometimes be wrong—and the bishops are engaged in different but complementary tasks. The primary task of the bishops is to proclaim the mysteries of faith, that of the theologians to penetrate the meaning of these mysteries as much as possible.

## TEACHING AUTHORITY IN THE CHURCH

Doctrine develops. "As the centuries succeed one another, the Church constantly moves forward towards the fullness of divine truth until the words of God reach their complete fulfilment in her" (*Dei Verbum* 8). "The body of the faithful as a whole anointed as they are by the Holy One, cannot err in matters of belief" (*Lumen Gentium* 12). This follows from the supernatural sense of faith, *sensus fidei*, aroused and sustained by the "Spirit of truth," which characterizes the people of God as a whole. Faith, however, does not consist totally or even primarily in assent to the *propositions* enunciated by the Creed, much less to those enunciated by the Roman magisterium,[14] but rather to the truth for our salvation they express, whose unfathomable riches can only be adequately expressed by the Word incarnate, and not by a proposition.

---

12. Accessible at www.papalencyclicals.net/greg16/g16mirar.htm.

13. *Inter Caetera* of Pope Alexander VI (1493) stated that any land not inhabited by Christians was available to be "discovered," and claimed by Christian rulers. This "Doctrine of Discovery" became the basis of all European claims in the Americas. Absurdly, First Nation people had only a right of occupancy, which could be abolished, http://www.let.rug.nl/usa/documents/before-1600/the-papal-bull-inter-caetera-alexander-vi-may-4-1493.php.

14. Sullivan, *Magisterium*, 14–23.

One aspect of the modern development of the term "magisterium" is that it is used almost exclusively—and to that degree, erroneously—to refer to the teaching office of the hierarchy. If in common catechesis, the bishops are considered the successors of the "apostles," they are not the successors of the "teachers," something abundantly clear for at least a thousand years. A similar reduction is evident in the use of the word "authentic" in reference to the magisterium. In modern English, "authentic" means "genuine." But the meaning of the Latin word *authenticum* is "authoritative," in the sense of "entitled to obedience." If that is not borne in mind, it might result in the absurd misunderstanding that only bishops can give a genuine interpretation of the word of God.

It is the Church as a whole that is maintained in the truth of the gospel by the Holy Spirit, consequently the bishops must "consult" the faithful, even in matters of doctrine, as classically expounded by J. H. Newman (1801–1890). In speaking of "consulting," Newman intended something substantive, organically and constitutively part of the process of deciding:

> The English word "consult" in its popular and ordinary use . . . is doubtless a word expressive of trust and deference, but not of submission. It includes the idea of enquiring into a matter of fact as well as asking a judgment.[15]

Some of the faithful are exegetes and theologians, people of faith who have spent years closely, and in many cases prayerfully, studying God's word. "Teachers" and "apostles" are distinct in Paul's lists of charisms. The successors of the "teachers" are not primarily the bishops, but the theologians, exegetes, and catechists. Their roles are no less ecclesial than that of the bishops.

Belief in the infallibility of the Pope and of the Church does not postulate a class of "infallible propositions." Infallibility is predicated not of propositions but of the teaching authority. But since it is impossible to formulate a statement about revealed truth which *a priori* is not open to a possible different or better reformulation, a dogmatic statement, as distinct from what it proposes, cannot be said to be unchangeable. No serious bishop or theologian, moreover, would argue from the abiding presence of the Holy Spirit to the conclusion that every development in Church organization has been beneficial or even legitimate.[16] Catholic

---

15. Newman, *On Consulting the Faithful in Matters of Doctrine*, 54.
16. "Not everything that exists in the church must for that reason be a legitimate

theologians who correctly uphold papal infallibility are well aware that Popes have made mistakes in the exercise of their teaching function—while never solemnly defining as infallible anything incompatible with the truth of the gospel. The definition of infallibility at Vatican I does not and cannot rule out the real dependence of papal definitions on the faith of the people of God. By contrast, it would be a gross misunderstanding to imagine that the certitude of our faith somehow depends on papal infallibility.

## RECEPTION: CO-CREATION OF MEANING

The role and responsibility of the people of God, moreover, are never reducible to merely passive obedience to formal authority, but include active participation in the dynamic by which the Church as a whole "clings without fail to the faith once delivered to the saints, penetrates it more deeply by accurate insights and applies it more thoroughly to life."[17] Reception of a teaching is always the creative reception on the part of active, living subjects. The recipients of a teaching become co-creators of its meaning.[18] No text, even one from Scripture, much less a subordinate text of interpretation or application, simply yields up its meaning entirely by itself. Its reception is seldom merely "take it or leave it as stated," but requires the dynamic of tradition.

Living tradition is the handing on and the receiving of the active presence of revelation in living subjects. Thereby, the recipients of a text become co-creators of its meaning as it is permanently retrieved and enriched through being re-interpreted in new contexts, on the basis of new experience and in answer to new questions. This is equally so in the re-evaluation of experience long present, but unrecognized, or in the facing up to questions long asked, but still lacking an engaged response.

In that regard, particular attention must be paid to the perspective of the poor and excluded, the first to hear the gospel. Since there is undeniable evidence of the silencing of the voice of women in Church affairs,

---

tradition.... [T]here is a distancing as well as a legitimate tradition, ... piety that is opposed to the spirit of Liturgy, ... casuistic and untheological morality ... *in statu viatorum*, tradition proceeds in a spirit of progress and ever deeper insight into faith, but there is also the possibility of a *deficere* and in fact the possibility is constantly being realized...." Ratzinger, "Dogmatic Constitution on Divine Revelation," 185.

17. *Lumen Gentium* 12.

18. Congar, *La Tadition et les traditions*, vol. 2, 81–93.

it is reasonable to posit a comparable hermeneutical privilege on their part within the theological conversation exploring these issues.[19] That dynamic is paramount in exploring the question of the admissibility of women to Holy Orders.

Non-infallible teaching certainly can be erroneous and, on occasion, actually *has been so;* not only can it need correction, but historically it *has been corrected. Lumen Gentium* 25 speaks of the *obsequium* due to non-infallible teaching, often translated as "submission," but perhaps more accurately by "due respect."[20] The crucial question arises again in this present study in the case of informed, faithful people who have prayerfully made an honest and sustained effort at "due respect" yet still find themselves unable to give sincere assent to some particular teaching of the magisterium. This certainly does happen and does so fundamentally because interior assent is a judgement of the mind and not primarily an act of the will. The mind cannot assent to a proposition unless it can accept it as true.

## THE APOSTLES AND THEIR SUCCESSORS

The second paragraph of the recent declaration on the "definitive" nature of the Roman magisterium's ban on the ordination of women begins with a statement that succinctly sums up comparable teaching in previous documents: "Christ wanted to give this sacrament to the twelve apostles, all men, who, in turn, communicated it to other men." In *Inter Insigniores*, the conclusion is drawn from the judgment that "Christ did not call any women to be part of the Twelve," that Jesus intended in principle to exclude women from the priestly ministry for all times and under all sociological conditions. In these and associated texts, the transition from the concepts of "apostle" and "the Twelve" to those of priest and bishop seems far too smooth to square with present-day knowledge of the origins, structure, and organization of the primitive Church.

Apart from the problems associated with a loss of eschatological perspective in the implied view of Church origins and history, including thereby a loss of the symbolic significance of the Twelve, as well as the implied assumption that we know in exhaustive detail exactly what

---

19. O'Brien, *Theology and the Option for the Poor*, 162–65.

20. On the translation of disputed terms used in Vatican II, cf. Butler, "Infallible; Authenicum; Assensus; Obsequium," 77–89.

happened at the Last Supper, there is the further difficulty of apparently equating the "Twelve" with the "apostles" as the latter are described throughout the New Testament. The official, canonical position leaps over difficult but fundamentally important questions, for the present discussion, about the concrete emergence of the Church and its origin from Jesus.

Quite obviously, Paul, never one of the Twelve, sees himself as an apostle. Ironically, if not sarcastically, describing himself as "the least of the apostles" (1 Cor 15:9), he immediately adds that, in that calling, he has worked harder than any of the others (v. 10). He has been appointed apostle not "by human beings," not even by the historical Jesus, but by the resurrected Christ (Gal 1:1), persecuted, crucified, and resurrected in his people (Acts 9:5). Many decisions about ministry and office in the early Church are similarly derived not from the *ipsissima verba Jesu* at a putatively reconstructed Last Supper but from developing, ecclesial practice animated by the presence and power of the resurrected Christ.

In addition to the Twelve, the New Testament explicitly mentions many other apostles, even apart from Paul. James, "the Lord's brother," and leader of the Jerusalem church, if considered different to James son of Alphaeus, is called apostle in Galatians 1:19; as is Barnabas in Acts 14:14. Apollos in 1 Corinthians 4:6–9 is not only called apostle, but Paul favorably compares Apollos' exercise of apostleship to his own. The apostleship of Timothy and Silvanus is implicit in 1 Thessalonians 1:1, as together with Paul, they are authoring and issuing that Epistle, and they are quite explicitly designated as apostles in 2:6. Epaphroditus, in Philippians 2:25, is called apostle, even though the word is variously translated in English. Two further unnamed apostles are referred to in 2 Corinthians 8:23. It is possible, though by no means certain, that one of them is Titus. Paul so esteems their apostleship as to call them "a glory to Christ." Finally, there are Andronicus and Junia, mentioned in Romans 16:7. There were even counterfeit "super-apostles" in Corinth, who made Paul's life so difficult (2 Cor 11:13–15).

## THE APOSTLES AND THE TWELVE

In the Synoptics, the common term for Jesus' immediate circle is "the Twelve," or "the disciples." Comparison of Luke 6:13 with the earlier Mark 3:13 is instructive. Luke reads: "he summoned his disciples and picked out twelve of them; he called them apostles." Mark reads: "He appointed twelve," with no mention of the word *apostle*. The wording of the parallel passage in Matthew 10:1, "he summoned his twelve disciples" (*tous dōdeka mathētas autou*), implies that the reader already knows about the choice of the Twelve. Matthew's next verse gives "the names of the twelve apostles." In the text of Luke 9:1, the word "apostles" is considered an addition to "the Twelve."[21] Although Jesus certainly "called" some "disciples" to a more intimate association with him and equally certainly "sent" them to proclaim the kingdom of God, from the available evidence, one can reasonably infer that the appellation "apostle" was one given by the very early post-resurrection communities.

Since it was well understood by the first readers of the Synoptics, the term was retrojected into the Gospel narrative and used to describe the Twelve, in practice, the first to be apostles, as the term, as well as the office and ministry it implied, was used in the early communities. Thus, the "twelve apostles" of the Gospel texts were truly apostles, but "the apostles" were not limited to "the Twelve," even if they almost certainly included them. When in catechesis, we say that the bishops are the successors of the apostles, they are not simply the successors of the Twelve alone, but of all those apostles who fulfilled in a foundational way, the call of the risen Christ to proclaim the good news to all creatures. On balance, it seems more likely that the term "apostle," widely used and well understood in the early communities, was read backwards and thereby memorialized in the call of the Twelve, than it was that this Greek word was historically first used of the Twelve and carried forward into the New Testament communities.

In 1 Corinthians 12:28 and Ephesians 4:11, Paul lists "apostleship" as the highest gift and calling for the building up of the body of Christ. "Apostles" are listed prior to "prophets," who, according to the Didache, presided at the Eucharist. Philip the evangelist, one of the Seven, "had four unmarried daughters who were prophets" (Acts 21:9). Paul's understanding of the charismatic nature of office in the Church does not conflict with the emergence of what would become a hierarchy. In fact, he distinguishes among the charismatic gifts precisely to demonstrate that not all are apostles or prophets or teachers. Likewise, not all are called to administer the Church. Each has his or her charismatic gift (Rom 12:6),

---

21. Luke took from Mark the primitive appellation of "the Twelve." Copyists either added or substituted "apostles." Metzger, *A Textual Commentary on the Greek New Testament*, 122.

but only those charismatically gifted to exercise a given office should be appointed to that office. Could one or more such apostles have been female?

## A CLOSER READING OF ROMANS 16:7

Against that background, it may prove instructive to read Romans 16:7 more closely:

> Greet Andronicus and Junia, my fellow-countrypeople and fellow-prisoners, who are notable among the apostles (*hoitines* [plural] *eisin epismoi en tois apostolois*) and who have been longer than I in Christ (*apo emou gegonan en Christō*).[22]

Here Andronicus and Junia are given the highest Pauline appellation of "apostle" (1 Cor 12:28; Eph 4:11). More, they are "notable" or "illustrious" or "outstanding" among the apostles, and have been so even before Paul's conversion to Christ.

There is no direct evidence that "they have been with us the whole time" (Acts 1:21), but they must come close to it. The flow of the verses before and after this one in Romans 16, suggests they were husband and wife, but as we have seen in considering 1 Corinthians 9:5, Junia was not by that fact any less a missionary or any less an apostle. She too is to be numbered "among the apostles" (*en tois apostolois*). Textually, the preposition ἐν ("among") followed by a noun in the dative case, normally signifies inclusiveness. The plural οἵτινές, moreover, suggests that both were apostles, and therefore Junia was herself an apostle. She was one of the apostles who brought the faith to Rome even before Paul arrived there.

Some have claimed that both these apostles were men, but this is highly unlikely. Paul writes Ἰουνιαν; accusative singular of the feminine name Ἰουνιά–'ας, the form found in all early authorities. The early church fathers universally understand Junia to be a woman. Joseph Fitzmyer lists sixteen Greek and Latin Christian writers of or around the first millennium who unambiguously accepted that Junia was a woman.[23] Origen develops the point: "How great the wisdom of this woman that she was

---

22. As rendered by Zerwick and Grosvenor, *A Grammatical Analysis of the Greek New Testament*, 496.

23. Including, Ambrosiaster, Jerome, Theodoret of Cyrrhus, Pseudo-Primasius, John Damscene, Haymo, Rabanus Maurus, Hatto, Ocumenius, Lanfranc, Bruno, Theophylect, Abelard, and Peter Lombard. Fitzmyer, "Romans," 738.

even deemed worthy of the apostle's title."²⁴ Furthermore, scholarship maintains that the masculine name Junias does not occur in any epigraph or literary work of the New Testament period whereas the feminine name Junia appears widely and frequently.²⁵ No Greek minuscule manuscript used the masculine *Iouniān*. At least twenty minuscule New Testament manuscripts use the feminine *Iounían*.²⁶ The putative masculine Ἰουνιας is attested *nowhere else*. The name is written Ἰουνιαν, in all modern critical Greek New Testaments. Greek uncial manuscripts of the New Testament were recopied in minuscule-type manuscripts in the seventh century. Before that the text was unaccented. The introduction of accents made for a clearer distinction between genders.

Giles of Rome (1247–1316), also known as Aegidius, was the first to turn Andronicus and Junia into "those honourable men (*viri*)."²⁷ He did so at the time when women were being written out of the history of ordained ministry. Martin Luther, to be followed by many continental translations, wrote "*den Junian*" (masculine) in 1552.²⁸ She became a man in English New Testament translations only in the Revised Version of 1881 and the masculine has been read from the second edition of the Nestle critical New Testament on. From the Revised Version until the New Living Translation (1996), twenty-one English translations have the masculine, while ten have the feminine.

Nineteenth-century opposition to *Junia's* apostleship, however, usually sprang not from textual criticism, but from the assumption that a woman *could not* be an apostle. Bruce Metzger reported both sides of the debate, and in writing of those who preferred a masculine interpretation of the name, stated: "some members considering it unlikely that

24. Ποση της γυναικος ταυτες ἡ φιλοσοφια, ὡς και της των αποστολων αξιωθηναι προσηγοριας. Origen, *In Epist. ad Rom.* XXXI, Migne, *PG*, 60, 669–70.

25. Belleville, "Women Leaders in the Bible," in *Discovering Biblical Equality*, 117.

26. Until H. Alford, (1849), who uses the masculine form but puts the feminine in the apparatus. Thirty-eight Greek New Testament editions, beginning with Erasmus (1516) through Eberhardt Nestle in 1920, use the feminine name *Iounían*. There was a shift from the Nestle version of 1927 through the UBS *Greek New Testament* of 1993, only one using the feminine and fourteen using the masculine. That trend is reversed with the 1994 Kurt Aland and the UBS 1998 versions, which return to the feminine, with no alternate reading.

27. Opera Exegetica. Opuscula I (Reprint of 1554/55 edition: Frankfurt, 1968), 97, as cited by Brooten, "Junia ... Outstanding among the Apostles," in [eds], Swidler and Swidle, "Women Priests," 141.

28. Thorley, "Junia, a Woman Apostle," 18.

a woman would be among those styled 'apostles,' understood the name to be masculine."²⁹ Thus, the view that Junia was not a female apostle is derived from *a prior assumption that women could not be apostles*, not because of any evidence in the text. Claiming the name is masculine is "mere conventional prejudice." According to the text, Junia was a woman and one of the apostles. Paul nowhere limits the apostolic company to the Twelve plus himself, as some have assumed. In 1 Corinthians 15:5–11, compare verse 5, "to the Twelve," with verse 7, "then to all the apostles." Clearly, "the Twelve" are distinct from "all the apostles." In Romans 16:7, Paul recognized Junia, a woman, as one of the apostles, one willing to suffer for the gospel she was active in spreading.

In the missal of the Byzantine Church, the *Liturgikon*, for May 17th, Junia is honoured as an apostle in the Monologian, a collection of the lives of the saints and commentaries on the meaning of feasts for each day of the calendar year.³⁰ In this light, the designation of Mary of Magdala as *apostola apostolorum* and that of Martha as a "confessor" of the faith take on a new depth of significance. From this perspective, the statement of the CDF that "Christ wanted to give this sacrament to the twelve apostles, all men, who, in turn, communicated it to other men," will have to be read in a more nuanced, expansive manner and cannot be absolutized in any exclusive sense.

## PHOEBE, PRISCILLA, AND A COUNCIL OF THE CHURCH AT ROME

When Paul confided the original manuscript of *Romans* to Deacon Phoebe, what exactly was he asking of her?³¹ To begin with, a journey; whether a dangerous land voyage of four weeks or an expensive sea voyage of five to ten days, depending on the weather. Deacon Phoebe was a benefactress and patroness (*prostatis*) to Paul and implicitly to the Church. Well known, reliable, and apparently wealthy, she could meet the expenses of the voyage and may even have subsidized the costs of producing the document she carried. To whom would she deliver it? Who was in charge? What did Paul expect them to do next?

29. Metzger, *A Textual Commentary on the Greek New Testament*, 475–76.
30. Eisen, *Women officeholders in Early Christianity*, 48.
31. Chapple, "Getting Romans to the Right Romans: Phoebe and the Delivery of Paul's Letter," 195–214.

Paul did not found the church at Rome nor had he ever visited it, though from Romans chapter 16, it seems clear that he knew its leaders, either personally or by reputation. The impression from the letter is of multiple house churches, possibly with occasional gatherings of a more general assembly. The letter insinuates Paul's need for funds, both for the poor Christians of Jerusalem, whom he intends to visit, as well as for his intended mission to Spain *en route* to which he will visit the church in Rome (Rom 15:22–33). The letter, which is not addressed to overseers/bishops, suggests that the central figure in the ensuing drama will be Phoebe. Tertius, given what he writes in 16:22, hardly accompanied her.

Secondly, the letter suggests that Phoebe's primary port of call was the house church presided over by Priscilla and Aquila. In both Pauline and Lukan texts, Priscilla whose name often precedes Aquila's, seems the more prominent figure. They are probably Paul's source of information about the situation in the Roman church. "Greet the community that meets at their house," suggests an assembly where the Eucharist was celebrated.[32] Priscilla, normally named first, was the likely presbyter.

Thirdly, we may infer that through them, Phoebe will address the letter to many other churches. That may have included copying the letter as well as dealing with the expenses involved: a classically diaconal task entrusted to one known as a deacon, who was capable of fulfilling it.

If that was followed either by a general assembly of the house churches in Rome (a kind of embryonic Synod of Rome addressed by an apostolic letter) or by a series of visitations of house churches on the authority of Paul—then who presented the letter, who read it, and with what nuances of tone, emphasis, and interpretation was it read? It seems probable that Paul entrusted this task to Phoebe: which is why he "commends" her, that the churches in Rome "may fittingly welcome her"—using technical, epistolary terminology to introduce a trusted co-worker. So she either did it herself or prepared someone else to do it. In this task, she was in all likelihood, facilitated by the leaders of the house churches in Rome whom the letter mentioned, many of whom were women, and in particular by Priscilla, the very first to be mentioned (Rom 16:3), after Phoebe herself.

At least seven of those Paul singles out as active in the ministry of the church in Rome are women: Prisca, Mary, Junia, Tryphaena, Tryphosa, Persis, and the mother of Rufus; and five are men. These are the

---

32. Fitzmyer, *Romans*, 736.

people Phoebe may call on for hospitality and assistance. Clearly, women were hugely significant and exercised key leadership roles in what was an event of fundamental importance for the church at Rome and even for the whole Catholic Church down to today, and for all who will meditate on *The Epistle to the Romans* in the Church of the future until the coming of the Lord. We are all nourished by the text that Phoebe, in a classic exercise of the ministry of deacon, brought to Rome and had disseminated there. Phoebe's ministry has proved hugely significant for the universal Church down through the centuries. The Church has always had its Marthas, its Phoebes, its Priscillas, its Junias, its Theosebias, and its Itas, as it has today, not least in those remoter places where women, whether religious or lay, have been selected, nominated, and installed to lead, guide, and minister to the people of God. Perhaps it is time to recognize their ministry and to consecrate it through ordination.

## GIVING ASSENT TO WOMEN'S ORDINATION

If it is not possible to establish that Jesus or the apostles forbade the ordination of women, for some, it is equally impossible to prove that they unambiguously endorsed it. In neither case is there unequivocal, direct proof. The truth of the matter may be inferred but not deduced. What is properly inferred, however, demands assent.

The act of reflective understanding grasps the sufficiency of the evidence for a prospective judgment. Before grasping that sufficiency of evidence, there is the task of marshalling and weighing it—what has been attempted in this study. Grasping the evidence as sufficient is "to grasp the prospective judgment as virtually unconditioned": it is conditioned, and the conditions are known and are fulfilled.[33] The link between the conditioned and its conditions is a judgment, product of a cognitional process, immanent and operative within that dynamic. How then does one properly affirm and give assent to the insight that, theologically speaking, suitable women may indeed validly receive Holy Orders?

Some may wish to short-circuit the process by declaring that since women have made excellent scientists, heads of state, communicators, and exegetes, so can they make excellent priests; or simply deduce from the acknowledged equality of women and men that no position may be closed to them. Such statements—compelling as they seem—do not

---

33. Lonergan, *Insight: A Study of Human Understanding*, 282.

answer all the questions that arise, as evidenced by the succession of documents from the Roman magisterium that argue differently. A seemingly compelling proposition is neither necessarily a correct one nor an incorrect one. Just as in sub-apostolic or in medieval theology so also today, many apparent certainties are a matter of cultural conditioning rather than insight into the truth. Yet just as there are rash judgments, so also there is mere indecision. Do the presuppositions and implications of the insight that women may be ordained, knit coherently with the presuppositions and implications of the other insights elucidated in this study, as we have argued they do? The sufficiency of the evidence, if sufficient it be, is not something merely external, but lies in the prior reflective grasp that compels reasonableness to assent.[34]

Assent occurs when a conception of something is judged to be true. It is the subjective and reflective part of judgment, the personal act committing the person, based upon an apprehension of the evidence, as including an awareness of its own validity. It is the fruit of wisdom, the virtue of right judgement through which we know the real as real, *en route* to a more complete act of understanding. It often occurs through inference.[35]

## INFERRING THE TRUTH

John Henry Newman's epistemology draws on what he named the "Illative Sense":[36] the mind's capacity to infer a truth from circumstantial evidence, as distinct from deduction from direct evidence. This illative sense is the intellectual counterpart of *phronesis*, the practical wisdom that enables discernment and correct judgment. In concrete life, formal, incontrovertible proof in favor of a decision is not always possible. More usually, there is a set of converging probabilities pointing to a conclusion. Logical certainty is not always possible to attain. The mind has the capacity to close a logic-gap in concrete situations and allow for assent. The "Illative Sense," the capacity to infer correctly, allows the mind to close that gap between converging probabilities and full assent.

---

34. Lonergan, *Insight: A Study of Human Understanding,* 279–83, 484.

35. Lonergan, *Verbum: Word and Idea in Aquinas,* 66–67.

36. As explained in Newman, *An Essay in Aid of a Grammar of Assent,* 266–98. The full text is accessible at Project Gutenberg, www.gutenberg.org/files/34022/34022-pdf.

For Newman, "antecedent probability is the real instrument of conviction." A "collection of weak evidences ... makes up a strong evidence," constituting "a converging evidence amounting to proof," while "prudent judgment" decides when "probability is sufficient for conviction." Rational faith is "the result of converging probabilities and a cumulative proof from cumulating probabilities." His illustration imagined "a cable which is made up of a number of separate threads each feeble, yet together as sufficient as an iron rod"; or the strength of a "bundle of sticks each of which ... you could snap in two if taken separately from the rest."

Inference and assent are distinct. Assent is unconditional while inference, even if demonstrative, is still conditional. Inference establishes a conclusion to which assent gives absolute recognition. But how is one justified in believing what one cannot prove, given that non-logical reasoning never rises above probability—as opposed to logical certainly, where assent immediately follows from demonstration—but where nonetheless the assent is still distinct from the inference. Newman appealed to *phronesis*—the *prudentia* enabling good judgment for practical action—for the wisdom in assembling and evaluating arguments and determining when we ought to be certain.

Historical precedent of itself does not establish theological truth. Syllogistic reasoning will not solve the problem of ascertaining the nature of inference and assent. Arguing that many concrete truths that cannot be demonstrated are nonetheless unconditionally accepted, Newman wrote that it is an accumulation of probabilities, which cannot be reduced to a syllogism, that leads to certainly in the concrete. Many certitudes depend on informal proofs whose reasoning is more or less implicit, grasped by a sort of instinctive perception of the legitimate conclusion in and through the premises. "Natural" inference proceeds not from proposition to proposition, but from concrete things to concrete things. This, for Newman, is our natural way of reasoning, and he concludes: "Judgment, in all concrete matters is the architectonic faculty and what may be called the Illative Sense or right judgment in ratiocination, is one branch of it." As the mind outstrips language, the "Illative Sense" determines the beginning, course, and term of an investigation.

This present study draws on such an accumulation of probabilities. Women in the early Church exercised ministries that today would be considered presbyteral. While the notion of deacon certainly developed, if the deaconate of later centuries can be legitimately traced to that of the apostolic era, the women deacons of that era were likewise truly deacons.

Nuanced, contextualized, New Testament exegesis indicates women in important Church offices and ministries that today would be considered presbyteral or episcopal. Examination of the massive, epigraphic evidence of ordained women during the first centuries cannot, as a whole, be explained away. It is reasonable to infer from the letter of Pope Gelasius prohibiting it, that bishops were ordaining women to the presbyterate.

Argumentation against the ordination of women was overwhelmingly canonical rather than theological. When medieval theologians sought to develop a more theologically coherent argumentation, they did so based on a flawed anthropology of gender. Up to the thirteenth century, many women in Church office would certainly be considered to have been ordained. Women who through serious and sustained living out of their incorporation into Christ through baptism, bear a supernatural resemblance to Christ, no less than men—that, in the order of grace, is a natural resemblance. Christ the eternal High Priest has, in resurrection, transcended gender difference. The priesthood of the order of the presbyterate, while ministerially distinct, and different in kind, is derived from and at the service of the priesthood of all believers, which is certainly not gender specific.

Consider Newman's illustration of how religious conviction is like a cable made up of a number of rods, each feeble, yet together solid as iron. In the same way, each of the arguments summed up here, if taken on its own, or disconnected from the others, as well as many more, might conceivably be considered inconclusive. But *taken together* they reinforce each other strong as iron to construct a set of converging probabilities, pointing to a conclusion. They constitute an accumulation of probabilities that leads to certainty in the concrete. Under these circumstances, it is not reasonable to withhold assent from what is thereby inferred, namely that *women can indeed be validly ordained in the Catholic Church*. At least one notable bishop has given his assent, not only in theory, but in fact.

## BISHOP FELIX DAVIDEK

When Felix Davidek (d. 1987), a charismatic local priest, returned home to Brno in then Czechoslovakia after a fifteen-year imprisonment for exercising his priestly ministry, he asked a committed, local Catholic woman, Ludmilla Javorova (b. 1932), to help him find candidates for a clandestine priesthood and to organise secret meetings to discuss theological issues and the Second Vatican Council. Davidek had made innovative and daring plans for the Church's underground survival under Czechoslovakian Communism. He soon gathered many committed Catholics around him. They called their group Koinotes (*koinonia*) and met regularly in secret, at night.

Ludmila Javorova had a happy childhood in a large Catholic family, the only girl among seven brothers. She felt a calling from an early age to dedicate her whole life to God, but her hopes of entering a religious order were thwarted due to restrictions imposed by the communist regime. She would eventually become Vicar-General of the underground Czech Bishop Felix Davidek.[37]

In 1967, Davidek was clandestinely consecrated bishop by Jan Blaha, whose episcopal ordination has been declared valid by the Vatican. Blaha in turn, had been clandestinely consecrated by Bishop Peter Dubovsky, a Jesuit. The apostolic succession of Dubovsky's episcopal ordination can be traced through a number of previous Jesuit bishops in Czechoslovakia and thence to Bishop Ritten, consecrated on 11 August 1935 by Cardinal Pacelli, the future Pius XII, himself ordained bishop by Pope Benedict XV, who in turn, was ordained bishop by Pius X. Bishop Davidek's apostolic succession can scarcely be doubted.

Bishop Davidek began to ordain priests, including married men, as they came under less suspicion from the political regime, which understandably expected priests to be celibate. In this way, *Koinotes* spread all over Czechoslovakia. During fifteen years in prison, when he had frequently been tortured, Davidek realized that while male prisoners could at least sometimes receive the sacraments secretly from imprisoned priests, the hundreds of nuns and other Catholic women prisoners, many of whom were tortured, could not: they were not allowed male visitors. Under these exceptional circumstances, Davidek was convinced that the

---

37. Winters, *Out of the Depths—The Story of Ludmila Javorova Ordained Roman Catholic Priest*. A positive review of this work may be found in Pongratz-Lippitt, *Czechoslovakia's Secret Church*, 6. A somewhat hostile version of the events is published in a review of *Out of the Depths* in *First Things* 115 (Aug-Sept 2001) 73–74. The argumentation there is *ad hominem*. It makes unsubstantiated allegations about Davidek's mental health and never mentions the testimony of Bishop Blaha—who was very close to Davidek until his death—that he was not in any way mentally ill. Cf. the report: "Yes, I am a Catholic Woman Priest!" by Ertel and Motylewicz (translated by Mary Dittrich) in *Kirche Intern* 9 (1995) 11, 18–19 (www.womenpriests.org) and the later interview with Ludmila Javorova by Rudolph Schermann entitled "We must Fight Patiently for the Ordination of Women," *Kirche Intern* 13 (1999) 6, 10–11.

underground Church needed women priests to visit women in prison and administer the sacraments to them secretly.

When Davidek summoned a pastoral synod in 1970, and brought the ordination of women into discussion, a number of people broke away from him. In the preparatory body there had been no dissenting voices, but when it came to the vote, some people turned away. Davidek initially suspended these auxiliary bishops he had ordained, who disagreed. Three months later however, he revoked the suspension.

## LUDMILA JAVOROVA

After a meeting of *Koinotes* in December 1970 from which Bishop Davidek, Bishop Blaha, and Ludmila Javorova were the last to leave, Ludmila went directly home. Later that evening, Davidek arrived. "He asked me if I were willing to receive ordination from his hands. He was prepared to do it. He said the decision was mine, but not to take too long to decide or delay in telling him." I wanted to know why he was in such a hurry. He replied: "Believe me, I cannot delay it, because I do not know what will happen with us." The times were so uncertain: "If we wait for a man to approve this," he said, "it will never happen, so we must go ahead without it." "But why have you chosen me?" He replied: "It is one minute to twelve." By this he meant that the issue of women priests was urgent and could no longer be ignored . . . ." "It is my responsibility to inform the Pope. I will investigate every possible way to inform him personally. Now let's pray to the Holy Spirit."

"In my heart, everything was clear . . . on the way home from work on December 28, I stopped in to see Felix, and I said, 'Yes, I will receive it.' '. . . I said yes to it, to receiving everything associated with it, to all of the consequences connected to it . . . I had no idea how to develop this charism, but I accepted it with faith, with a feeling of responsibility, and with love." Around 10:00 p.m. that evening, Ludmila went to Bishop Davidek's place ready to receive the sacrament of Holy Orders. Prior to presbyteral ordination, she was ordained a deacon. In the late night hours of December 28, 1970, Ludmila Javorova was ordained a priest by Bishop Felix Maria Davidek in the presence of his brother, Leo, who witnessed the ordination. The liturgy for ordination to the priesthood was from the Rite of Ordination according to the Roman Pontifical. Following ordination,

Ludmila celebrated Mass simply, quietly, together with Bishop Davidek and his brother Leo.

One of the conditions of her ordination was to tell no one. Ludmila kept her secret. "A major problem for me at the time was how would I celebrate Mass so that no one at home would see it? For the first few days, I went to Felix's place or Felix came to mine and we would celebrate together. Because he usually came every day, nobody was surprised or suspected anything. Later, I celebrated alone when everyone was sleeping."

In a 1995 interview she first declared publicly: "Yes, I am a Catholic priest!" She says that she had long prayed for that meeting, and that she saw in it a work of the Holy Spirit. Some three years earlier, during an interview, she was asked if she was an ordained priest. "I evaded the question, because the matter was not meant for publication. But it kept on worrying me, which is why I invited you here today."

Her priestly ordination was met with mistrust on the part of her male colleagues. At Eucharistic celebrations, she concelebrated; but she was never the principal celebrant among male priests. "On the surface they accept it, because they know that I am ordained, but internally they can't cope with it. That's the two thousand year old tradition of a male church (*sic*), which can't be changed overnight." She herself set forth the circumstances of her ordination in a letter to Pope John Paul II, to which she never received a reply. She stresses that the reason for Bishop Davidek's decision was necessity. "He saw the need. He saw in that a sign of the times. Communication with Rome was not possible. He acted according to his conscience."

Ludmila knows names and addresses of other ordained women. One worked as a nurse in the Brno area. For her work as Vicar-General and priest in the underground church, Ludmila got no recognition, nor payment of any kind. She regards herself as someone who has to offer her life in this cause: "In battle the first line always falls, so that the second line can get through." For Ludmila, "[t]he fundamental question is: How does the church—both its leadership and the people—accept the pastoral involvement of women? Are women respected in this regard in your circles . . . ? As for fundamental acceptance by the People of God, I'm not worried. The difficulties tend to be in the hierarchy."

## CHURCH PRACTICE BUT NOT TRADITION

One cannot simply construct as monolithic, clearly defined, universally accepted, and immutable, the narrative assumed by modern Church authorities. Exegesis shows positive evidence in the New Testament that ministries were shared by various groups in which women did in fact exercise roles and functions later associated with priestly ministry. Arguments adduced against the admission of women to priestly ministry, putatively based on the praxis of Jesus and the apostles, cannot be sustained. The New Testament evidence, while not decisive by itself, points toward the admission of women to ministry and office that today would be considered diaconal, presbyteral, and episcopal.

The relegation of women's ministry, in the sub-apostolic period, happened not out of conscious fidelity to the praxis of Jesus, but for reasons of apologetics and cultural adaptation. First-millennial, historical evidence likewise points to women exercising ordained ministry. Patristic and scholastic doctors opposing women's ordination do so overwhelmingly on the basis of a time-bound, socially constructed, untenable assumption of female inferiority. The scholastics do so in terms of priesthood considered as rank more than as ministry. "Natural" resemblance to Christ, moreover, is theological rather than simply biological.

The non-ordination of women is the customary practice of the Church but it is not "Tradition" in the strong sense of the term. It is not a "Tradition" unmistakably "received" from Christ and the apostles which immutably reveals the will of God for his Church for all ages. It is not one of those "things without which the deposit [of faith] cannot be properly safeguarded and explained." The practice and presumption of the non-ordainability of women is a matter of ecclesiastical law and not one of divine precept. That law is reformable. Women have been and can be ordained in the Catholic Church.

# Select Bibliography

Abrahamsen, Valerie Ann. "Women at Philippi: The Pagan and Christian Evidence." *Journal of Feminist Studies in Religion* 3.2 (1987) 17–30.
Aland, Kurt, ed. *Synopsis of the Four Gospels*. 10th ed. Stuttgart: German Bible Society, 1983.
Aquinas, Thomas. *Summa Theologiae*, III. Latin text and English translation, introductions, notes, appendices, and glossaries. 61 vols. London: Eyre & Spottiswoode, 1965–75.
Bailey, Lisa. "The Strange Case of the Portable Altar: Liturgy and the Limits of Episcopal Authority in Early Medieval Gaul." *Journal of the Australian Early Medieval Association* 8 (2012) 31–51.
Bareille, G. "Collyridiens." In *Dictionaire de Théologie Catholique*, vol. 3, edited by A. Vacant and E. Mangeuot, 369–70. Paris: Letouzet & Ané, 1911.
Barthes, Roland. *S/Z*. Translated by R. Miller. Oxford: Blackwell, 1974.
Belleville, Linda. "Women Leaders in the Bibl." In *Discovering Biblical Equality*, edited by Ronald Pierce and Rebecca Merrill Groothuis, 110–25. Downers Grove, IL: InterVarsity Press, 2005.
Belo, Catarina. "Some Considerations on Averroes' Views Regarding Women and Their Role in Society." *Journal Of Islamic Studies* 20.1 (2009) 1–20.
Bradshaw, Paul F. *Anglican Ordinal*. London: SPCK, 1971.
Brooten, Bernadette. "Junia: Outstanding among the Apostles." In *Women Priests: A Catholic Commentary on the Vatican Declaration*, edited by Leonard Swidler and Arlene Swidler, 141–44. New York: Paulist, 1977.
Brown, Peter. *The Body and Society: Men, Women and Sexual Renunciation in Early Christianity*. New York: Columbia University Press, 1988.
Brown, Raymond E. *Priest and Bishop*. New York: Paulist, 1970.
———. "Roles of Women in the Fourth Gospel." *Theological Studies* 36.4 (1975) 688–99.
Burke, T. Patrick. "Monarchical Episcopate at the End of the First Century." *Journal of Ecumenical Studies* 7.3 (1970) 499–518.
Burns, P., ed. *Butler's Lives of the Saints*. Vol. 1. Collegeville, MN: Liturgical, 1995.
Butler, B. C. "Infallible; Authenicum; Assensus; Obsequium: Christian Teaching Authority and the Christian's Response." *Doctrine & Life* 313 (1981) 77–89.
Butler, Sara. "Quaestio Disputata: In Persona Christi." *Theological Studies* 56.1 (1995) 61–80.

Byrne, Brendan. "The Letter to the Philippians." In *New Jerome Biblical Commentary*, edited by Raymond E. Brown, Joseph A. Fitzmyer, Roland E. Murphy, 791–97. Englewood, NY: Prentice Hall, 1990.

Carlson, Mary. "Can the Church Be a Virtuous Hearer of Women?" *Journal of Feminist Studies in Religion* 32.2 (2106) 21–36.

*Catechism of the Catholic Church*. Rome: Libreria Editrice Vaticana, 2012.

Catholic Biblical Association of America Task Force. "Women and Priestly Ministry: The New Testament Evidence." *Catholic Biblical Quarterly* 41.4 (1979) 608–11.

Céitinn, Seathrún. *Foras Feasa ar Éirinn: An Treas Leabhair* (1634). Edited by P. S. Dineen. London: Irish Texts Society, 1908.

Chapple, Allan. "Getting Romans to the Right Romans: Phoebe and the Delivery of Paul's Letter." *Tyndale Bulletin* 62.2 (2011) 195–214.

Chrysostom, John. *Homilies on Philippians*. Translated by John A. Broadus. In *Nicene and Post-Nicene Fathers* First Series, Vol. 13, edited by Philip Schaff. Buffalo, NY: CLC, 1889.

Clement of Alexandria. *Stromata*. In *Ante-Nicene Fathers*, Vol. 2, Book 3. Translated by Philip Schaff et al. Edinburgh: T. & T. Clark, 1870.

Coffey, David. "The Whole Rahner on the Supernatural Existential." *Theological Studies* 65 (2004) 95–118.

Collins, John N. *Are All Christians Ministers?* Collegeville, MN: Liturgical, 1992.

———. *Deacons and the Church: Making Connections between Old and New*. Harrisburg, PA: Morehouse, 2002.

———. *Diakonia: Re-interpreting the Ancient Sources*. New York: Oxford University Press, 1990.

———. "Reinterpreting *Diakonia* in Germany." *Ecclesiology* 5 (2009) 69–81.

Congar, Yves. "The Holy Spirit in the Sacraments." In *I believe in the Holy Spirit*, Vol. 3, 217–67. London: Chapman, 1983.

———. "Note sur une valeur des termes ordinare, ordination." *Revue des sciences religieuses* 58 (1984) 7–14.

———. "La Réception comme Réalité Ecclésiologique." *Revue des Sciences philosophiques et théologiques*, 56.3 (1972) 369–403.

———. "A Semantic History of the Term 'Magisterium.'" In *Readings in Moral Theology*, no. 3, "The Magisterium and Morality," edited by C. Curran and R. McCormick, 297–313. New York: Paulist, 1982.

———. *La Tadition et les traditions*. Vol. 2. Paris: Seuil, 1963.

———. *Vraie et fausse réforme dans l'Église*. Paris: Cerf 1950.

Congregation for the Doctrine of the Faith. *Inter Insigniores: On the Question of Admission of Women to the Ministerial Priesthood*. 15 October 1976. Acta Apostolicae Sedis 67 (1975) 98–116.

———. *Mysterium Ecclesiae*. Acta Apostolicae Sedis, vol. 65 (1973) 396–408.

———. *Sacerdotium Ministeriale*. Acta Apostolicae Sedis, vol. 75 (1983) 1001–9.

Connell, Desmond. "Women Priests: Why Not?" *L›Osservatore Romano* (Eng. ed.) No. 10, 7 March 1988, 6–8, 10.

Cook, John Granger. "1 Cor 9:5; The Women of the Apostles." *Biblica* 89.3 (2008) 352–68.

Cross, F. L., and E. A. Livingstone, eds. *The Oxford Dictionary of the Christian Church*. 2nd ed. Oxford: Oxford University Press, 1978.

D'Alton, A. "Limerick." In *Catholic Encyclopedia*, vol. 9, 262. New York: Appleton, 1910.

Diehl, E. *Inscriptiones Latinae Christianae Veteres*. Zurich: Weidmann, 1970.
Duschene, L. "Lovocat et Catihern; Prêtres Bretons du temps de Sainte Melaine." *Revue de Bretagne et de Vendée* 57 (1885) 5–18.
Eisen, Ute E. *Women Officeholders in Early Christianity: Epigraphical and Literary Studies*. Collegeville, MN: Liturgical, 2000.
Ferrara, Dennis Michael. "The Ordination of Women: Tradition and Meaning." *Theological Studies* 55.4 (1994) 706–19.
———. "A Reply to Sara Butler." *Theological Studies* 56.1 (1995) 61–91.
Fink, Peter E. "The Sacrament of Orders: Some Liturgical Reflections." *Worship* 56.6 (1982) 482–502.
Fiorenza, Elisabeth Schüssler. "A Feminist Critical Interpretation for Liberation: Martha and Mary: Lk 10:38–42." *Religion and Intellectual Life* 3.2 (1986) 21–36.
Fitzmyer, Joseph. *Romans*. The Anchor Yale Bible. New Haven: Yale University Press, 1993.
Gadamer, H-G. *Truth and Method*. 2nd rev. ed. Translated by J. Weinsheimer and D. G. Marshall. New York: Crossroad, 2004.
Gaillardetz, R. "The Reception of Doctrine: New Perspectives." In *Authority in the Roman Catholic Church*, edited by B. Hoose, 95–114. Farnham, UK: Ashgate, 2002.
———. "Towards a Contemporary Theology of the Diaconate." *Worship* 79.5 (2005) 419–38.
Gibaut, John. "Sequential Ordination in Historical Perspective: A Response to J. Robert Wright." *Anglican Theological Review* 77.3 (1995) 367–91.
———. *Sequential or Direct Ordination? A Return to the Sources*. Joint Liturgical Studies 55. Bramcote, UK: Grove, 2003.
Gibson, Joan. "Could Christ Have Been Born a Woman? A Medieval Debate." *Journal of Feminist Studies in Religion* 8.1 (1992) 65–82.
Gilbert of Limerick. "De statu ecclesiae." In *The Whole Works of the Most Rev. James Ussher*. Dublin: Elrington and Todd, 1847–64.
Gryson, R. *Le ministère des femmes dans L'Église ancienne*. Gembloux: Duculot, 1972.
Guarducci, Margherita. *The Tomb of St. Peter*. Portland: Hawthorn, 1960.
Gwynn, Aubrey, and R. N. Hadcock. *Medieval Religious Houses in Ireland*. Dublin: Irish Academic Press, 1988.
Gwynn, Aubrey. *The Irish Church in the 11th and 12th Centuries*. Dublin: Four Courts Press, 1992.
Haddan, A. H., and W. Stubbs. *Councils and Ecclesiastical Documents Relating to Great Britain and Ireland*. Oxford: Clarendon, 1871.
Harrington, C. *Women in a Celtic Church: Ireland 450–1150*. Oxford: Oxford University Press, 2002.
Hentschel, Anni. *Diakonia im Neuen Testament: Studien zur Semantik unter besonderer Berücksichtigung der Bode von Frauen*. Tübingen: Siebeck, 2007.
Holland, Martin. "Gille (Gilbert of Limerick)." In *Medieval Ireland: An Encyclopedia*, edited by Seán Duffy, 198–99. Abingdon, UK: Routledge, 2005.
International Theological Commission. *From the Diakonia of Christ to the Diakonia of the Apostles (2002)*. San Francisco: Ignatius, 2009.
Jedin H. *A History of the Council of Trent, Volume I: The Struggle for the Council (1951)*. Lexington, KY: American Council of Learned Societies, 2008.

Just, Arthur A. Jr. "The Apostolic Councils of Galatians and Acts: How First-Century Christians Walked Together." *Concordia Theological Quarterly* 74.3–4 (2010) 261–88.

Karras, Valerie A. "Female Deacons in the Byzantine Church." *Church History* 73 (2004) 272–316.

Kelly, J. N. D. *Early Christian Doctrines*. London: Black, 1989.

LaCelle-Petersen, Kristina. *Liberating Tradition: Women's Identity and Vocation in Christian Perspective*. Grand Rapids: Baker Academic, 2008.

Ladaria, Luis (Prefect of the CDF). *A proposito di alcuni dubbi: Il carattere definitivo della dottrina di «Ordinatio sacerdotalis.»* Rome: L'Osservatore Romano, 2018.

Larkin, E. *The Roman Catholic Church in Ireland and the Fall of Parnell: 1888–1891*. Liverpool: Liverpool University Press, 1979.

Laurance, J. D. "The Eucharist as the Imitation of Christ." *Theological Studies* 47 (1986) 286–96.

Legrand, Hervé. "La Présidence de l'Eucharistie selon la Tradition Ancienne." *Spiritus* 69 (1977) 409–31.

———. "*Traditio perpetuo servata*? The Non-ordination of Women: Tradition or Simply an Historical Fact?" *Worship* 65.6 (1991) 482–508.

Lienhard, Joseph T., trans. *Origen: Homilies on Luke; Fragments on Luke*. Washington, DC: Catholic University of America Press, 1996.

Lodt, J. "Un Ancien Usage de l'Église Celtique." *Revue Celtique* 15 (1885) 92–93.

Lonergan, B. J. F. *Insight: A Study of Human Understanding*. London: Longmans, 1957.

———. *Method in Theology*. London: Darton, Longman & Todd, 1971.

———. *Verbum: Word and Idea in Aquinas*. South Bend, IN: University of Notre Dame Press, 1967.

MacDonald, Sarah. "Artifacts Show That Early Church Women Served as Clergy." *National Catholic Reporter*, July 13, 2019.

MacGregor, Kirk R. "1 Corinthians 14:33b–38 as a Pauline Quotation-Refutation Device." *Priscilla Papers* 32.1 (2018) 23–28.

Macy, Gary. "The Ordination of Women in the Early Middle Ages." *Theological Studies* 61.3 (2000), 481–507.

Marshall, Jill, E. "The Recovery of Paul's Female Colleagues in Nineteenth Century Feminist Biblical Interpretation." *Journal of Feminist Studies in Religion* 33.2 (2017) 21–36.

Martin, John Hilary. "The Injustice of not Ordaining Women: A Problem for Medieval Theologians." *Theological Studies* 48.2 (1987) 303–16.

Mawdudi, Maulana. *Purdah and the Status of Women in Islam*. Lahore, Pakistan: Islamic Publications, 1939.

McElwee, Joshua J., and Brian Roewe. "Amazon Synod Calls for Married Priests: Pope to Reopen Women Deacons Commission." *National Catholic Reporter*, October 26, 2019.

Meier, John P. "Biblical Reflections: The Conflict at Antioch (Gal 2:11f.)." *Mid-Stream* 35.4 (1996) 471–75.

———. "On the Veiling of Hermeneutics" (1 Cor 11:2–16)." *Catholic Biblical Quarterly* 40.2 (1978) 212–22.

Metzger, Bruce M. *A Textual Commentary on the New Testament*. Stuttgart: United Bible Societies, 2001.

Migne, J. P., ed. *Patrologia Latina*, vols. 88, 112, 159. Paris, 1844–55.

Miller, Amanda C. "Cut from the Same Cloth: A Study of Female Patrons in Luke-Acts and the Roman Empire." *Review & Expositor* 114.2 (2017) 203–10.
Montes-Peral, Luis Ángel. "El comportamiento de las mujeres discípulas en la pasión de Marcos."*Estudios eclesiasticos* 88.344 (2013) 3–44.
Morris, Joan. *The Lady Was a Bishop.* New York: Macmillan, 1973.
———. 'Women and Episcopal Power,' New Blackfriars 53 (1972) 205–10.
Newman, John Henry. *An Essay in Aid of a Grammar of Assent.* London: Burns & Oates, 1874.
———. *On Consulting the Faithful in Matters of Doctrine.* London: Chapman, 1859.
Nolan, Michael. "What Aquinas Never Said about Women." *First Things,* November 1998, 11–12.
O'Brien, John. "The Authority of the Poor." In *Authority in the Roman Catholic Church,* edited by B. Hoose, 217–30. Farnham, UK: Ashgate, 2002.
———. *The Construction of Pakistani Christian Identity.* Lahore, Pakistan: University of Lahore, 2006.
———. "The Danger in Dining with Jesus." *Focus* 22.3 (2002) 258–76.
———. "Ecclesiology as Narrative." *Ecclesiology* 4.2 (2008) 148–65.
———. *Theology and the Option for the Poor.* Collegeville, MN: Liturgical, 1992.
O'Connell, Gerard. "Pope Francis Says Commission on Women Deacons Did Not Reach Agreement." *America,* May 7, 2019.
O'Malley, J. "The Hermeneutic of Reform: A Historical Analysis." *Theological Studies* 73.3 (2012) 517–46.
———. "Vatican II: Did Anything Happen?" *Theological Studies* 67 (2006) 3–33.
Örsy, Ladislaus. *The Church: Learning and Teaching.* Dublin: Dominican, 1987.
———. *Theology and Canon Law: New Horizons for Legislation and Interpretation.* Collegeville, MN: Liturgical, 1992.
Otranto, Giorgio. "Note sul sacerdozio femminile nell'antichità in margine a una testimonianze di Gelasio 1." *Vetera Christianorum* 19 (1982) 341–60.
Payne, Philip B. *Man and Woman, One in Christ: An Exegetical and Theological Study of Paul's Letters.* Grand Rapids: Zondervan, 2009.
Peppiatt, Lucy. *Women and Worship at Corinth: Paul's Rhetorical Arguments in 1 Corinthians.* Eugene, OR: Cascade, 2015.
Perry, Gregory R. "Phoebe of Cenchreae and 'Women' of Ephesus: 'Deacons' in the Earliest Churches." *Presbyterion* 36.1 (2010) 9–36.
Picken, Elizabeth J. "If Christ Is Bridegroom, the Priest Must Be Male?" *Worship* 67.3 (1993) 269–78.
Pierce, Ronald W., Rebecca Groothuis, and Gordon Fee, eds. *Discovering Biblical Equality.* Downers Grove, IL: InterVarsity Press, 2005.
Plummer, Carolus, ed. *"Vitae Sanctorum Hiberniae."* 2 vols. Oxford: Clarendon, 1910.
Pongratz-Lippitt, Christa. "Czechoslovakia's Secret Church." *Tablet,* April 9, 2011, 6–7.
Pontifical Biblical Commission. "The Interpretation of the Bible in the Church." *Origins,* January 6, 1994, 497–524.
Pope Francis. *Evangelii Gaudium.* Acta Apostolicae Sedis 105 (2013) 1019–1137.
———. *Video Message to Participants in the International Theological Congress, Buenas Aires 3-9-2015.* Acta Apostolicae Sedis 108, 997–980.
Pope Leo XIII. *Aterni Patris.* Acta Sanctae Sedis 12 (1879) 97–115.
———. *Saepe Nos,* (ASS 21 1888 3–5).

Pope John XXIII. *Veterum Sapientia: On the Promotion of the Study of Latin.* Acta Apostolicae Sedis 53 (1961) 785–803.
Pope John Paul II, *Christifideles laici.* (December 30, 1988) Acta Apostolicae Sedis 81 (1989) 393–584.
———. *Mulieris Dignitatem.* Acta Apostolicae Sedis 80 (1988) 1653–1727.
———. *Ordinatio Sacerdotalis.* Acta Apostolicae Sedis 86 (1976) 545–48.
Pope Paul VI. "Address on the Role of Women in the Plan of Salvation." (January 30, 1977.) *Insegnamenti di Paulo Sexto*, XV. Rome: Libreria Editrice Vaticana, 1977.
———. *Response to the Letter of His Grace the Most Reverend Dr. F. D. Coggan, Archbishop of Canterbury, concerning the Ordination of Women to the Priesthood.* (November 30, 1975). Acta Apostolicae Sedis 68 (1976) 599.
Pope Pius XII. *Sacramentum Ordinis*, A.A.S. (1948) 5–7
Rahner, Karl. *Concerning the Relationship between Nature and Grace*, Theological Investigations, Vol. 1, (London: Darton, Longman, Todd, 1961) 297–318.
———. "The Dispute concerning the Church's Teaching Office." In *Theological Investigations* 14, 85–88. London: Darton, Longman & Todd, 1978.
———. *Foundations of Christian Faith: An Introduction to the Idea of Christianity.* London: Darton, Longman & Todd, 1978.
———. "Monogenism." In *Sacramentum Mundi*, 974–77. London: Burns & Oates, 1973.
———. "Original Sin." In *Sacramentum Mundi*, 1148–55. London: Burns & Oates, 1973.
———. "The Theology of the Restoration of the Diaconate." In *Theological Investigations* 5, 268–314. Baltimore, MD: Helicon, 1966.
———. "Women and the Priesthood." In *Theological Investigations* 20, 35–47. London: Darton, Longman & Todd, 1981.
Ramelli, Illiaria. "Theosebia: A Presbyter of the Catholic Church." *Journal of Feminist Studies in Religion* 26.2 (2010) 79–102.
Raming, Ida. *A History of Women and Ordination: The Priestly Office of Women: God's Gift*, vol. 2, Toronto: Scarecrow, 2004.
Ratzinger, Joseph (later Pope Benedict XVI). "Dogmatic Constitution on Divine Revelation." In *Commentary on the Documents of Vatican II*, vol. 3, edited by H. Vorgrimler, 155–272. New York: Herder, 1969.
——— (Cardinal, Prefect, Congregation for the Doctrine of the Faith). *Letter Concerning the CDF Reply Regarding Ordinatio Sacerdotalis: Reply of the Congregation for the Doctrine of the Faith to a dubium*, Rome, 28 October 1995.
Reynolds, Roger E. "*Virgines Subintroductae* in Celtic Christianity." *Harvard Theological Review* 61 (1968) 547–66.
Rossi, Mary Ann. "Priesthood, Precedent, and Prejudice: On Recovering the Women Priests of Early Christianity." *Journal of Feminist Studies in Religion* 7.1 (1991) 73–94.
Ryan, Gregory A. *Hermeneutics of Doctrine in a Learning Church: The Dynamics of Receptive Integrity*, (Leiden: Brill, 2020).
Salmon, George. "Collyridians." In *A Dictionary of Christian Biography*, edited by W. Smith and H. White, 596. London: Murray, 1877.
Schermann, Rudolph. "We Must Fight Patiently for the Ordination of Women." *Kirche Intern* 13.6 (1999) 10–11.

Schillebeeckx, E. *Christ, the Sacrament of the Encounter with God.* New York: Sheed and Ward, 1963.
Schmitt, Albert. "Gilbert V. Limerick." In *Lexikon für Theologie und Kirche*, vol. 4, edited by Michael Buchberger, 4:890. Freiburg: Herder, 1957–68.
Shannon, Thomas A. "A Scotist Aside to the Ordination of Women." *Theological Studies* 56 (1995) 353–54.
Shaver, Stephen R. "A Eucharistic Origins Story," Part 1; "The Breaking of the Loaf." *Worship* 92 (May 2018) 204–22; part 2: "The Body and Blood of Christ." *Worship* 92 (July 2018) 298–317.
Sparstot, Francis. "Aristotle on Women." *The Society for Ancient Greek Philosophy Newsletter* 8, 1983.
Strand, Kenneth A. "The Rise of the Monarchical Episcopate." *Andrews University Seminary Studies* 4 (1966) 65–88.
Sullivan, F. *Magisterium: Teaching Authority in the Catholic Church.* Dublin: Gill & Macmillan, 1985.
Sunberg, Carla D. *The Cappadocian Mothers: Deification Exemplified in the Writings of Basil.* Eugene, OR: Pickwick, 2017.
Tanzella-Nitti, Giuseppe. "The Aristotelian-Thomistic Concept of Nature and the Contemporary Debate on the Meaning of Natural Laws." *Actaphilosophica* 6.2 (1997) 237–64.
Thorley, John. "Junia, a Woman Apostle." *Novum Testamentum* 38.1 (1996) 18–29.
U. S. National Bishops' Conference. *Human Life in Our Day.* Glen Rock, NJ: Paulist, 1969.
Viecher, Lukas. "The Problem of the Diaconate: An Analysis of Early Christian Sources." *Encounter* 25.1 (1964) 84–104.
Walsh, Lora. "Ecclesia Reconsidered: Two Pre-Modern Encounters with the Feminine Church." *Journal of Feminist Studies in Religion* 33.2 (2017) 73–91.
Wijngaards, J., *The Ordained Women Deacons of the Church's First Millennium* (Norwich: Canterbury Press, 2011, 2nd ed.)
Winters, M. *Out of the Depths—The Story of Ludmila Javorova Ordained Roman Catholic Priest.* New York: Crossroad, 2001.
Wippel, J. F. "Thomas Aquinas and the Condemnation of 1277." *Modern Schoolman* 72 (1995) 233–72.
Wood, Susan K. *Sacramental Orders.* Collegeville, MN: Liturgical, 2000.
Wright, John H. "Patristic Testimony on Women's Ordination in *Inter Insigniores*." *Theological Studies* 58.3 (1997) 516–26.
Zagano, Phyllis. "Remembering Tradition: Women's Monastic Rituals and the Diaconate." *Theological Studies* 72.4 (2011) 787–811.
Zerwick, M., and M. Grosvenor. *A Grammatical Analysis of the Greek New Testament.* Rome: Biblical Institute, 1981.

www.ingramcontent.com/pod-product-compliance
Lightning Source LLC
Chambersburg PA
CBHW021730220426
43662CB00008B/785